THE INVISIBLE WORLD

Lectures from the Wordsworth Summer Conference

and Wordsworth Winter School

by

JONATHAN WORDSWORTH

Selected transcribed and edited by Richard Haynes

Copyright © 2015 Richard Haynes

All rights reserved.

ISBN: 1503290259
ISBN-13: 978-1503290259

For Giles, Helen and Jonathan

Front Cover Photograph: Tree at Tarn Hows

CONTENTS

	Introduction	vii
	Acknowledgments	xxx
	Abbreviations	xxx
1	Revolutionary Wordsworth	1
2	What is *The Excursion*?	24
3	Sympathetic Imagination	51
4	Keatsian Imagination	76
5	Double Bicentenary	116
6	Doors of Perception	143
7	Two Strangers and a Pair of Wild Eyes	173
8	Blake and the Imagination	202
9	Wordsworthian Transformations	226
10	Understanding Blake; *The First Book of Urizen*	254

INTRODUCTION

> Imagination – lifting up itself
> Before the eye and progress of my song
> Like an unfathered vapour, here that power,
> In all the might of its endowments, came
> Athwart me! I was lost as in a cloud,
> Halted without a struggle to break through;
> And now, recovering, to my soul I say
> 'I recognize thy glory.' In such strength
> Of usurpation, in such visitings
> Of awful promise, when the light of sense
> Goes out in flashes that have shown to us
> The invisible world, does greatness make abode,
> There harbours whether we be young or old.
> Our destiny, our nature, and our home,
> Is with infinitude, and only there...
>   (*Prelude* 1805 VI 525-39)

Students of Romanticism will find these lectures a fertile source of critical ideas and perspectives. Letters, prose-writing, literary criticism, historical detail, philosophy, journalism are variously used *inter alia* to offer the reader greater understanding of the poetry and period. There is much variety. There are four lectures on Wordsworth, one on Coleridge, three on Blake, one on Keats and one on Burns and Macpherson's Ossian; and there are references to Shelley and Byron interspersed. Some lectures are quite specific; the last chapter for instance is a detailed look at Blake's *The First Book of Urizen*. Others are more general; though Chapter Four begins with a detailed look at the verse-letter to

Reynolds of the 25th March 1818, the lecture expands to consider much broader issues touching upon Keatsian 'Imagination'. There is a prevailing tendency in some of the lectures to steer the arguments towards discussion of the Romantic Imagination so it seemed appropriate to draw this book's title from one of Wordsworth's relevant major passages. In some there is a wish to explore what 'Imagination' means for individual poets and what we mean when we use the word 'Romanticism'. Acknowledging that a group of six major poets might be viewed 'anarchic', there are sometimes, it is argued, important shared features. All in one way or other, it may be said, are Platonic writers and all value the concepts of 'loss of self' and 'oneness', even if for Byron such writing was a momentary experience. Students tend to turn to Coleridge for a 'theory' of the Romantic Imagination but Blake, who is often overlooked, is argued to have formed the earliest.

Each chapter is a transcription of a lecture given either at the Wordsworth Summer Conference or Wordsworth Winter School held annually in Grasmere. In view of the importance of that location to the poetry Jonathan Wordsworth would contemplate no other. For almost half of his life he was a central figure at these gatherings and towards the end of it he was Director choosing themes, inviting guest speakers from around the world, selecting papers, chairing debates and overseeing general administration. The lectures vary in style and this reflects the fact that they were given to different audiences at different times and sometimes for different purposes. Most of them were recorded and the recordings deposited in the Library of The Wordsworth Trust. Some have already been published. But for the most part they were not and the recordings have been left to languish on the shelves. The death of Jonathan Wordsworth in 2006 seemed an opportunity to reopen that archive, to transcribe the best of those previously unpublished and make them available in print for the first time

It should be born in mind that the lectures are sometimes not delivered in the writing style of their author; occasional casual interjections, comments or commentary should be expected. There is little doubt that had Jonathan Wordsworth prepared them for publication he would have scrupulously revised them. The full arguments of the lectures however are carefully crafted nonetheless and are mostly subtle and extended and will repay attentive reading. The following summaries are an attempt to give quick reference points only for the contents of each chapter though in most cases no summary could be adequate.

In **'Revolutionary Wordsworth'** Wordsworth is shown to be a 'revolutionary' poet in many different ways. There is the political poet who is defended against the criticism he betrayed his earlier revolutionary sympathies. He visits France first in 1790 (*Prelude* 1805 VI) just after the Revolution has begun and is uplifted by idealism and hope for the future of mankind. On his second visit in 1791-2 (*Prelude* 1805 X) he is aware of menace (Paris seemed 'a wood where tigers roam') and senses that Revolutionary violence will become cyclical like a horse in 'manage' ('the wind / Of heaven turns round and treads in his own steps'). But his meeting with the army officer and nobleman Michel Beaupuy confirms for him the original objectives of the Revolution. Empty pomp and tyranny will be abolished and the democratic principle firmly established where ordinary people will have a strong hand in the making of their own laws. Wordsworth has a sense of the 'substance or corporeality of emotion'; he feels the potential violence of Paris as 'a substantial dread' (*Prelude* 1805 X 66), is able to feel things 'with a weight of pleasure' (*Prelude* 1805 II 178). And in 1793 Wordsworth's unpublished 'A Letter to the Bishop of Llandaff' justifies the necessity of the execution of Louis XVI which had taken place in January of that year. Ultimately however support for the course of the Revolution became untenable but, as Jonathan Wordsworth argues, the poet's support for the revolutionary spirit continued.

The emotional turbulence of these years is illustrated by the two episodes of praying in an English church ('like an uninvited guest') for the defeat of the English army at the hands of the French and the hauling of himself metaphorically before the criminal bar to answer what are self-questionings over his revolutionary sympathies and his acceptance of Godwinian reasoning. What results, we are told, is something akin to a nervous breakdown in which sister Dorothy's role is central to his recovery back to his true vocation – nature and poetry. The Revolutionary passion becomes itself revolutionized. The poem 'Old Man Travelling' marks the turning point where Wordsworth demonstrates his new priorities; what was an intensity generated by Revolutionary passion now turns inward to value the individual, however humble in life. There is a new sense of calm in the poetry; the Old Man's 'settled quiet' is at the centre of the poem.

Wordsworth comes to accept what he later calls, 'The Mind of Man' as 'the haunt and main region of [his] song'. 'There was a Boy' is part of this development where the mind and imagination are shown at work. The poet has discovered a way to discuss the complexities of mind and heart by ascribing to them the features of 'internal space'. The lakeside and all its attendant sights and sounds are received by the mind and heart just as they are 'received into the bosom of the steady lake'. The truly revolutionary nature of the poetry is that Wordsworth has found a language for the subconscious.

'**What is *The Excursion*?**' asks 'What was *The Recluse* to be?' since *The Excursion* was to be a part. The question is placed in its historical context against the backdrop of the French and

American Revolutions. It was a time of political despair. Wordsworth and Coleridge in 1798 are searching for a literary alternative to these political failures which will bring hope to mankind and which nurtures the individual and the community in ways these revolutions did not. The French Invasion (Spring 1798) of the Swiss Republic was a devastating blow to such hopes. And both Wordsworth in 'Not Useless do I deem' (March 1798) and Coleridge in his 10th March 1798 letter to brother George are seeking a solution to social strife through akin concepts of the 'pure principle of love', the 'active principle' common to animate and inanimate and 'the elevation of the imagination' which is attuned to 'the beauty of the inanimate impregnated...as with a living soul'. The sense of there being a kind of life shared by all men and things was to offer hope for harmony between men and between men and the natural world.

Three stages of *The Excursion* are outlined. The first is from 1798 in Wordsworth's '1300 lines' later incorporated into the work of 1814 which stress 'Nature, Man and Society', including the poem known separately as 'The Ruined Cottage'. The second is the published work of 1814 into which that poem and 'The Pedlar' are inserted amongst its nine books. And the third is the later *Excursion* from 1845 onwards revised to include conventional Christian thinking following Christopher North's criticisms. The 1814 version has special value; it is true to the ideals of 1798 and it is the major work of Wordsworth by which he is known for the whole of the nineteenth century.

The theme of community is stressed. The poet includes not just human society but the total 'community' of the animate and inanimate, the sense of a shared existence with all things. The '1300 lines' from 1798 gave hope by demonstrating Margaret's resilience, an example of the human capacity to endure tragedy derived from the stabilising influence of natural surroundings; the character of the Pedlar showed how the human mind could be 'educated' by Nature and how he lived the 'One Life'. Other forms of Wordsworthian self-portraiture, The Wanderer and the Solitary, stress the importance of 'community' and the dangers of too much hope, of hardening of the heart against experience following pain and of solitariness as a way of responding to it. There is further analysis of contemporary evils; in addition to the French Revolution, the Industrial Revolution too had turned out badly. British commercial success did not compensate for the destruction of family life or the deaths of children from industrial disease. And the treasured rivers, hills and valleys were being harnessed to provided water power to drive machinery.

The Excursion nevertheless offers hope and vision. There is a new Wordsworthian landscape voice in Book IX where the 'two-fold image' of the ram, whose picture is reflected, is received by the water in a way analogous to the imaginative mind's receptiveness. And there is the New Jerusalem of Book II which entails a vision of a 'grand imaginative community' of men, minds and natural world. And there is finally, also in Book IX, the vision from Loughrigg Terrace in which, as throughout *The Excursion*, communion is advocated and celebrated alongside community. There the evening sun, masked by cloud, has initially disappointed the group of walkers but suddenly they are uplifted by a breaking through of sunlight into the sky. As Jonathan Wordsworth puts it, the 'clouds separately poized' 'emblemize' the individual possibilities of the human soul and of the human imagination in the context of togetherness, sublime natural beauty, hope and love.

'Sympathetic Imagination' concerns the poet's ability to identify intuitively with the feelings of others. Wordsworth's early life is sketched, concluding that dearth of early experience with women did not prevent him writing perspicaciously about them.

Keats's derogatory remarks concerning the nature of Wordsworth's 'poetical character' are disputed. All poets have a mode in which they speak of themselves (the 'egotistical sublime') as Keats himself demonstrated in 'Ode to a Nightingale'. But Wordsworth was just as capable of being the 'camelion poet'. The argument is linked to Hazlitt's essay 'On Gusto' which is related but distinguished because of its concern with painting. Keats, whose 'camelion poet' is continually 'filling some other body' and living 'in gusto be it foul or fair' is not so far away from the Wordsworthian poet of the Preface to *Lyrical Ballads* who may wish sometimes to enter an 'entire delusion' of being someone else and 'even to confound and identify his feelings with theirs'. The Betty Foy portrait from 'The Idiot Boy' shows how the poet confounds his identity with his female subject. Her happiness and pleasure are described with intimate understanding; they are at times tender and ridiculous simultaneously.

Analyses are offered of 'The Mad Mother', 'Goody Blake and Harry Gill', 'The Idiot Boy' and 'The Thorn'. The appropriate sections from the Preface are discussed in detail. Wordsworth is almost always writing about the mind (unlike Keats or Hazlitt) and particularly obsessive states. He wishes to 'trace the maternal passions through many of its more subtle windings'. 'The Thorn' poses 'complex questions about association and mental process'. There is a discussion of repetition and habit and how 'feelings and ideas are associated in a state of excitement'. And there is an acknowledgement of the influence of guilt in the poetry which is linked to the predicament in which Wordsworth left Annette Vallon on leaving France in December 1792.

The last poem discussed in detail is 'The Complaint of the Forsaken Indian Woman'. It is an example of the 'sympathetic imagination' and a stream of consciousness of feelings and ideas where moods and voices alternate rapidly. Wordsworth confounds his own identity with the woman's and offers an intuitive understanding of her own feelings as she approaches the moment of death but the poem is not about that alone. The 'perfect' example of the sympathetic imagination is given as the woman remembers the expression on the face of the child as he is taken from her. In that moment 'a most strange something did I see / As if he strove to be a man / That he might pull the sledge for me.' The 'powerful imprecision' of 'something' is commented on and related to 'something far more deeply interfused' of 'Tintern Abbey'. Finally, 'death in the opening lines had had the 'numinous beauty' of assimilation into the world of the northern lights'. As the poem closes the wolf's approach (referred to as 'he' not 'it') is not totally unwelcome. The processes of nature take over as night falls and the 'not wholly unfriendly' animal draws near against the starlit backdrop.

'Keatsian Imagination' is a searching analysis of the qualities of Keatsian image-making as well as a comparative essay on the concepts of 'oneness' and 'loss of self' shared by all six Romantic poets.

The verse-letter to Reynolds of the 25th March 1818 is asserted as central to the great period of enquiry by Keats into the nature of Imagination which begins with the letter to Bailey of the 22nd November 1817 (claiming Beauty seized by the Imagination to be Truth and that Imagination can be compared to Adam's dream) and ends with the letter to Reynolds of the 3rd May 1818 ('mansion of many apartments')(although such parameters may be debated). The biographical context is sketched in.

The prose letter to Reynolds of the 3rd May reveals something of Keats's practice as a letter-writer. He 'must be free of [generous with] tropes and figures...crown a white with a black, or a black with a white and move as far and near' as he pleases.

Things are chosen for the pleasure of their incongruity. Keats is talking about fantasy, what Coleridge would call Fancy rather than Imagination. But in doing so, he is concerned with the workings of the mind, 'patterns and pictures thrown up by the unconscious and with their relation to creativity' whilst engaged with the entertainer's pleasure in fantasy and the search for truth and beauty.

Hazlitt's *On Gusto* lies behind the reference to 'Titian's colours' in the verse-letter. To perceive the colours brought alive ('touched into real life') is the achievement of Wordsworth's 'higher mind' (*Prelude* 1805 XIII 90). Though Hazlitt singled out Claude as not having 'gusto', Keats chooses to incorporate in his verse-letter reference to Claude's *The Enchanted Castle* and to invest it with 'gusto', the ideal of imaginative intensity.

Keats engages with Wordsworth and Shakespeare. Wordsworth had yearned to invest Peele Castle with 'the gleam, / The light that never was…..The consecration, and the Poet's dream'. It seems Keats may have had this in mind in the verse-letter when, addressing Phoebus, he wishes he had 'thy sacred word' and could show his own castle 'in fair dreaming wise'. Each poet wishes to paint his castle 'in the gleam of imagination'. Shakespeare's sonnets are admired. They are 'full of fine things said unintentionally…in the intensity of working out conceits'. Keats celebrates being carried along by 'song' and in 'When I have Fears' speaks of 'tracing shadows with the magic hand of Chance' causing Woodhouse to comment that this gave some 'insight' into Keats's working method, Keats believing that if poetry did 'not come naturally it had better not come at all'. 'Song' and 'the magic hand of Chance' it is suggested might have availed Keats a line of defence against some (not all!) of Croker's criticisms which are discussed.

Keats 'is an associationist of ideas' and sometimes rewrites himself. The 'golden galley' in 'silken trim' anticipates the heifer's 'silken flanks' of the Grecian Urn. Its movement into the middle of the poem echoes the gracefulness of Wordsworth's White Doe. The 'mystery of the unknown' which it brings is akin to the 'numinous distancing' of the nightingale as its 'plaintive anthem fades.....up the hill-side'. The ineffective 'verdurous bosoms of those isles' is rewritten by Keats in stanza four of Ode to a Nightingale's 'verdurous glooms'.

In the letter to Bailey (22nd November 1817) Keats's complex statement concerning Adam's dream offers a definition of the Imagination which 'closely resembles the higher reaches of Coleridge's Primary Imagination'. Between April 1817 and January when he finalizes Endymion, Keats 'alchymizes' the poetry. Imaginative achievement of 'chief intensity' is associated with 'fellowship divine', 'fellowship with essence'.

The sunset is for Keats symbolic of a realm of pure imagination. It possesses the 'chief intensity'. Keats yearns for it in the verse-letter when he wishes that 'our 'dreamings / Would all their colours from the sunset take; / From something of material sublime'. Wordsworth had used the image in 'Tintern Abbey' when speaking of the pantheist life-force 'whose dwelling is the light of setting suns' and in the 'Immortality Ode'. The closest Wordsworth gets to Keats is in the sunset of 'Stepping Westward' where the poetry is 'unusually free of the Wordsworthian palpable design upon us'. But Keats is always at risk of the 'moods of one's mind' when the intensity of the Imagination sees 'into the core / Of an eternal fierce destruction'.

Keats's 'Soul-making' has affinities with the other Romantic poets. Blake would have accepted the statement 'Atoms of perception' (which could 'so easily be the Coleridge of 1795') 'they know and they see and they are pure, in short they are God'. And Wordsworth comes close to this in a manuscript of 1799.

There is a discussion of the affinities with Coleridge's 'Destiny of Nations' 1795 and Chapter 13 of *Biographia*.

Keats relies upon the shared Romantic concepts of 'oneness' and 'loss of self'. Wordsworth loses bodily awareness and becomes 'a living soul' in 'Tintern Abbey' which had drawn its 'more theological moments' from Coleridge's 'Religious Musings'. Differences of rhetoric conceal positions that are shared. Keats is drawn to 'a sort of oneness' that has an equivalent in Blake of 'fourfold vision' and that Coleridge presents in 'Frost at Midnight' and Wordsworth in 'The Pedlar', Shelley in 'Adonais' and Byron, briefly, in 'Childe Harold'.

In 'Double Bicentenary', there is an account of how, in part, Romanticism evolved in Britain and an explanation of the central importance of Macpherson's Ossian and Burns both of whom died in 1796. There is an assessment of popular reading of the time. Then we are offered a definition of Romanticism: 'the full flowering...of the quest for origins and abiding human values that is implied in eighteenth century primitivism...asserting the simple, the permanent and the sublime'.

Why was Macpherson's Ossian so popular? Hazlitt, despite knowing it was fake, described it as 'a feeling and a name that can never be destroyed'. It is suggested that success was founded on the tone of 'tender melancholy', on its primitivism and, with the Scots, because it was a national epic. Hugh Blair authenticates the fake and advocated its tenderness and sublimity. David Hume was reluctant to declare it ungenuine because it exhibited the 'highest beauties' and had 'enthusiasm and vehemence'. Even the young Wordsworth was charmed by it.

But the adult Wordsworth could not accept it. In Nature 'everything is distinct' and nothing is defined or obvious. In Ossian it is the reverse! Dr Johnson researched the claim that Ossian is ancient Scots epic on his tour of the Western Isles but could not find proof of authenticity putting the claims down to absurd Scots pride. Scott on behalf of the Highland Committee undertakes a full examination of the evidence but cannot support Macpherson's claims though remains proud of Ossian's international influence. Its success, despite being a fake, was because it expressed that need of the moment to go back to a fresher primitive voice in poetry.

It was left to Burns however to provide the literary lift exploited by Wordsworth. Blair's influential *Lectures* advocated poetry as song, as the language of passion, the native effusions of the heart (Lecture thirty five). The earlier the poetry was written the greater the fidelity to the emotion expressed. This contrasted with many contemporary poets composing 'coolly in their closets'. But Blair, we are told, is always looking backward, regarding the greatest poetry to have been written before civilization. Burns is 'a striking example of native genius bursting through the obscurity of poverty and the obstructions of labouring life' and brings primitivism up to date.

Just over a decade after Burns's first edition, Wordsworth, who probably knew a great deal of Burns by heart, is writing 'The Ruined Cottage' and about 'low and rustic life' (with indebtedness to Blair) and 'The Pedlar', 'his eye flashing fire he would repeat the songs of Burns'. Coleridge had taken Blair's lectures out of the Bristol Public Library. Blair had offered the theoretical basis of the Preface and Burns an example of the poetry of ordinariness lit by 'a spark of nature's fire'.

The timing of these influences had been critical; all seemed convergent on that important Wordsworthian year of 1797-8.

'The Doors of Perception' is a far ranging discussion on the nature of Romanticism and the Romantic imagination. The lecture is concerned with what the great writers of the period have in common. Blake's statement ('If the doors of perception were cleansed every thing would appear to man as it is: infinite) is 'pure Platonism' where two worlds are implied; the world of pure spirit from which we are barred by our limited sensual perception and the lower world which we in fact inhabit. Blake suggests we can remove the barrier and access the world of pure spirit. These words from 1790, it is argued, 'offer the first great definition of Romantic Imagination', which Wordsworth referred to as 'another name for absolute strength / And clearest insight' (*Prelude* XIII 168-9), which Coleridge in *Biographia* claims enables us 'to lose and find all self in God' and which Shelley in *Defence of Poetry* sees as 'the interpenetration of a diviner nature through our own'.

But there are many different forms of Platonism. Blake, in the 'Marriage' playfully denies (Plate 14) that 'man has a body distinct from his soul'. His view is that man is a spiritual being which he would know if he had not closed himself up and limited his sensual perception. Man should be able to see the infinite but has accepted limitation. Improved sensual enjoyment leads directly to the cleansing of the 'doors' of imagination leading to the return to an earlier unfallen state in which the senses were expansive, 'all-flexible' (*Urizen* Plate 3).

The Millenium underlies the optimism of Romanticism. Belief in it was widespread despite established theories of evolution. Archbishop Ussher's arithmetic placed the creation of the world at 4004 B.C. Since it was to last six thousand years, the Millenium (which was to herald in another one thousand years of Christ's reign on earth) would begin in 1996. Blake refers to it in the 'Marriage' (Plate 14) when the world will be 'consumed in fire at the end of six thousand years'. Cowper also refers to it in *The Task* (vi 729-736). Some thought events in America and France heralded the event. Wordsworth speaks movingly of the French Revolution; Hazlitt too writes of his youth when 'the sun of Liberty rose upon the sun of Life' and Southey wrote of it 'nothing was dreamt of but the regeneration of the human race'.

Coleridge conflated the Millenium with the French Revolution in 'Religious Musings'. Thinking in terms of the Book of Revelation, he sets out an apocalyptic vision of Christ's Second Coming together with a radical political agenda 'based on the sharing of love in hearts that are appropriately self-governed'. The Millenium will be a time of 'entering the state of pure intellect' which, it is argued, is akin to Blake's 'infinite'.

Thomas Taylor, the dominant Platonic voice of the time, believed that Platonism was 'coeval with the universe'. Blake 'probably' knew him personally; Coleridge noted his translations among his 'darling studies'. A wide range of writers of the time thought in terms of the 'infinite' (Goethe, Wollstonecraft, Madame Roland) and there were many places where readers could gain Platonic insights (Cudworth, Shaftesbury, Pope). Thomson anticipates Romantic Platonism in *The Seasons* 1730 ('Spring' 849-855) when he refers to God being the 'All-conscious Presence in the Universe / Nature's vast ever-acting Energy').

The conflict between Platonism and materialism is outlined. Priestley had offered a 'materialist Platonism': 'We have our existence in God as material beings powered by his energy'. Man is only body, matter, has no soul and no means of attaining the infinite except, at God's pleasure, he may rise from the dead. Keats's 'sparks of divinity, 'schooled' by suffering, offer a different form of the body-soul dualism; they have the capacity to become part of the 'infinite' – another form of Blake's 'cleansing' of the doors.

Coleridge's position is more complicated. In a letter to Southey he goes 'farther than Hartley and believe(s) in the corporeality of thought, namely that it is motion'. It is suggested that the idea featured in conversation at Alfoxden and is behind

Wordsworth's use of the word in 'Tintern Abbey' where the divine presence is said in part to be 'a motion and a spirit'; and further verbal correspondencies are noted.

Sensual awareness is for Wordsworth a first stage to perception of the divine life force in 'Tintern Abbey'. But for Coleridge it is a barrier; those who have been educated 'through the constant testimony of their senses…contemplate nothing but parts…the Universe to them is but a mass of little things'. Though Blake shares Coleridge's fear of smallness and division he saw, unlike Coleridge, sensual enjoyment as the means by which man could access the infinite.

All the cited writers and thinkers were Platonists in one form or another, all 'questing' for the oneness of existence, sometimes defined as 'beauty' or 'truth'. Wordsworth sometimes called it 'knowledge'. The exact nature of the term used does not matter. Imagination is that divine quality which enables man to glimpse the higher world. Two crucial concepts are 'loss of self' and 'creative perception' referred to, for example, in Coleridge's "Tis the sublime of man, / Our noontide Majesty to know ourselves / Parts and proportions of one wond'rous whole' ('Religious Musings' 131). No single definition suffices. But there are many examples; Wollstonecraft was able to 'supply' Nature with an 'animating soul' and thus 'converse with her God' and Shelley could write that the wind and melody of the flowing brooks and the rustling of the reeds beside them 'by their inconceivable relation to something within the soul awaken the spirits to a dance of breathless rapture….' (*On Love*)

'Two Strangers and a pair of wild eyes' not only entails a thorough and extended comparison of 'Frost at Midnight' with Coleridge's source, Cowper's 'Winter Evening' from *The Task*, but also shows how Coleridge expands his concerns beyond Cowper's into a demonstration of Fancy, the Secondary and then the

Primary Imagination at work (though these terms had not been forged in 1798).

Hazlitt remembered hearing Coleridge's sermon at Wem in January 1798, a month before the writing of 'Frost at Midnight' in which Coleridge speaks of the 'living spirit in our frame' transfusing into all its own delights, 'its own volition, sometimes with deep faith and sometimes with fantastic playfulness'. Poetry was the means by which he would make his Unitarian faith in the One Life within us and abroad available to others.

Cowper's 'frost', his playfully imagined houses and towers, the gloom which 'suits the thinking or unthinking mind', his 'stranger', the poet's self consciousness are all motifs of Coleridge's later poem. They become his own frost, 'this populous village', the solitude which suits abstruser musings, the stranger on the bars of the grate, and Coleridge's 'self-watching subtilizing mind'.

But new elements of memory and time enter 'Frost at Midnight'. Coleridge is able to 'transfuse' into the stranger (i.e. the 'film' on the grate) and convert it into a 'companionable form'; the moment is 'numinous'; 'hold commune' and 'dim sympathies' have a spiritual dimension. Coleridge begins with the transformation of nature with which Cowper closes. And unlike, Cowper, he has a child present.

The later 'Frost at Midnight' text is distinguished. The earlier self (1798) is generous, 'the living spirit in our frame' has a tendency to 'transfuse' its delights into other things. The later self (1834) is egotistical, moral and offers an 'uneasy companionship'.

Coleridge moves on from Cowper to make larger claims for the human mind and human imagination. The child's imaginative credentials become his subject. Association, which for Cowper had been arbitrary, becomes for Coleridge personal. From loneliness and superstition comes a faith which Cowper did not envisage. Memory provides reassurance. And the child by his side represents the future. Coleridge wants his child to know intuitively the 'eternal language of God'. Little Hartley becomes the spirit-child of his father's musings and a definition of the Imagination.

The three stages of the imagination, the Primary and Secondary Imaginations and Fancy, cited in *Biographia* in descending order – are depicted in the poem in ascending order – from 'fantastic playfulness' to deep faith to transfusing into an ordinary child a perception of the Oneness of Nature of Coleridge's Unitarian creed. Coleridge borrows the concept of 'ministry' from Cowper who had implied a Director into the natural world and turned the snow into a blessing which offered tenderness and a sharing at the personal level. Coleridge has adopted a 'priestlike' role in addressing the child Hartley whose spirit God would mould with the gift of imaginative sharing in the One Life.

At the end of the poem Coleridge is still working with his source in the verbal echo 'pendulous'. But the identity of Hartley is the dominant closing idea; though he has been depicted as Coleridge's spirit-child he is also afforded the status of being an entirely free self.

'Blake and the Imagination' begins by informing us that Blake has his own 'theory' of Imagination. Students tend to head for Coleridge's *Biographia* (1817) when they want a definition or possibly Wordsworth's *Preludes* or Keats's Adam's dream or Shelley's 'Mont Blanc'. Though Blake is often ignored, he had a clear idea of the Imagination earlier than any of the other major poets and which, by remarkable coincidence since his works were largely unknown, is resembled by them.

In 'The Marriage' (1790) at Blake's dinner party we hear that man ought to be able to be part of the infinite but has willfully condemned himself to live in the cavern of his skull; unlike Isaiah and Ezekiel his senses need cleansing and thus cannot perceive eternity. *Europe* (1794) is more optimistic; the Fairy, who goes on to dictate the poem, observes something similar except that the senses are described as 'windows' through which man might escape from mortality by apprehending the infinite. The Fairy has 'knowledge', a vision of eternity, and commands respect as a supernatural being. Blake's question - what is the material world and is it alive? - causes the Fairy to respond that every particle of dust breathes forth its joy. Parallels are cited; Wordsworth's 'every flower / Enjoys the air it breathes' and the Pedlar's 'in all things / He saw one life and felt that it was joy'; Coleridge is concerned with the same question 1794-5 and in 'The Ancient Mariner' 1797-8; Shelley is drawn to an 'active universe' and Byron and Keats 'turn over the possibilities'. But here Blake insists that man's limitation is self-willed; humanity has a preference for the 'fallen' because 'stolen joys are sweet….and bread eaten in secret pleasant'!

Passages from *Milton* (1802-3) show how time can be reassessed, not as the passage of moments which confirm our mortality but as a means of imaginatively accessing eternity; the lark rising from the cornfield and disappearing into the sky in song is symbolic of the capacity of imaginative man to raise himself up and grasp eternal truths: it is a 'moment' when time and eternity touch.

Milton seeks 'self-annihilation' which means both that he himself will be doing the annihilating and that he will be annihilating himself because he must rid himself of 'selfhood'. Coleridge had been concerned in 'Religious Musings' with the isolated 'smooth savage'; 'sacred sympathy' was an imaginative path through life which would enable man to escape that confinement.

In the last of the selected passages, from *Jerusalem*, Blake observes that eighteenth century rationalism and unimaginative artistry are the 'destroyers of Jerusalem'. Imagination is for Blake the 'Divine Body of Jesus'. Affinities with Coleridge are observed whilst carefully distinguishing him.

In **'Wordsworthian Transformations; The Pitcher at the Fountain'** the 'pitcher at the fountain' and the 'golden bowl' (from *Ecclesiastes* 12:6) are transformed into the 'fragment of a wooden bowl' in 'The Ruined Cottage'. The biblical sublime is recreated on a domestic level; or is 'naturalised'. Broken bowl and well suggest life cut off at its source; formerly they had possessed a social function of 'ministering' refreshment to passers-by. The bowl is almost a chalice and the water a sacrament.

There is also transformation of epic. In *Paradise Lost* (Bk IX) Eve is seen to be stooping 'to support / Each flower of slender stalk' and is described as 'fairest unsupported flower / From her best prop so far'. This is transformed into the garden of 'The Ruined Cottage' where Margaret herself is suggested in the lines '...unwieldy wreathes / Had dragged the rose from its sustaining wall / And bent it down to earth'. The imagery of the immense conception of The Fall of Man is used to evoke the pathos of a cottage woman.

In 'The Thorn', Burger's Gothic tale 'The Lass of Fair Wone' is transformed into an associationist poem *inter alia* in which Wordsworth explores mental process and how the mind returns obsessionally to what De Quincey termed its 'involutes'. In considering the thorn tree, Wordsworth wished to make it 'permanently an impressive object'. The two cardinal points of poetry from *Biographia* (Chap XIV)(exciting sympathy by faithful adherence to the truth of nature and creating 'novelty' by the modifying colours of the imagination) can be combined by weather ('accidents of light and shade', moonlight , sunset diffused over a familiar landscape). Weather is 'analagous' to the imagination; each has transforming power. There is an extended discussion of how 'The Thorn' transforms its Gothic source.

In 'Lucy Gray' 'the wild' seems to have been transformed from an ordinary heathland into another realm of experience. Lucy becomes, like the girl on Penrith beacon with the pitcher on her head, 'a lovely apparition, ghostlike'. Momentarily she is associated with 'the fawn at play' or the 'hair upon the green'. The dawn and the day-moon are significant. We are invited to see the child as an act of imagination. By the end of the poem the 'identity' of Lucy has been through many transformations beginning with a girl seen while the poet was crossing the wild and ending with an existence as a kind of 'solitary song', which in itself transforms into the 'whistling' in the wind. Wordsworth has also transformed his source, the Halifax anecdote told him by Dorothy, in 'spiritualising' the character.

In 'The Immortality Ode', 'simple' childhood experience is transformed into a sacred time. Wordsworth presents childhood in biblical terms; 'common sights' were for him 'apparelled in celestial light'. Simple childhood is not celebrated; thanks are not given for 'delight', 'liberty' and 'new-born hope'. Instead childhood is transformed into and presented as a time when pain and fear are central to the child-poet's education. The boy Wordsworth experiences 'blank misgivings', 'fallings from us', vanishings'; the Fenwick note is introduced as clarification that these are times when he fell into 'an abyss of idealism' and needed to grasp a wall or tree ('the ballast of familiar life') to 'recall' reality. The boat stealing episode (from *Prelude* 1799 i 119-29) is related where that experience leads to 'darkness', 'solitude', 'blank desertion'. 'Blank misgivings' are further transformed in 'The Ode' into 'High instincts'; the image of Hamlet's guilty surprised father features in the background. The prevalence of light imagery is discussed, as is the image of the 'fountain'. The last transformation is of the poem itself as the poetry is lifted into 'a quite different realm of experience', talking in terms of the 'purely numinous'.

'Understanding Blake: *The First Book of Urizen*' is an example of how we might read Blake as a whole. Blake poses special problems and we are not helped in that he despises consistency. In his most difficult works we are rarely certain of interpretation; we proceed through parallels and recognitions. How can we understand his relationship with the Divine? The lyric Blake of The Songs of Innocence and Experience offers beauty we recognize but how do we value the more difficult prophecies which make fewer and fewer concessions to their audience when easier, more attractive features of the poetry are left behind?

Urizen (1794) is written between the *Songs* and the starting point for the great prophecies (1797). The poem demonstrates a series of evolutions; of the character (a not wholly appropriate term) of Urizen, the hero (a similarly inappropriate term); of Blake's myth of the Fall into Creation; of the human form and the globe of earth; of sexual division and of the 'Net of Religion'.

Satan's Fall in *Paradise Lost* is distinguished. Milton had placed it in the context of time passing, as part of human history, and thus was able to structure his poem as narrative. Blake goes further back, placing the Fall of Urizen before time, where it should be, in the mind of God. Urizen, originally part of the divine Mind (collectively 'the Eternals') splits himself off, is 'brooding', 'unprolific, self-closed, all-repelling'. In wrenching himself away he splits the Divine Mind and irreversibly self-wounds. In doing so he transmutes into landscape ('desolate mountains') which can speak; into priest/prophet establishing a kind of Mosaic Law; into sulphurous liquid.

Having divided the Eternal Mind he then self-divides. The

Romantics have it in common that they strive for wholeness, oneness. But 'Times on times he divided'. The attempt to contain division and restore unity becomes a central theme. In the 'character' of Los, the blacksmith, Blake introduces the means by which Urizen is to be contained. Los embraces Imagination and is ranged against Urizen who represents reason.

The poetry becomes openly satirical. Urizen challenges the Eternals and becomes a parody of the Holy Spirit (from *Paradise Lost* Bk. I) brooding over chaos. The Primeval Priest, Urizen, mimics Moses laying down the Seven Deadly Sins as he unfolds darkness with the 'Book of eternal brass' containing laws of 'peace, of love, of unity'. As he does so, Earth is severed from Eternity ('Eternity rolled wide apart / Wide asunder rolling').

As a defence to the Eternals' anger Urizen hides by digging mountains; then he creates the globe of earth with 'rivers in veins / Of blood' pouring down the mountains which appears to the Eternals as a 'black globe' 'like a human heart, struggling and beating'. Urizen's fall is seen as Creation. Urizen has made and/or turned into the earth itself. Los, an unfallen Eternal, forges new chains and numbers the links as 'hours, days and years' denoting how the fallen world is now subject to time.

The second major Fall is productive of the human form. Los binds Urizen's changes with rivets of iron and brass. The process is presented to us as a parody of the seven days of Creation. The chains and rivets form a vast spine with ribs, so that the 'chain' of time is associated with the 'chain' of the human body. Then the heart, eyes, ears, nostrils and stomach are created ending with the legs and arms.

The third major Fall is productive of sexual division. Los falls this time through pity at Urizen's enchainment. Pity produces division in Los who becomes human and thus creates the female principle, Enitharmon, who becomes pregnant producing Orc. The

Fall is thereby perpetuated; each generation 'will now mark a further stage from the original harmony'. At some point Enitharmon is a form of Nature; Orc digs his way to the surface of the earth (replicating the child's emergence from the mother's womb and the worm's coming to the surface of the soil) as he is born and simultaneously kinds of fish, bird and beast also give birth.

The poem ends with Los's Oedipal jealousy of his son Orc who is chained to the top of a mountain beneath Urizen's shadow. Enitharmon bears an enormous race which Urizen curses because he knows he can devise no law which can contain flesh and spirit. Urizen's last bequest to his children beyond the fact that life lives upon death is the 'Net of Religion' which is said to be so 'suited to humanity that its cords and meshes are knotted like to the human heart', or a spider's web.

By the end of this commentary, Jonathan Wordsworth has not only engaged us with some of the most vivid imagery of the book but has shown us ways of interpreting it. Logical questions rightly asked but which have no answers (such as when or where is this taking place?) are not allowed to frustrate our understanding of 'characters' 'concepts' or 'events' even though there is no normal narrative sequence or consistent representation.

ACKNOWLEDGEMENTS

I wish to thank the following: Jessica Wordsworth for permission to publish the lectures; David Wilson former Director of The Wordsworth Trust for early discussions and support; Jeff Cowton and The Wordsworth Trust at Grasmere for kindly allowing me access to the recordings from their Library; Geoffrey Blake for making the original recordings. Thanks are due additionally to Duncan Wu who has given encouragement and guidance throughout the long process of this book's gestation; also to David Chandler and Paul Betz whose enthusiasms for the project were equally undimmed. Thanks also to Thomas Haynes who suggested the title and H.H. for constantly supporting, questioning and correcting and saving me from countless infelicities. All remaining mistakes are of my own making.

ABBREVIATIONS

Allott	*Keats The Complete Poems* ed. Miriam Allott (Longman 1970, fifth impression 1980)
BL	*Biographia Literaria: The Collected Works of Samuel Taylor Coleridge 7* ed. James Engell and W. Jackson Bate; Bollingen Series lxxv (Princeton 1983)
BOV	*William Wordsworth: The Borders of Vision* by Jonathan Wordsworth (Clarendon Oxford 1982, reprinted 1984)
Byron	*Byron Poetical Works* Oxford Standard Authors (Oxford 1967)

Cornell Ex	*The Excursion by William Wordsworth* ed. Sally Bushell, James A. Butler and Michael C. Jaye with the assistance of David Garcia (Cornell 2007)
Cornell LB	*Lyrical Ballads and Other Poems 1797-1800* ed. James Butler and Karen Green (Cornell 1992)
Cornell 2 Vol	*Poems in Two Volumes and Other Poems 1800-1807* ed. Jared Curtis (Cornell 1983)
EHC	*Coleridge : Poetical Works* ed. Ernest Hartley Coleridge : (London, OUP 1912 reprinted 1967)
Erdman	*The Complete Poetry and Prose of William Blake* Newly Revised Edition ed. David V. Erdman (Anchor Books 1988)
Ex.Woodstock	*William Wordsworth: The Excursion 1814* Facsimile edition (Woodstock Books, Oxford and New York 1991)
EY	*The Letters of William and Dorothy Wordsworth* ed. E. de Selincourt, 2nd edn., *The Early Years* revised by Chester L. Shaver (Clarendon Oxford 1967 reprinted 2000)
Fowler	*Paradise Lost* ed. Alastair Fowler (Longman 1971 republished 1984)
Griggs	*The Collected Letters of Samuel Taylor*

	Coleridge ed. E. L. Griggs (6 vols., Oxford 1956-71)
Hutchinson	*Shelley Poetical Works* ed. Thomas Hutchinson (Oxford 1968)
FN	*The Fenwick Notes of William Wordsworth* ed. Jared Curtis (London 1993)
FT	William Wordsworth, *The Prelude: The Four Texts 1798, 1799, 1805, 1850* ed. Jonathan Wordsworth (Penguin 1995)
JDW	*Journals of Dorothy Wordsworth* ed. E. de Selincourt 2 vols (London MacMillan 1952)
KJV	*Holy Bible*, King James Version
Lamb L	*The Letters of Charles and Mary Ann Lamb* ed. Edwin W. Marrs 2 vols. (Ithaca, New York, Cornell University Press 1975)
LB 1798 & 1800	*Lyrical Ballads 1798* William Wordsworth and Samuel Taylor Coleridge (Woodstock 2002); *Lyrical Ballads 1800* (Woodstock 1997)
MM	*William Wordsworth: A Biography* by Mary Moorman (2 vols. (Oxford 1957 reprinted 1967)
MOH	*The Music of Humanity* by Jonathan Wordsworth (Nelson 1969)
Norton	*The Prelude 1799 1805 1850* William

	Wordsworth ed. Jonathan Wordsworth, M. H. Abrams and Stephen Gill Norton and Company (New York 1979)
OS	*The Prose Works of William Wordsworth* ed. W. J. B. Owen and Jane Worthington Smyser (3 vols. Oxford 1974)
Penguin Romantic Poetry	*The New Penguin Book of Romantic Poetry* ed. Jonathan and Jessica Wordsworth (Penguin 2001)
PW	*Wordsworth's Poetical Works* ed. E. de Selincourt (5 vols Oxford 1940 reprinted 1963)
Rollins	*The Letters of John Keats* ed. Hyder Edward Rollins (2 vols Cambridge 1958)
STC I and II	*Coleridge Collected Works 16* ed. J.C.C. Mayes; Bollingen. *Poetical Works 1 Poems* (Reading Text) 2 vols. and *Poetical Works II Poems* (Variorum Text) 2 vols. (Princeton 2001)
Ward	Thomas de Quincey *Confessions of an English Opium Eater and Other Writings*, ed. Aileen Ward (New York 1966)
WC	*The Poems of William Cowper* ed. Baird and Ryskamp 3 vols. (Oxford 1980-95)
WS	*The Collected Poems of Wallace Stevens* (New York 1968)

Wu(1)   *The Selected Writings of William Hazlitt* ed. Duncan Wu 9 vols. (London 1998)

Wu(2)   *Romanticism: An Anthology* ed. Duncan Wu 3rd edn. (Blackwell 2006)

1   REVOLUTIONARY WORDSWORTH[1]

In Book X of *The Prelude*, Wordsworth is on his way home in September/October 1792. He is in a splendid Parisian mansion, up near the roof, a place which he says would have pleased him in different times and wasn't wholly without pleasure on this occasion. But it is a place of terror. The Revolution in which he passionately believes has turned, after a surprisingly long time, to violence. The French Revolution was initially peaceful and constitutional, in spite of the storming of the Bastille in which its commander was nastily killed. Its early history saw very little bloodshed. Two months before Wordsworth's return to Paris from Blois and Orleans, however, it had got out of hand. He is looking back now over recent events, particularly the September Massacres when the prisoners of Paris were summarily executed in barbarous acts of mob justice. There were prisoners of both sexes, largely innocent of any crime against the Revolution, though many were ordinary criminals.

He is in Dove cottage or the woods nearby in 1804, as he writes on this time in Paris:

> My room was high and lonely, near the roof
>
> Of a large mansion or hotel, a spot

---

[1] First delivered as a lecture to The Wordsworth Winter School 1989

That would have pleased me in more quiet times –

Nor was it wholly without pleasure then.

With unextinguished taper I kept watch,

Reading at intervals. The fear gone by

Pressed on me almost like a fear to come.

I thought of those September massacres,

Divided from me by a little month,

And felt and touched them, a substantial dread ...

'The horse is taught his manage, and the wind

Of heaven wheels round and treads in his own

                                                    steps;

Year follows year, the tide returns again,

Day follows day, all things have second birth;

The earthquake is not satisfied at once!'

And in such way I wrought upon myself

Until I seemed to hear a voice that cried

To the whole city 'Sleep no more!' To this

Add comments of a calmer mind, from which

I could not gather full security,

But at the best it seemed a place of fear

> Unfit for the repose of night,
>
> Defenceless as a wood where tigers roam. [2]

The voice is apocalyptic or prophetic and the last image is quite unlike anything else in Wordsworth. He is a revolutionary poet in many ways, the most important of which was his ability to make extraordinary poetry out of ordinary events in what was, in many ways, a very ordinary life. But occasionally he creates poetry not based on everyday experience.

I shall start by looking at the political Wordsworth. The 'wood where tigers roam' is a moment of heightened imagination that is appropriate to this unusual experience. Thinking of that September's events, he produces an extraordinary image; he holds his hand out; he feels and touches them, 'a substantial dread'. Wordsworth often demonstrates his sense of the substance, of the corporeality, of emotion, in this case of 'dread'. He can feel things, for instance, with a 'weight of pleasure'[3]. Like doubting Thomas, he reaches out to touch the Revolution with this appalling 'dread' of what has become of the beautiful and inspiring thing that he has believed in. The lines that follow are based on the behaviour of a horse, the steps taught in a riding school. The urgency and grandeur of his thinking is important as he tells us of his dread that once the Revolution has turned to bloodshed, it will become recurrent, cyclical[4]. We are inside the

---

[2] *Prelude* 1805 X 57-82; FT 400-402
[3] *Prelude* 1805 II 178; FT 82-4
[4] 'Reliving his substantial dread of the Massacres, Wordsworth produces five sudden purely apocalyptic lines of interior monologue that are quite unlike anything else he ever wrote…The horse is schooled by man against its nature to turn upon the spot (as Danton may induce spontaneous bloodshed to come round), and 'the wind of heaven', that should be freer still, wheels in its steps, constricted to the movements of a horse. In his nightmare reverie the poet can turn anything to evidence of cyclical return. Years, tides, days, add their more

mind of the poet Wordsworth in 1804 looking back inside the mind of the poet Wordsworth in Paris in October 1792. This is all, in many ways, revolutionary. No poet had been able to write like this, indeed none ever has since.

It is necessary to stay with the political scene to substantiate the overall pattern I wish to make. This is Wordsworth's second visit to France. The first which he looks back on is the visit when he lands in France at Calais on July 13th 1790. It is his last long vacation at Cambridge. He is setting out on a great tour that takes him through France and the Alps and back again in a journey of six weeks largely on foot. He lands in France on the day before the anniversary of the fall of the Bastille. It seems quite extraordinary, but nothing he tells us – and he is our only informant as to most of this – suggests that he chose to do so or that he had a considerable interest in politics at this moment. Looking back though, he offers us 'Bliss was it in that dawn to be alive / But to be young was very heaven!'[5] and from Book VI:

> But 'twas a time when Europe was rejoiced,
>
> France standing on the top of golden hours
>
> And human nature seeming born again.[6]

It wasn't just the poet's sensibility that made him sense the Revolution as beautiful and moving; many experienced it. As Southey put it, looking back in 1824, 'Old things seemed passing away and nothing was dreamt of but the regeneration of the

---

obvious corroboration, till the argument so commonly and tendentiously used for the Christian afterlife ('all things have second birth') betrays us suddenly into the power of insatiable violence: 'The earthquake is not satisfied at once'. (BOV 254)

[5] *Prelude* 1805 X 692-3; FT 440
[6] Ibid VI 352-5; FT 226

human race'[7]. Its tone might be mildly ironic because of its hindsight, but it was serious.

> Bound, as I said, to the Alps, it was our lot
>
> To land at Calais on the very eve
>
> Of that great federal day; and there we saw,
>
> In a mean city and among a few,
>
> How bright a face is worn when joy of one
>
> Is joy of tens of millions. Southward thence
>
> We took our way, direct through hamlets, towns,
>
> Gaudy with relics of that festival,
>
> Flowers left to wither on triumphal arcs,
>
> And window-garlands. On the public roads –
>
> And once, three days successively, through paths
>
> By which our toilsome journey was abridged –
>
> Among sequestered villages we walked
>
> And found benevolence and blessedness
>
> Spread like a fragrance everywhere[8]

This is the mood of a moment. Looking back, it had its political dangers. The 'great federal day' was when the King took a pledge

---

[7] *The Correspondence of Robert Southey with Caroline Bowles*, ed. Edward Dowden (Dublin, 1881) 52.
[8] *Prelude* 1805 VI 355-369; FT 226

of allegiance to the new constitution at the Fete de la Federation in Paris at the Champ de Mars. It was a day of public rejoicings as Wordsworth and his student friend Jones walked through France. The treacherous king had signed an oath which bound him to act constitutionally but had no wish to do so and his wife, Marie Antoinette, daughter of the House of Austria, could bring the armies of powerful relations to the banks of the Rhine to besiege France. The King and royal family later make a desperate attempt to reach that boundary and are brought back in ignominy. Though the situation looks optimistic, there are major political problems.

At this stage (December 1791) Wordsworth goes to Paris and pockets a relic of the Bastille. This is Wordsworth as tourist!

> Where silent zephyrs sported with the dust
>
> Of the Bastille I sat in the open sun,
>
> And from the rubbish gathered up a stone
>
> And pocketed the relic in the guise
>
> Of an enthusiast;[9]

Wordsworth can be humorous and extremely self-knowing. He understands exactly the sort of empty gesture he was originally making. He was doing the Revolutionary sights;

> ...yet, in honest truth,
>
> Though not without some strong incumbences,
>
> And glad – could living men be otherwise? –
>
> I looked for something which I could not find

---

[9] Ibid. IX 63-7; FT 350

> Affecting more emotion than I felt.[10]

It is precise, witty poetry. Wordsworth doesn't talk about 'silent zephyrs' meaning the winds sporting with stones; he talks about rocks and stones and trees in quite another voice. This is playful, more like the Pope of the *Rape of the Lock*. He is deliberately using eighteenth century diction to mock gently his former self, just to show the emptiness of the tourist's feeling about the Revolution's great events. As a young British tourist, he did not yet care.

Wordsworth mixed with military officers at Blois. The army, though subject now to the constitution, is royalist and has royalist officers who are therefore divided in their loyalties. There comes a moment when it is necessary to let them leave France for the Rhine, even if they come back with invading troops, rather than have them stay. It is a curious turning of the tide but importantly Wordsworth found among those stationed at Blois just one with whom he could talk. Wordsworth's 'revolutions' depend above all on something within himself. On the other hand, several people exerted influence on his life – an influence you could term 'revolutionary'. One is Michel Beaupuy who is a member of the nobility and an army officer and might thus be expected to be a royalist. But he believes in the Revolution. From him Wordsworth learns to see the Revolution for what it is and for what it might have been:

> Among that band of officers was one,
>
> Already hinted at, of other mould –
>
> A patriot, thence rejected by the rest...[11]

---

[10]Ibid. IX 67-71

>   And when we chanced
>
>   One day to meet a hunger-bitten girl,
>
> [they are walking along the Loire]
>
>   Who crept along fitting her languid self
>
>   Unto a heifer's motion – by a cord
>
>   Tied to her arm, and picking thus from the lane
>
>   Its sustenance, while the girl with her two hands
>
>   Was busy knitting in a heartless mood
>
>   Of solitude – and at the sight my friend
>
>   In agitation said, "Tis against *that*
>
>   Which we are fighting!' I with him believed
>
>   Devoutly that a spirit was abroad
>
>   Which could not be withstood; that poverty,
>
>   At least like this, would in a little time
>
>   Be found no more; that we should see the earth
>
>   Unthwarted in her wish to recompense
>
>   The industrious and the lowly child of toil
>
>   (All institutes for ever blotted out
>
>   That legalized exclusion, empty pomp

---

[11] Ibid. IX 294-6; FT 362

> Abolished, sensual state and cruel power,
>
> Whether by edict of the one or few);
>
> And finally, as sum and crown of all,
>
> Should see the people having a strong hand
>
> In making their own laws – whence better days
>
> To all mankind.[12]

It is important to notice the origin of this passionate political statement. Wordsworth (at twenty one, possibly twenty two) is deeply influenced by friendship with Beaupuy, who is considerably older at thirty-two. Beaupuy is offering him the idealism of the Revolution. But what Wordsworth remembers of the moment (a 'spot of time' if you like in the context of the *Prelude*) is that he is personally confronted by individual human suffering, or as he puts it in the 'Prospectus', it is the human being piping 'solitary anguish'[13] that touches Wordsworth's heart and which through his poetry so often touches ours. His great political passion is that the individual shall be able to lead the life which seems happy and useful. They are quite humble objectives but they have a grandeur in the larger context. The girl is starving, leading a heifer along a lane where it can get a great deal of good food because it is spring or early summer. She on the other hand is getting very little. She is in a heartless mood, lonely, knitting, indifferent and 'hunger-bitten'. It prompts Beaupuy into the statement ''Tis against *that* / Which we are fighting' and it prompts Wordsworth all that time later to look back on his former self and give him utterly his due. It is sometimes argued that

---

[12] Ibid IX 512-34; FT 374
[13] 'Prospectus to the Recluse' l.77. Cornell Ex 40

Wordsworth changed and by 1804 was no longer a believer in the Revolution. It is true but only in the sense that nobody could have been; it was impossible to be a believer in the French Revolution in 1804. Nevertheless, he continued to be a believer in the Revolutionary spirit as it had originally touched him. It was a deep and passionate humanitarian concern.

I wish to refer to two more important passages from the *Prelude*. In the first, Wordsworth talks of his harsh predicament when back in London, probably in early December 1792. His personal position is that he is separated from Annette Vallon and their child Caroline who by now has been born and baptised in Orleans Cathedral in her father's absence. Wordsworth had left France in a worsening political situation. Englishmen in Paris were being arrested and, as a result of the September Massacres, the bloodthirsty side of the Jacobins was getting the upper hand. On the 21st January 1793 Louis XVI is guillotined. At that moment political loyalties split. Wordsworth was back in England in 1792. In this context he publishes two poems – probably updating them considerably, *An Evening Walk* and *Descriptive Sketches*. His next writing though is entirely political. It is *A Letter to the Bishop of Llandaff* which he doesn't publish – possibly due to his publisher, Joseph Johnson. In it Wordsworth was prepared to say that the execution of the King of France was a necessary event. He lines himself up with the position Milton would certainly have taken in 1649, not as active regicide but one who thought that a Revolution which was to bring about the happiness of mankind might require initial violence. Wordsworth's reasoning for that position was that there was no time to educate people to receive power. But as he watched from England he must have, following the period January 1793 (execution of Louis XVI), gradually become aware that the cause in which he had so passionately believed was in fact lost. But he does not surrender it.

The next passage, belonging probably to 1794, shows him of all places in church – a symbol of community – sitting alone 'like an uninvited guest / Whom no one owned'. He is politically contaminated, has endured the revolutionary experience but everyone else has the innocence which can lead them to pray for British victories. He is forced to pray for French victory against his own people hoping it would lead to revolution in England and thus bring about happiness in both countries. It is a stern test of his belief in the possibility of a benign revolution:

>   I who with the breeze
>
> Had played, a green leaf on the blessed tree
>
> Of my beloved country – nor had wished
>
> For happier fortune than to wither there –
>
> Now from my pleasant station was cut off
>
> And tossed about in whirlwinds. I rejoiced,
>
> Yes, afterwards (truth painful to record)
>
> Exulted in the triumph of my soul
>
> When Englishmen by thousands were o'erthrown,
>
> Left without glory on the field, or driven,
>
> Brave hearts, to shameful flight. It was a grief –
>
> Grief call it not, 'twas anything but that –
>
> A conflict of sensations without name,

> Of which he only who may love the sight
>
> Of a village-steeple as I do can judge,
>
> When in the congregation bending all
>
> To their great Father, prayers were offered up
>
> Or praises for our country's victories,
>
> And, mid the simple worshippers perchance
>
> I only, like an uninvited guest
>
> Whom no one owned, sat silent – shall I add,
>
> Fed on the day of vengeance yet to come![14]

He has, as Keats said, this capacity to 'think into the human heart'[15] as Milton did not; but not just into the human heart, he thinks into extraordinarily conflicting human emotions in different situations and with a passionate truth and intensity which is unparalleled. Here we have him quite clear in 1804 that he was, ten years earlier, feeding on the day of vengeance *against* his own country.

It was not to be. Those lines concern the end of 1794. In the late summer of that year, Robespierre had been guillotined and in the following passage of the *Prelude* Wordsworth tells of his 'glee…/ In vengeance and eternal justice'[16]. He hears of the death of Robespierre as he is crossing Morecambe Sands. 'Glee'

---

[14] *Prelude* 1805 X 253-74; FT 414
[15] Keats's letter to Reynolds 3rd May 1818. Rollins i 282 Letter 80
[16] Great was my glee of spirit, great my joy
  In vengeance, and eternal justice, thus
  Made manifest.   *Prelude* 1805 X 539-11; FT 430

indicates no sympathy or compassion for Robespierre; it is glee in eternal justice and 'vengeance' precedes 'justice'. At that moment, he hopes the Revolution will revert to its proper course in the hands of the Girondins[17]. But it turns France into an aggressive and imperialist nation. British radicals could still sympathize with the principles of the French. But they couldn't any longer say that the Revolution had got into the wrong hands because Robespierre and followers were now dead. Wordsworth and other radicals are gradually forced to withdraw sympathy for France as a political fact. France as a symbol, an embodiment of a powerful political hope, could still continue.

In the Spring of 1796 Wordsworth experiences something which might normally referred to as a nervous breakdown. But we only know what he tells us and the letters of this period give no indication of this kind. He has been at Racedown for about six months, a beautiful house in West Dorset and is with Dorothy; they are poor, but happy in broad terms. But Wordsworth cannot be entirely happy with a merely personal situation. He is trying to reconcile political events with his own ideals and is forced into a painful confusion about moral values. My suspicion is that a catalyst for this is a reading of the second edition of Godwin's *Political Justice* (1796):

Time may come

When some dramatic story may afford

Shapes livelier to convey to thee, my friend,

What then I learned, or think I learned, of truth,

---

[17] Their madness is declared and visible—
Elsewhere will safety now be sought, and earth
March firmly towards righteousness and peace.   ibid 550-2.

> And the errors into which I was betrayed
>
> By present objects, and by reasonings false
>
> From the beginning, inasmuch as drawn
>
> Out of a heart which had been turned aside
>
> From nature by external accidents,
>
> And which was thus confounded more and more
>
> Misguiding and misguided.[18]

The heart itself is 'misguiding' him – a very strange thing for Wordsworth to admit or to see within himself. He is 'misguided', I take it, by William Godwin who had offered an extreme form of rationalism welcomed by many English radicals after the execution of Louis XV1th. The book was published exactly at that moment in February 1793 (first edition) and seemed to offer reason why the human race was going to be all right in the longer run. It offered an innate rationality as the cornerstone of future progress. People grasped at it because the political situation was so bad. Wordsworth seems to have believed in it particularly as things got out of hand at the death of Robespierre late in 1794. At this stage he meets Godwin about ten times, though there is no record of their talks. The important fact here is that Wordsworth has turned aside from Nature briefly. He has believed that the human mind is capable of an abstract rather than an intuitive 'reason', which is a higher imaginative form of feeling, a kind of very Wordsworthian sympathy, and which is the support of his greatest poetry. When Wordsworth speaks of 'my friend', it is Coleridge. And he is speaking of the period after the Revolution

---

[18] *Prelude* 1805 X 878-888; FT 450

when he refers to the time when he learned, or thought he learned, of truth. 'Reasonings false / From the beginning' are probably Godwinian reasonings.

Wordsworth continues with the extended metaphor – one of the grandest he ever used, – of the moment at which he hails his emotions to the Bar, treats them as culprits, asking them to establish their credentials. This is 'reason' sitting as judge over his emotions, with disastrous results:

> Thus I fared,
>
> Dragging all passions, notions, shapes of faith,
>
> Like culprits to the bar; suspiciously
>
> Calling the mind to establish in plain day
>
> Her titles and her honours; now believing,
>
> Now disbelieving; endlessly perplexed
>
> With impulse, motive, right and wrong, the ground
>
> Of moral obligation – what the rule,
>
> And what the sanction – till, demanding proof,
>
> And seeking it in everything, I lost
>
> All feeling of conviction, and (in fine)
>
> Sick, wearied out with contrarieties,
>
> Yielded up moral questions in despair,
>
> And for my future studies, as the sole

Employment of the enquiring faculty,

Turned towards mathematics, and their clear

And solid evidence. Ah, then it was

That thou, most precious friend – about this time

First known to me – didst lend a living help

To regulate my soul. And then it was

That the beloved woman in whose sight

Those days were past (now speaking in a voice

Of sudden admonition, like a brook

That does but cross a lonely road; and now

Seen, heard and felt, and caught at every turn,

Companion never lost through many a league)

Maintained for me a saving intercourse

With my true self. For, though impaired and
                            changed

Much, as it seemed, I was no further changed

Than as a clouded, not a waning moon.

She, in the midst of all, preserved me still

A poet, made me seek beneath that name

My office upon earth, and nowhere else.[19]

It is one of the many great tributes to Dorothy. It is touching that he brings Coleridge and his memory into the scene; he did not know Coleridge at this time but he merely imaginatively wishes to thank him too as the source of imaginative strength and restoration. But Dorothy is central; it is she who makes him seek his 'office upon earth' as a poet 'and nowhere else'.

I want to redefine 'revolution'. Wordsworth is then a political revolutionary in the sense that he is a passionate sympathiser with the ideal of revolution. There is no proof that he was ever a political activist though we have scant knowledge of him from about early 1793 to the end of 1795. There are times in London with a very radical crew of friends. He must have been talking to people who passionately hoped that there would be a revolution in England. But whether he did anything about it, we cannot know and Pitt was an extremely successful repressive Prime Minister. The 'revolution' that comes next comes with the help of Dorothy and then a little later of Coleridge as Wordsworth finds a true revolutionary self. In the Preface to *Lyrical Ballads*, a great deal which is revolutionary about Wordsworth's poetry is spelt out, very much with the help of Coleridge. It is important to emphasize that Wordsworth has this very strong resurgence before Coleridge features as the dominant force in Wordsworth's thinking in *Tintern Abbey* and the *Prelude*, for example. Part of the original version of 'The Old Cumberland Beggar' is 'Old Man Travelling' written probably in May 1797:

> The little hedgerow birds,
>
> That peck along the road, regard him not.
>
> He travels on, and in his face, his step,

---

[19] *Prelude* 1805 X 888-920; FT 450-4

> His gait, is one expression; every limb,
>
> His look and bending figure, all bespeak
>
> A man who does not move with pain, but moves
>
> With thought – He is insensibly subdued
>
> To settled quiet: he is one by whom
>
> All effort seems forgotten, one to whom
>
> Long patience has such mild composure given,
>
> That patience now doth seem a thing, of which
>
> He hath no need. He is by nature led
>
> To peace so perfect, that the young behold
>
> With envy, what the old man hardly feels.[20]

Wordsworth has gone from one extreme to another, but in a controlled way. The passion now is subdued to something like a 'settled quiet'. Within the poetry there is a strange and powerful intensity. It is the intensity of Wordsworth's revolutionary ability to enter into what he elsewhere terms 'the Mind of Man / My haunt and the main region of my song'[21]. It is the mind of man at its least prepossessing. This is an old man who is probably not thinking. And yet his mind is valuable. In the political context he could be seen as the 'hunger-bitten girl', an outcast of society who would be bettered through political revolution which offered self-determination. That is how Wordsworth would have thought a few years previously perhaps. But he is not thinking that way

---

[20] Cornell LB 110
[21] Cornell Ex 40; PW v 4

now. He is thinking about this man as an essentially valuable human being. And is that not revolutionary?

'There was a Boy' from the end of 1798 takes us into the peculiar intensities of Wordsworth's own boyhood experienced at Hawkshead. He regarded the poem as a means by which he could talk about the imagination. It is referred to by Wordsworth in the 1815 Preface. De Quincey too thought this poem particularly magnificent. He speaks of that wonderful moment when the noise of the owls penetrates into Wordsworth's consciousness in terms of a 'flash of sublime revelation'[22]. Both of them pick the poem for its imaginative power. I have chosen it not only for that but for its quite ordinary state of affairs. A schoolboy is standing on the side of a lake making ridiculous noises, rather skilfully. Owls answer him across the water. We could be nostalgic about it but we can hardly think about it as a large political event:

> There was a Boy, ye knew him well, ye Cliffs
>
> And Islands of Winander! – many a time,
>
> At evening, when the stars had just begun
>
> To move along the edges of the hills,
>
> Rising or setting, would he stand alone,
>
> Beneath the trees, or by the glimmering lake,
>
> And there, with fingers interwoven, both hands
>
> Press'd closely palm to palm and to his mouth

---

[22] ' This very expression, 'far', by which space and its infinities are attributed to the human heart, and to it capacities of re-echoing the sublimities of Nature, has always struck me as with a flash of sublime revelation' . From *Tait's Magazine* 1839; reprinted in *De Quincey as Critic*, ed. John E. Jordan RKP (1973) 443

> Uplifted, he, as through an instrument,
>
> Blew mimic hootings to the silent owls
>
> That they might answer him. And they would shout
>
> Across the wat'ry vale, and shout again
>
> Responsive to his call, with quivering peals,
>
> And long halloos, and screams, and echoes loud
>
> Redoubled and redoubled, a wild scene
>
> Of mirth and jocund din. And, when it chanced
>
> That pauses of deep silence mock'd his skill,
>
> Then, sometimes, in that silence, while he hung
>
> Listening, a gentle shock of mild surprize
>
> Has carried far into his heart the voice
>
> Of mountain torrents, or the visible scene
>
> Would enter unawares into his mind
>
> With all its solemn imagery, its rocks,
>
> Its woods, and that uncertain heaven, receiv'd
>
> Into the bosom of the steady lake[23].

Wordsworth himself was impressed by the poem in its ability to talk about the way the mind interacts with the natural scene by mistake. De Quincey relates a long story when Wordsworth was

---

[23] Cornell *LB* 139-40

up on Dunmail Raise listening for the mail coach; he has laid his ear to the ground and, on rising up, is suddenly struck by the beauty of a star[24]. Wordsworth seems to be saying 'Don't think you can be imaginative if you try, you can't. Lead the life in which it is a possibility, in which you give it a chance. Do the other things, blow mimic hootings to the owls, take pleasure in that and perhaps in that silence something quite different will happen'. And the something quite different that does happen is the transference, the moment when he receives into himself the beauty, power and sublimity of the scene: received not just into himself but carried 'far' into his heart is 'the voice of mountain torrents'. And, as De Quincey puts it, it is that same expression 'far' that strikes him with the sense of 'sublime revelation'. It is the Wordsworthian ascribing of internal space, what we would now call, using the same internal metaphor, the subconscious.

Stepping Westward is a personal poem which shows Wordsworth's ability to take the imagination one stage further. He and Dorothy are on a walking tour in Scotland:

> While my Fellow-traveller and I were walking by the side of Loch Ketterine, one fine evening after sunset, in our road to a Hut where, in the course of our Tour, we had been hospitably entertained some weeks before, we met, in one of the loneliest parts of that solitary region, two well-dressed Women, one of whom said to us, by way of greeting, 'What, you are stepping westward?'

Wordsworth is making extraordinary poetry out of very ordinary events. On this occasion he is struck how one of these well-dressed women uses the salutation, 'What, you are stepping

---

[24] *De Quincey as Critic* ed. John E. Jordan; RKP (1973) 442-3

westward?' He plays like Donne with the concept of 'west'. Donne's disciple Henry King in his *Exequy* talks about our 'west of life' and Wordsworth (who talks about 'Clouds that gather round the setting sun / Do take a sober colouring from an eye / That hath kept watch o'er man's mortality'[25]) is also playing with the concept of our 'west of life', the sunset, mortality. On this occasion he is playing with an extraordinary tenderness and offering that glimpse into the higher possibilities of the imagination, that crossing of the border into a spiritual realm that cannot be explored by the human mind but it can tentatively reach out towards.

'What, you are stepping westward?' - 'Yea.'

'Twould be a wildish destiny,

If we, who thus together roam

In a strange Land, and far from home,

Were in this place the guests of Chance:

Yet who would stop, or fear to advance,

Though home or shelter he had none,

With such a Sky to lead him on?

The dewy ground was dark and cold;

Behind, all gloomy to behold;

And stepping westward seem'd to be

---

[25] 'Ode Intimations of Immortality' 197-199; Cornell 2 Vol 277

A kind of *heavenly* destiny:

I liked the greeting; 'twas a sound

Of something without place or bound;

And seem'd to give me spiritual right

To travel through that region bright.

The voice was soft, and she who spake

Was walking by her native Lake:

The salutation had to me

The very sound of courtesy:

Its power was felt; and while my eye

Was fixed upon the glowing Sky,

The echo of the voice enwrought

A human sweetness with the thought

Of travelling through the world that lay

Before me in my endless way.[26]

---

[26] Cornell 2 Vol 186

2 WHAT IS *THE EXCURSION*?[1]

In Book I of *The Excursion*, The Sage, who is the Wanderer and whose earlier incarnation as the Pedlar told the story of *The Ruined Cottage* (1797), makes a number of very important statements:

> 'To every Form of Being is assigned,'
>
> Thus calmly spake the venerable Sage,
>
> 'An *active* principle: – howe'er removed
>
> From sense and observation, it subsists
>
> In all things, in all natures: in the stars
>
> Of azure heaven, the unenduring clouds,
>
> In flower and tree, in every pebbly stone
>
> That paves the brooks, the stationary rocks,
>
> The moving waters, and the invisible air.
>
> Whate'er exists hath properties that spread
>
> Beyond itself, *communicating good*,
>
> A simple blessing, or with evil mixed;

---

[1] First delivered as a lecture to The Wordsworth Winter School 1992

> Spirit that knows no insulated spot,
>
> No chasm, no solitude;

and then again, very importantly:

> from link to link
>
> It circulates, the Soul of all the Worlds.
>
> This is the freedom of the Universe;
>
> Unfolded still the more, more visible,
>
> The more we know; and yet is reverenced least,
>
> And least respected in the human Mind,
>
> Its most apparent home.[2]

The formation of this poetry has been through different stages, written, as so much of the great poetry of *The Excursion*, in March 1798. It was written within days of the following passage from Book IV 'Despondency Corrected' and there is no reason why they should not run together into a single statement:

> For the Man
>
> Who, in this spirit, communes with the Forms
>
> Of Nature, who with understanding heart,
>
> Doth know and love, such Objects as excite
>
> No morbid passions, no disquietude,

---

[2] *The Excursion* ix 1-17; This and all other quotations from *The Excursion* are taken from Cornell Ex (the 1814 version) except where the 1850 version is quoted when PW is referred to.

> No vengeance, and no hatred, needs must feel
>
> The joy of that pure principle of love
>
> So deeply, that, unsatisfied with aught
>
> Less pure and exquisite, he cannot choose
>
> But seek for objects of a kindred love
>
> In Fellow-natures, and a kindred joy.
>
> Accordingly, he by degrees perceives
>
> His feelings of aversion softened down;
>
> A holy tenderness pervade his frame.
>
> (iv 1201-1214)

Leaving that for a moment, I want to take you back to the place where we originally knew this passage – Coleridge's Letter of the 10th March 1798 to his elder brother George. George Coleridge is a father figure and Coleridge, wishing to please him, tends to put his thoughts in a way more acceptable for an Anglican priest, as his father and brother had been in succession at Ottery St. Mary. Consequently he plays down his Unitarianism. But it is a letter of very great importance;

> I have snapped my squeaking baby-trumpet of Sedition and the fragments lie scattered in the lumber-room of Penitence.

Coleridge was nothing if not preposterous and when he wanted to turn on the self-abasement he could do it! The snapping of the 'squeaking baby-trumpet of Sedition' is coming at an important moment because in March 1798 he is thinking of the recent French invasion of Switzerland, the oldest Republic in Europe. And he is also thinking in terms which he formulates in *France: an Ode*, Coleridge's great political recantation of this moment. Coleridge continues by telling George of his own present frame of mind; what follows is an interesting statement because everything is stressing 'community' or the 'social' in the strict sense of the word:

> I devote myself to such works as encroach not on the antisocial passions, in poetry to elevate the imagination and set the affections [*emotions*] in right tune by the beauty of the inanimate impregnated, as with a living soul, by the presence of Life

then he moves over from poetry:

> ...in prose, to the seeking with patience and a slow, very slow mind,...What our faculties are and what they are capable of becoming.

This is all very Wordsworthian. It is the stuff of the *Prelude*. It is even more the stuff of *The Excursion*:

> I love fields and woods and mountains with almost a visionary fondness – and because I have found benevolence and quietness growing within me as that fondness has increased, therefore I should wish to be the means of implanting it in others – and to destroy the bad passions not by combating them, but by keeping them in inaction.[3]

He continues by quoting poetry which is not his own, it is

---

[3] Letter to George Coleridge 10th March 1798. Griggs i 397

Wordsworth; and Wordsworth it is who is formulating this doctrine – and it is the passage quoted from *The Excursion* IV. This is its original form not on this occasion very different:

>Not useless do I deem
>
>These shadowy Sympathies with things that hold
>
>An inarticulate Language: for the Man
>
>Once taught to love such objects, as excite
>
>No morbid passions, no disquietude,
>
>No vengeance and no hatred, needs must feel
>
>The Joy of that pure principle of Love
>
>So deeply, that, unsatisfied with aught
>
>Less pure and exquisite, he cannot chuse
>
>But seek for objects of a kindred love
>
>In fellow natures, & a kindred Joy.[4]

This is a philosophy being put across by Coleridge and Wordsworth jointly in early March 1798 and which brings together the love of nature and the love of man in a way which is beautiful and highly appropriate and it is to do with a language of sympathy with that which is in its nature apparently inarticulate.

    The date of March 1798 is important because it is the time when it all happens. Four days earlier, Wordsworth had written to James Watts Tobin with the statement which is rightly taken as

---

[4] Ibid. 397-8

the announcement of *The Recluse*:

> I have written 1300 lines of a poem in which I contrive to convey most of the knowledge of which I am possessed. My object is to give pictures of Nature, Man and Society. Indeed I know not anything which will not come within the scope of my plan.[5]

'Pictures of Nature, Man and Society' are stressed.

The question 'What is *The Excursion*?' links back to the question 'What is *The Recluse*?' I have written on this in the Epilogue of *The Borders of Vision*; a statement can be found there which is painstaking and accurate. The *need* for *The Recluse* is perhaps more important in this context. Why do Wordsworth and Coleridge in March 1798 have this idea of producing a great philosophical poem that will shape the history of mankind? This is where the snapping of the 'squeaking baby-trumpet of sedition' becomes important because *The Recluse* is being projected in a moment of political despair, of going back (and finally for Coleridge) on earlier hopes in the French revolution. Wordsworth in the *Prelude* talks of:

> France standing on the top of golden hours
>
> And human nature seeming born again.[6]

It is easy to ridicule them for feeling in those terms. But they did. Southey looked back in 1824 reflecting on how great a period it had been and on the initial hopes of the French Revolution. 'Nothing was dreamt of but the regeneration of the Human race'[7].

---

[5] EY 212
[6] *Prelude* 1805 vi 353-4. FT 226
[7] 'Few persons but those who have lived in it, can conceive or comprehend what the memory of the French Revolution was, nor what a visionary world

What Wordsworth and Coleridge were trying to do was to find that alternative to the political situation which hadn't worked. Both believed in the principles behind not just the French Revolution but its precursor the American Revolution. But those principles had not in practice produced an egalitarian society, not the 'liberty equality fraternity' that was proclaimed. For this reason and because they were both poets they turned to the hope of producing a literary masterpiece that would provide a basis for hope. Coleridge, as a Unitarian, emerges first as the spokesman of that 'active principle' alive 'in all things' and it is he, no doubt, who takes us on to the second stage in which the existence of that principle is the guarantee of the possibility of the fraternity of man within his own race and across the border into other forms of life and the apparently inanimate.

So what was *The Recluse* going to be? The '1300 lines' include undoubtedly *The Ruined Cottage*, that is to say the original poem in its form as *The Excursion* Book I. *The Ruined Cottage* offers us two things. Firstly there is the original tragic story which is the product of the summer of 1797 in which we see Margaret's suffering, her heroic endurance and her hope. This is Wordsworth's answer to the problem, from one aspect of a great tragic writer, that there is something in the human capacity to endure that is so impressive that it allows us hope even in a situation which is inherently black. Secondly there is that aspect that comes with the development of the character of the Pedlar which is present in the extended version of *The Ruined Cottage* and for a short time becomes in Wordsworth's mind a separate

---

seemed to open upon those who were just entering it. Old things seemed passing away, and nothing was dreamt of but the regeneration of the human race.' *Correspondence of Robert Southey with Caroline Bowles*, ed. Dowden (Dublin 1881) 52.

poem. There is quite a sharp separation in *The Excursion* Book I between what is thought of as the philosophical verse spoken by the poet about the character and philosophy of the Pedlar and the central story.

In *The Music of Humanity* I discuss *The Ruined Cottage* and attempt to show Wordsworth's extremely rare intuition into the tragedy of human suffering. It is an intuition which leaves an appalling blank and as he developed that poem into *The Excursion* and then revised *The Excursion* he slightly changed his views as to how the human race should cope with suffering. Briefly, the last part of *The Excursion* Book I points to the fact that Wordsworth does not at his stage (when *The Excursion* is published in 1814) look for that larger Christian message which he will later offer:

> The Old Man ceased: he saw that I was moved;

The poet is urging his audience to express its own emotion and also offering the central value statement of Wordsworth's poetry:

> From that low Bench, rising instinctively
>
> I turn'd aside in weakness,...

it is weakness to go too far:

> ....nor had power
>
> To thank him for the Tale which he had told.
>
> I stood, and leaning o'er the Garden wall,
>
> Reviewed that Woman's sufferings; and it seemed
>
> To comfort me while with a Brother's love

> I blessed her – in the impotence of grief.

This is society working. He is blessing somebody, who he does not know and has never met, with a brother's love:

> At length towards the Cottage I returned
>
> Fondly, – and traced with interest more mild,
>
> That secret spirit of humanity
>
> Which, mid the calm oblivious tendencies
>
> Of Nature, mid her plants, and weeds, and flowers,
>
> And silent overgrowings, still survived….

Then comes Wordsworth's very great statement:

> 'My Friend! enough to sorrow you have given,
>
> The purposes of wisdom ask no more: (952-968)

The Excursion is really about 'the purposes of wisdom', what they ask and in what they consist:

> Be wise and cheerful; and no longer read
>
> The forms of things with an unworthy eye.
>
> (969-970)

The 'forms of things' are the surfaces, the outer shapes which it is necessary to penetrate to reach the essential:

> She sleeps in the calm earth, and peace is here.
>
> I well remember that those very plumes,

> Those weeds, and the high spear-grass on that wall,
>
> By mist and silent rain-drops silver'd o'er,
>
> As once I passed, did to my heart convey
>
> So still an image of tranquillity,
>
> So calm and still, and looked so beautiful
>
> Amid the uneasy thoughts which filled my mind,
>
> That what we feel of sorrow and despair
>
> From ruin and from change, and all the grief
>
> That passing shews of Being leave behind,
>
> Appeared an idle dream, that could not live
>
> Where meditation was. I turned away
>
> And walked along my road in happiness.' (971-984)

Wordsworth revises *The Excursion* at the end of his life for a specific reason, the criticism of Christopher North / John Wilson in 1842;

> In the story of Margaret containing we believe more than four hundred lines….there is not except one or two weak lines that seem to have been afterwards purposely dropped in one single syllable about religion. Was Margaret a Christian? Let the answer be yes – as good a Christian as ever kneeled in the small mountain chapel in whose churchyard her body now waits for the resurrection…If she was, then the picture painted of her

and her agonies is a libel not only on her character but on the character of all other poor Christian women in this Christian land. Placed as she was for so many years in the clutches of so many passions she surely must have turned sometimes aye often and often and often else had she sooner left the clay towards her Lord and Saviour.[8]

You could argue that he didn't read it terribly well to put her in that churchyard. It is a form of Victorian piety and Wordsworth who is always responsive to criticism (though he hated it, he was always responsive to it, and sometimes mistakenly) adds lines to *The Excursion* where instead of 'that could not live where meditation was' he writes,

> that could maintain,
>
> Nowhere, dominion o'er the enlightened spirit
>
> Whose meditative sympathies repose
>
> Upon the breast of Faith. [9]

Margaret is one

> Who in her worst distress, hath ofttimes felt
>
> The unbounded might of prayer; and learned, with
>
> soul
>
> Fixed on the Cross, that consolation springs,

---

[8] *Recreations of Christopher North* vol ii 58; first pub. 1842, new edition 1844 pub. William Blackwood and Sons Edinburgh; see PW v 415, note to lines 934-55.
[9] PW v 39 952-955.

> From sources deeper far than deepest pain,
>
> For the meek Sufferer.[10]

There are three stages now. That is the last stage (1845 and onwards) and is therefore for most purposes the standard text of *The Excursion*. But there is also *The Excursion* of 1814, the great poem read by Wordsworth's contemporaries, some of whom disparaged it but none of whom ignored it. And it was read at a period when all of them were coming to see Wordsworth grudgingly as the great poet of his age.

The first stage was 1798 which I keep insisting upon. *The Excursion* was predictable from that early moment. Wordsworth was going to attempt to write a poem based on the *The Ruined Cottage*. It would have a narrative structure and a dramatic structure, as he called it, with several story-tellers interacting. And from that moment on, the germ of *The Excursion* is in his mind as part, at least, of *The Recluse*. The part that he struggles with and never succeeds in writing is the central philosophical core which Coleridge imposes on him and which he could never write. He had attempted it in *Home at Grasmere*, which is the most unphilosophical poem yet very beautiful, and Coleridge must have thrown his hands up in despair when he saw it in April 1800. It was so extremely unlike the philosophical piece that he thought necessary to present to the human race as a basis for optimism.

But in *The Excursion* of 1814 Wordsworth is true to the ideals of 1798. It is a poem which does not have the stature of the *Prelude*. I doubt if it is commonly done to give five days to *The Excursion* but I think it should be[11]. But it is not the *Prelude*, which

---

[10] PW v 39 935-939

[11] The Wordsworth Winter School, at which this lecture was delivered, lasted for

is the greatest long poem in the language other than *Paradise Lost* and which carries us to heights and depths of poetry and understanding that *The Excursion* does not. On the other hand, this is a very impressive poem in its own right and it is the work which preserves much great writing from 1798, in many ways Wordsworth's most inspired creative period. Also it is the poem known to his contemporaries, which is immensely important. *The Excursion* is published in 1814 during Wordsworth's lifetime. The *Prelude* is not published, though completed in May 1805, till July 1850, Wordsworth having died on 23rd April 1850. Had the *Prelude* been published as it could have been in 1806 literary history would have been very different and *The Excursion* would not have been the important poem that it is. A great deal of its importance resides in the simple fact that it is the major work of Wordsworth for thirty-five years[12]. And it is not just those years, because by the time the *Prelude* is published it takes another thirty, forty or fifty years to win through because it is so belated. People have got used to the Wordsworth they know. The *Prelude* is not the Wordsworth they know. They do not instinctively take to it. So *The Excursion* is really Wordsworth's greatest poem for the whole of the nineteenth century. It must therefore have our due respect.

What does Wordsworth do to make *The Ruined Cottage* into *The Excursion*? (March is an important month for Wordsworth and Coleridge too I think. Curiously, they are active at certain parts of the year and quite passive at other times. Apart from 'Tintern Abbey' in July 1798 there is precious little great Wordsworth writing in the summer. He is a winter/early spring

---

five days in 1992; *The Excursion* was that year's topic.
[12] From about the time of publication to the year of Wordsworth's death (1814-1850)

writer.) The continuity which is important is to be seen in the character of the Wanderer. Wordsworth adds to the existing structure two further versions of himself. They are notoriously all versions of himself as his contemporaries were quick to point out. I think ventriloquism is a very good idea. His *Letter to a friend of Robert Burns*[13] pays tribute to Burns for creating out of his own character figures in his poetry who will in spirit recommend his opinions. It is a good way of writing. It needs interaction and some degree of variety. *The Excursion* has this. It had it originally in *The Ruined Cottage* in the interaction which is very moving between the poet and the Pedlar which becomes that between the poet and the Wanderer. The Solitary is added to *The Excursion* and is also very important. The Pastor is not as important; he is introduced at the beginning of Book V (the last two books belong to the Wanderer) so that he is really just there, as it were, at the half way mark and the next two books. He is a version of the Priest of 'The Brothers' but far less successful. The Priest of that poem is very charmingly ironised; the conversation in the churchyard is successful in a way that that aspect of *The Excursion* never is. The Pastor represents Wordsworth moving on into the 1810 period as not wholly successful. One might compare the story of Ellen in Book VI and the story of Margaret in Book I. Ellen is a saint's tale from the start. She suffers not with her eye 'fixed on the cross' but in an appalling Christian resignation; she suffers and suffers and finally dies saying that he who imposed this suffering on her will know when to relieve her of it. That aspect of *The Excursion* is not greatly successful. However, again and again

---

[13] 'Not less successfully does Burns avail himself of his own character and situation in society, to construct out of them a poetic self,—introduced as a dramatic personage—for the purpose of inspiriting his incidents, diversifying his pictures, recommending his opinions, and giving point to his sentiments'. *Letter to a Friend of Robert Burns*. OS iii 125.

it is rescued by the presence of the Wanderer which shows Wordsworth as very much true to himself.

The Solitary's importance is threefold. Initially he is seen in a state of sadness. He incorporates the story of the deaths of Catherine[14] and Thomas Wordsworth[15] and Wordsworth's own sorrow is brought out very movingly:

> But at once
>
> From some dark seat of fatal Power was urged
>
> A claim that shattered all. - Our blooming Girl
>
> Caught in the gripe of Death, with such brief time
>
> To struggle in as scarcely would allow
>
> Her cheek to change its colour, was conveyed
>
> From us, to regions inaccessible;
>
> Where height, or depth, admits not the approach
>
> Of living Man, though longing to pursue.
>
> – With even as brief a warning – and how soon
>
> With what short interval of time between,
>
> I tremble yet to think of – our last prop,
>
> Our happy life's only remaining stay –
>
> The Brother followed; and was seen no more.

---

[14] Wordsworth's daughter, born 1808, died 1812 of a seizure.
[15] Wordsworth's son, born 1806, died 1812 of pneumonia.

(III 645-658)

Then there is the terrible effect on the mother, which must be to some extent the effect on Mary Wordsworth:

> Calm as a frozen Lake when ruthless Winds
>
> Blow fiercely, agitating earth and sky,
>
> The Mother now remained;

The frozen lake is totally incapable of responding but around it there is this turbulence:

> as if in her,
>
> Who, to the lowest region of the soul,
>
> Had been erewhile unsettled and disturbed,
>
> This second visitation had no power
>
> To shake; but only to bind up and seal;
>
> And to establish thankfulness of heart
>
> In Heaven's determinations, ever just. (III 661-667)

Mary's piety was, interestingly, much greater, or far more orthodox, than the poet's and it may be that that is a biographical statement. So the Solitary at first exhibits extreme sadness and the warning that you mustn't go too far. 'The purposes of wisdom ask no more'[16]. Wordsworth is the poet above all who values human emotion, but not in extremes, in depths, in silent sorrow but not in that kind of abstracted grief that makes the heart no

---

[16] *The Ruined Cottage* ii 509: MOH 48

longer responsive. So that is the first danger of the Solitary.

The second danger, as in the French Revolution, is of too much hope. We go straight on from the grief into:

> From that abstraction I was rouzed, – and how?
>
> ……For, lo! the dread Bastile,
>
> With all the chambers in its horrid Towers,
>
> Fell to the ground: – by violence o'erthrown
>
> Of indignation; and with shouts that drowned
>
> The crash it made in falling. From the wreck
>
> A golden Palace rose, or seemed to rise,
>
> The appointed Seat of equitable Law
>
> And mild paternal Sway.

Wordsworth is a much more skilful ironist than he is given credit for and the tones here are important:

> The potent shock
>
> I felt: the transformation I perceived,
>
> As marvellously seized as in that moment
>
> When, from the blind mist issuing, I beheld
>
> Glory – beyond all glory ever seen,
>
> Confusion infinite of heaven and earth,
>
> Dazzling the soul! (III 714-731)

So the second great importance of the Solitary, the cautionary tale if you like, is of too much political hope. Wordsworth had experienced it, and not he alone.

The third danger of the Solitary is precisely that of his name; solitude as a temptation. The poem has its roots in 'Despondency Corrected' Book IV, which looks back to Coleridge and March 10th 1798. It is a poem about community and communion. Solitude and the business of being a solitary is a danger. It is the danger not of solitude but solipsism, of abstracted going-back into the self. And Wordsworth is extremely conscious of it. And the great poetry that warns us of it in the Solitary is extremely important. Wordsworth had experienced the French Revolution at first hand in 1790 and 1792 in France and maybe thought he knew more about it than the majority of his contemporaries. But *The Excursion* is a public, not a private poem and I would adduce the fact of its quarto publication in an elegant and rather massive style as another aspect of it being a public statement. It has been shaken and dominated and in many ways inspired by the French Revolution.

There is the other revolution, the alternative hope in what was not then called the Industrial Revolution. *The Excursion* puts the positive side first. There is reference to the greatness of Britain, the Empire and a sort of pride perhaps:

> - Hence is the wide Sea peopled, – and the Shores
>
> Of Britain are resorted to by Ships
>
> Freighted from every climate of the world
>
> With the world's choicest produce. Hence that sum

Of Keels that rest within her crowded ports,

Or ride at anchor in her sounds and bays;

(VIII 134-139)

It is impressive; Wordsworth is not unthoughtful about what is going on. On the other hand my theme, and his theme, of communion and community is utterly devastated by the Industrial Revolution, the depopulation of the countryside, the masses going into the towns and also the towns coming out to the masses. The Industrial Revolution can go on anywhere where there is water. It is a revolution of water power. And the valleys which Wordsworth particularly loves all have rivers and streams which are capable of becoming industrialised and horrifying centres of impersonal work that break down the structures of community, village and family. There is the particular horror of night work as well as day. It is the horror of a revolution which has gobbled them all up (and the metaphor is Wordsworth's) with such insatiability that it devours human beings and human lives by night as well as by day. These are the night workers taking over:

Disgorged are now the Ministers of day;

And, as they issue from the illumined Pile,

A fresh Band meets them, at the crowded door, –

And in the Courts – and where the rumbling

Stream,

That turns the multitude of dizzy wheels,

Glares, like a troubled Spirit, in its bed

> Among the rocks below. (VIII 176-182)

This is like Blake and quite unlike Wordsworth and is late, about 1810. But it is a tortured mountain stream, recalling the mountain stream that is forced to 'dimple down...a channel paved by the hand of man' in Book IV of the *Prelude*[17]. Now we have a mountain stream, equally a 'froward brook'[18], but it is being tortured and forced to be the power of the Industrial Revolution.

Wordsworth also offers the picture of the family destroyed:

> How art thou blighted for the poor Man's heart!
>
> Lo! in such neighbourhood, from morn to eve,
>
> The Habitations empty!...

'the habitations empty' refer to *Isaiah* and the apocalyptic prophecy of the coming of destruction:

> ...or perchance
>
> The Mother left alone, no helping hand
>
> To rock the cradle of her peevish babe;
>
> No daughters round her, busy at the wheel,
>
> Or in dispatch of each day's little growth
>
> Of household occupation; no nice arts
>
> Of needle-work; no bustle at the fire,
>
> Where once the dinner was prepared with pride;

---

[17] *Prelude* 1805 iv 43ff. FT 142
[18] ibid 40

> Nothing to speed the day, or cheer the mind;
>
> Nothing to praise, to teach, or to command.
>
> (VIII 266-277)

And finally there is the child sent into the factory:

> Behold him – in the school
>
> Of his attainments? no; but with the air
>
> Fanning his temples under heaven's blue arch.
>
> His raiment, whitened o'er with cotton flakes,
>
> Or locks of wool, announces whence he comes.
>
> (VIII 308-312)

He is outside, where he should be, but his clothes tell of the life he actually leads and the disease that will speedily kill him (echoing Shakespeare's schoolboy):

> Creeping his gait and cowering – his lip pale –
>
> His respiration quick and audible;
>
> And scarcely could you fancy that a gleam
>
> From out those languid eyes could break, or blush
>
> Mantle upon his cheek. Is this the form,
>
> Is that the countenance, and such the port,
>
> Of no mean Being? One who should be clothed
>
> With dignity befitting his proud hope;

> Who, in his very childhood, should appear
>
> Sublime – from present purity and joy!
>
> (VIII 313-322)

Interesting how the poetry reinforces one's sense of the Wordsworth of the *Prelude*.

There is also the new landscape voice in Wordsworth that is the other great aspect of *The Excursion*. We see it briefly in the image of the ram. They are walking in Grasmere now:

> Thus having reached a bridge, that overarched
>
> The hasty rivulet where it lay becalmed
>
> In a deep pool, by happy chance we saw
>
> A two-fold Image; on a grassy bank
>
> A snow-white Ram, and in the crystal flood
>
> Another and the same! Most beautiful,
>
> On the green turf, with his imperial front
>
> Shaggy and bold, and wreathed horns superb,
>
> The breathing Creature stood; as beautiful,
>
> Beneath him, shewed his shadowy Counterpart.
>
> Each had his glowing mountains, each his sky,
>
> And each seemed centre of his own fair world:
>
> Antipodes unconscious of each other,

> Yet, in partition, with their several spheres,
>
> Blended in perfect stillness, to our sight!
>
> (IX 440-454)

It blends the life of actuality and the life of the imagination, the life of the mind, of imaginative receptiveness as the image is received by water which was seen earlier in 'There was a Boy' belonging to the end of 1798. That is still central to Wordsworth and it is very much the message of the *Prelude* but also in a large degree of *The Excursion*.

Then there is the Solitary's great vision of the New Jerusalem in Book II;

> The Appearance, instantaneously disclosed,
>
> Was of a mighty City – boldly say
>
> A wilderness of building, sinking far
>
> And self-withdrawn into a wondrous depth,
>
> Far sinking into splendour – without end!
>
> Fabric it seemed of diamond and of gold,
>
> With alabaster domes, and silver spires,
>
> And blazing terrace upon terrace high
>
> Uplifted; here, serene pavilions bright,
>
> In avenues disposed; there, towers begirt
>
> With battlements that on their restless fronts

>Bore stars – illumination of all gems!   (ll 869-880)

Perhaps this is not the climbing of Snowdon! That passage (found in Book XIII of the 1805 *Prelude* and is in a much reduced form in Book XIV of the 1850 *Prelude*) stands for all time in a way that perhaps this doesn't. On the other hand this does have new qualities. It is dazzling in its array of gems, jewels, in its willingness to be Miltonic in a very powerful and elusive manner. And I think the new voice has something which all of us should value. Skipping a little way:

> O, 'twas an unimaginable sight!
>
> Clouds, mists, streams, watery rocks and emerald
>
> turf,
>
> Clouds of all tincture, rocks and sapphire sky,
>
> Confused, commingled, mutually inflamed,
>
> Molten together, and composing thus,
>
> Each lost in each, that marvellous array
>
> Of temple, palace, citadel, and huge
>
> Fantastic pomp of structure without name…
>
>   (ll 887-894)

This grand style speaks of things blending, 'molten together', forming a grand imaginative community in heaven which is the counterpart of the grand imaginative community which you see on earth and particularly in the relation of the mind and the natural world.

Finally Book IX; this is a much less well-known vision. But it is also much closer to us. You can walk up to Loughrigg terrace[19] today and pray to see such an impressive sight. Wordsworth doesn't overdo it. There is nothing as big as the Solitary's initial vision. On the other hand there is something shared. All are there and watch it from Loughrigg Terrace across the lake; it is a wonderful blending – but also something a little bit more;

> Soft heath this elevated spot supplied,
>
> With resting-place of mossy stone; – and there
>
> We sate reclined – admiring quietly
>
> The frame and general aspect of the scene;
>
> And each not seldom eager to make known
>
> His own discoveries; or to favourite points
>
> Directing notice, merely from a wish
>
> To impart a joy, imperfect while unshared.
>
> (IX 580-587)

That is the hope for the human race in muted form, 'to impart a joy, imperfect while unshared';

> That rapturous moment ne'er shall I forget
>
> When these particular interests were effaced
>
> From every mind! – Already had the sun,
>
> Sinking with less than ordinary state,

---

[19] A terrace overlooking Grasmere Lake

> Attained his western bound;...

(Many of Wordsworth's images follow an anticlimax – the sun 'sinking with less than ordinary state' has gone down and they have not had a decent sunset!):

> ...but rays of light –
>
> Now suddenly diverging from the orb
>
> Retired behind the mountain tops or veiled
>
> By the dense air – shot upwards to the crown
>
> Of the blue firmament – aloft – and wide:
>
> And multitudes of little floating clouds,
>
> Pierced through their thin etherial mould, ere we,
>
> Who saw, of change were conscious, had become
>
> Vivid as fire –

The sun is out of sight, behind the mountain and yet he is creating imaginatively a scene that transfuses the prospect in front of them and offers not just a large landscape but individual clouds which emblemize the individual possibility of the human soul, the human imagination:

> clouds separately poized,
>
> Innumerable multitude of Forms
>
> Scattered through half the circle of the sky;
>
> And giving back, and shedding each on each,

> With prodigal communion,...

This is love;

> ...the bright hues
>
> Which from the unapparent Fount of glory...

this is not God sitting there dealing out his dictates and giving his blessings, it is an 'unapparent Fount of glory', something vastly more Wordsworthian, closer to the Wordsworth of 1798, tentative, mysterious, beautifully 'unapparent';

> They had imbibed, and ceased not to receive.
>
> That which the heavens displayed, the liquid deep
>
> Repeated; but with unity sublime!   (IX 588-608)

3 SYMPATHETIC IMAGINATION[1]

When it came to writing about women, Wordsworth was short on experience. His mother died when he was seven. Ann Tyson with whom he lodged for eight years, while going to school at Hawkshead, was in her seventies and eighties and not in a relationship from which he could learn a great deal. School was all male, as was Cambridge[2]. Though breathing his first fond vows to Mary Hutchinson[3] in Dorothy's company at the age of seventeen he saw very little of her for the next eight and a half years and rather forgot his vows when aged twenty one he met Annette Vallon in France in the Spring of 1792. To judge from Caroline's birth[4] just after he left for England in early December he must have known Annette for a little over nine months after which there were letters but the war prevented them meeting again till the Peace of Amiens in 1802[5]. Dorothy was of course the woman whom Wordsworth knew best. Separated from her at their mother's death[6], he came to know her in 1787 just before going up to Cambridge. In April 1794 they were together for six weeks

---

[1] First delivered as a lecture to The Wordsworth Summer Conference 1993
[2] WW attended the Grammar School Hawkshead 1779-87 and St. John's College Cambridge 1787-90.
[3] WW married Mary Hutchinson October 4th 1802.
[4] In 1792, Wordsworth's illegitimate daughter, Caroline Wordsworth, was born to Annette Vallon and baptised at Orleans on December 15th.
[5] WW was in France from November 1791 till December 1792.
[6] Died 1778

at Windy Brow[7]. And from Sept 1795, when he was twenty five and she was twenty three, they were able to stay together. It may be significant that Mary Hutchinson re-enters Wordsworth's life at the end of 1796 when she pays a six month visit to Dorothy at Racedown.[8]

Though he had a five year old daughter[9], Wordsworth, when he came to write *Lyrical Ballads*, had never seen mother and child together. Despite this, the women of the 1798 *Lyrical Ballads* (Betty Foy, Martha Ray, the nameless Mad Mother and Forsaken Indian Woman[10]) are all seen in a mother-child relationship, three out of four in a relationship with infants. Annette's letters (most of which Wordsworth did not receive) would no doubt have given him insight into the peculiar tenderness of this bond but we are dealing here primarily with the poet's imagination. Keats had the nerve to talk about Wordsworth's 'egotistical sublime'. To what other genre could one possibly ascribe the 'Ode to a Nightingale'? And he complicated matters by placing a barrier between this 'Wordsworthian' mode and the 'poetical character' defined by Keats as 'that sort of which, if I am any thing, I am a Member'. He presumably knew, however, that most poets, himself included, have both an 'egotistical sublime' when they talk in high-sounding terms about themselves and an alternative non-egotistical mode when they enter the feelings of others. His comments should be thought of not as a Keatsian discovery or an extension of the

---

[7] A house near Keswick, Cumbria.
[8] WW was loaned a house near Lyme, Dorset by the Pinney family from 1795-7 where he and DW lived together for the first time (apart from Windy Brow) since their mother's death.
[9] Caroline, see n. 4.
[10] From 'The Idiot Boy', 'The Thorn', 'The Mad Mother' and 'The Complaint of a Forsaken Indian Woman' respectively in *Lyrical Ballads* 1798.

discussion (tiresome at the best of times) of 'negative capability' but as a definition of the sympathetic imagination:

> As to the poetical Character itself, (I mean that sort of which, if I am anything, I am a Member; that sort distinguished from the wordsworthian or egotistical sublime; which is a thing per se and stands alone) it is not itself – it has no self – it is every thing and nothing – It has no character – it enjoys light and shade; it lives in gusto, be it foul or fair, high or low, rich or poor, mean or elevated. It has as much delight in conceiving an Iago as an Imogen. What shocks the virtuous philosopher, delights the camelion Poet. It does no harm from its relish of the dark side of things any more than for its taste for the bright one; because they both end in speculation. A poet is the most unpoetical of anything in existence; because he has no Identity – he is continually in for [informing] – and filling some other Body – The Sun, the Moon, the Sea and Men and Women who are creatures of impulse are poetical and have about them an unchangeable attribute – the poet has none; no identity – he is certainly the most unpoetical of all God's Creatures.[11]

Keats's words can best be described as a reverie on 'gusto'. Hazlitt in his Round Table essay on the subject had thought mainly as a painter singling out memorably the hands of Correggio's women, the forms of Michael Angelo, the colouring of Titian[12]. Claude's landscapes are granted perfection but denied

---

[11] Letter to Woodhouse 27th October 1818; Rollins i 387
[12] 'Gusto in art is power or passion defining any subject. – It is not so difficult to explain this term / in what relates to expression (of which it may be said to be the highest degree) as in what relates to things without expression, to the natural appearances of objects, as mere colour or form. In one sense, however, there is hardly any object devoid of expression, without some character of power

'gusto' on the grounds that his eye lacked imagination. Rembrandt by contrast shows 'gusto' in all that he does. Everything in his pictures has a tangible character. When 'he puts a diamond in the ear of a Burgomaster's wife, it is of the first water; and his furs and stuffs are proof against a Russian winter'[13].

Keats knew Hazlitt and it is likely they would have talked about 'gusto' in its literary application. Whether they had or not Keats's use of the term makes clear an indebtedness while significantly moving the discussion into an area covered by Wordsworth in the Preface to *Lyrical Ballads*. For Keats, the 'poetical character', that is to say *his* kind of non-Wordsworthian poet, 'lives in gusto be it foul or fair, high or low, rich or poor'. The poet has no character himself because he is perpetually entering into some one or thing else. Wordsworth had written in his 1802 additions to the Preface – republished in the 1815 volume which Keats no doubt used:

> it will be the wish of the Poet to bring his feelings near to those of the persons whose feelings he describes, nay, for short spaces of time, perhaps, to let himself slip into an entire delusion and even confound and identify his own feelings with theirs[14].

The sole proviso that Wordsworth adds is that the language which suggests itself to the poet in his 'entire delusion' will be modified in accordance with the principle that poetry is written in order to give 'pleasure'[15]. There will be no necessity to trick out or

---

belonging to it, some precise association with pleasure or pain; and it is in giving this truth of character from the truth of feeling, whether in the highest or lowest degree, but always in the highest degree of which the subject is capable, that gusto consists' : From Hazlitt's 'On Gusto' see Wu (1) ii 79
[13] Ibid 80.
[14] OS i 138

to elevate nature. But the painful and distasteful it is the poet's responsibility to remove.

Wordsworth, master of the 'egotistical sublime' in 'Tintern Abbey', nonetheless exemplifies the Keatsian 'poetical character' as he enters the mind for instance of the cottage woman Betty Foy. Betty dotes on her son Johnny and proudly sends him off on horseback to fetch a doctor for her neighbour. Unable to comprehend her instructions, he is lost but then found again in a scene which is at once tender and ridiculous:

> She looks again – her arms are up –
>
> She screams – she cannot move for joy;
>
> She darts as with a torrent's force,
>
> She almost has o'erturned the horse,
>
> And fast she holds her idiot boy.
>
> And Johnny burrs and laughs aloud,
>
> Whether in cunning or in joy,
>
> I cannot tell; but while he laughs,
>
> Betty a drunken pleasure quaffs,
>
> To hear again her idiot boy.
>
> And now she's at the pony's tail,

---

[15] Ibid.

> And now she's at the pony's head,
>
> On that side now, and now on this,
>
> And almost stifled with her bliss,
>
> A few sad tears does Betty shed.
>
>
> She kisses o'er and o'er again,
>
> Him whom she loves, her idiot boy;
>
> She's happy here, she's happy there,
>
> She is uneasy every where;
>
> Her limbs are all alive with joy.[16]

Who told Wordsworth what it would feel like to be a mother 'quaffing' a 'drunken pleasure' at the inarticulate 'burrings' of a child? Or that, 'almost stifled with her bliss', she would at a particular moment shed 'a few sad tears'? Or that extreme happiness was akin to physical unease and that it was possible for limbs to be 'all alive with joy'? Wordsworth had, it has to be admitted, startling intuition. One might add he had already a comic genius and an astonishing tact.

It would be convenient to be able to hold up the Preface to *Lyrical Ballads* as in general a guide to the poetry it is supposed to introduce. Though containing much that is thoughtful, it is nevertheless a curmudgeonly work. Wordsworth writes a heavy, dogged prose and working at least partly from Coleridge's notes he adopts the Coleridgean manner at once assertive and

---

[16] 'The Idiot Boy'; from *Lyrical Ballads* 1798 p.174; PW ii 78

defensive about the critical issues of the day. There is however much that is useful; the discussion, for instance, about underlying purpose that leads into Wordsworth's brief comments on 'The Idiot Boy', 'Mad Mother' and 'Forsaken Indian Woman':

> I have said that each of these poems has a purpose. I have also informed my Reader what this purpose will be found principally to be: namely to illustrate the manner in which our feelings and ideas are associated in a state of excitement. But speaking in less general language, it is to follow the fluxes and refluxes of the mind when agitated by the great and simple affections of our nature.[17]

Wordsworth seems to feel in this case the need to translate. His translation into less general language, however, does not make things a great deal easier. It may be best to continue the quotation and then come back to its complexities:

> This object I have endeavoured in these short essays to attain by various means; by tracing the maternal passion through many of its more subtle windings as in the poems of The Idiot Boy and the Mad Mother; by accompanying the last struggles of a human being at the approach of death, cleaving in solitude to life and society, as in the Poem of the Forsaken Indian; by shewing as in the Stanzas entitled We Are Seven, the perplexity and obscurity which in childhood attend our notion of death.[18]

But what is all this about illustrating 'the manner in which our feelings and ideas are associated in a state of excitement'? And how much does it have to do with the following of 'fluxes

---

[17] Preface to *Lyrical Ballads* 1800; OS i.126.
[18] Ibid.

and refluxes' (an inelegant phrase) within the mind? Only two pages earlier, Wordsworth had been talking about 'tracing [in 'the incidents of common life']...the primary laws of our nature: chiefly as far as regards the manner in which we associate ideas in a state of excitement'[19]. To be so repetitive suggests that the words had a sort of magic for him. They were precious because they stood, whether or not they communicated to anyone else, for what he was trying to do or be as a poet. To quote his own shrewd perception in the note to 'The Thorn':

> ....an attempt is rarely made to communicate impassioned feelings without something of an accompanying consciousness of the inadequateness of our own powers, or the deficiencies of language. During such efforts there will be a craving in the mind, and as long as it is unsatisfied the speaker will cling to the same words, or words of the same character[20].

Repetition of the words may begin to give them the kind of emotional importance which they had for Wordsworth as he wrote.

On a rather simple level one can illustrate what he meant from the copybook associationist poem 'Strange Fits of Passion' – 'fits' of passion meaning shifting emotional states or moods. Fixing his eye on the moon (as the boy Wordsworth fixes his eye on the 'craggy ridge'[21] in the boat-stealing episode of the *Prelude*) the lover rides towards Lucy's cottage. Leaving the open ground, 'the wide lea', and mounting the hill on which the cottage stands causes the moon to drop, just as rowing out from the shore

---

[19] Ibid. 122-4
[20] End of volume note to 'The Thorn' *Lyrical Ballads* 1800: PW ii 513
[21] *Prelude* 1799 i 100. FT 10: *Prelude* 1805 i 398. FT 58

causes the hidden peak to rise[22]. Finally, as the planet drops behind the roof, an unspoken association in the lover's mind between the moon and Lucy brings in the terrifying thought of her death. It is all beautifully worked out but leaves rather little to the imagination. The *Prelude* lines, by contrast, refuse to tell us of the association in the boy's head as the huge peak rises 'as if with voluntary power instinct' and are much more powerful for not doing so.

'Strange Fits of Passion' is one of the poems which tells us the tricks of a poet's trade. Wordsworth wants to write about the mind and, as a follower of Hartley, thinks of it as working associatively (like Freud). But his intuitions take him into a realm of experience that cannot be explained in objective terms. His response, again like that of both Hartley and Freud, was to reach for a determinism; what cannot be explained has no doubt been ordained. Associating ideas 'in a state of excitement' is associated by Wordsworth with the 'primary laws of our nature', closer to Freud than Hartley who would have said 'with the laws of God'. Wordsworth's definition of poetry starts from spontaneity;

> ...all good poetry is the spontaneous overflow of powerful feelings[23]

It is an outflowing of emotion that has been neither prompted nor checked by the conscious will resembling, to take an obvious example, the Mariner's blessing of the water-snakes[24]. It would have been convenient to rest here; many people quoting the

---

[22] *Prelude* 1799 i 81-129. See also BOV 44-48.
[23] Preface 1800; OS i 126
[24] 'The Rime of The Ancient Marinere' ; 'A spring of love gusht from my heart, / And I bless'd them unaware'. Cornell LB 778

Preface do. But Wordsworth knows he can't. 'But though this be true', he adds the proviso that to produce good poetry the inspired poet must be 'possessed of more than usual organic sensibility' and have 'also thought long and deeply'[25]. Later in the Preface the concept of spontaneity will be qualified, the creative act consists not of the original emotion but of that emotion imaginatively re-experienced. But for the moment Wordsworth is heading us for a situation in which the poet can be said to write in a blind and mechanical obedience to habit:

> at length, if we be originally possessed of much organic sensibility, such habits of mind will be produced that by obeying blindly and mechanically the impulses of those habits we shall describe objects and utter sentiments of such a nature and in such connection with each other, that the understanding of the being to whom we address ourselves, if he be in a healthful state of association, must necessarily be in some degree enlightened, his taste exalted, and his affections ameliorated[26].

The poet obeys 'impulses'. He utters sentiments which, as long as the reader has built up the right associations – an element that Wordsworth will worry about later in *Essay Upon Epitaphs* – inevitably have a beneficial effect. It seems a little pat. The poet can slip into his 'entire delusion', 'confound and identify'[27] his feelings with those of his characters.

Keats is not so concerned with the moral outcome and does not use the mechanistic language of Hartley and his followers. But essentially we are back again with the 'camelion

---

[25] Preface 1800: OS i 126
[26] Ibid.
[27] Preface 1800; OS i 138

poet' who in the creative act surrenders his identity. As Stevens puts it:

> Then we,
>
> As we beheld her striding there alone,
>
> Knew that there never was a world for her
>
> Except the one she sang and, singing, made.[28]

The major difference between Wordsworth and Keats is that Wordsworth is less concerned with 'the diamond in the ear of a Burgomaster's wife'[29]. 'Gusto' for Keats, as for Hazlitt, is very often invested in inanimate detail – 'the sculptured dead' of 'The Eve of St. Agnes' aching in their 'icy hoods and mails'[30]; or the carpets in the same poem rising 'along the gusty floor'[31]—the 'gusto' and 'gustiness' connected in Keats's mind at some level.

Wordsworth, whether his idiom is the 'egotistical sublime' or self-surrendering narrative poetry, is almost always writing about the mind. The earliest of his *Lyrical Ballads*, 'Goody Blake and Harry Gill' and 'The Thorn', take as their subject the surrender of self, blind obedience to impulse. But it is within minds that are *not* 'possessed of more than usual organic sensibility', *haven't* prepared themselves by thinking 'long and

---

[28] 'The Idea of Order at Key West'; WS 129-30.
[29] 'On Gusto', Hazlitt. Wu (1) 80
[30] The sculptured dead, on each side, seem to freeze,
Imprisoned in black, purgatorial rails,
Knights, ladies, praying in dumb orat'ries,
He passeth by; and his weak spirit fails
To think how they may ache in icy hoods and mails. 'The Eve of St. Agnes' ii 14-18; Allott 454
[31] The arras, rich with horseman, hawk, and hound,
Fluttered in the besieging wind's uproar;
And the long carpets rose along the gusty floor. Ibid xl. Allott 477-8

deeply'. It matters to Wordsworth that Harry Gill's story is based on fact. Either he, or more probably Coleridge, must have come upon it presented as a medical case in Erasmus Darwin's *Zoonomia* 1794-6. None of Wordsworth's poems is written in a more business-like way. And none is written at a time when he is more concerned that his poetry should embody a serious 'purpose'. In early March 1798, the week in which his grand poetic scheme for *The Recluse* is announced, Wordsworth asks Cottle to send him *Zoonomia* subtitled *The Laws of Organic Life* (notice the word 'laws') from the Bristol Public Library. A week later Dorothy returns it with the comment that it has 'answered the purpose'[32].

'Goody Blake and Harry Gill' has been written as it should be read, very fast; it is Wordsworth's most dramatic poem. What matters to him chiefly is Harry's delusion. Harry is a young and vigorous farmer. He has seized the aged Goody as she steals firewood from his hedge, and Goody has cursed him:

> And fiercely by the arm he took her,
>
> And by the arm he held her fast,
>
> And fiercely by the arm he shook her,
>
> And cried, 'I've caught you then at last!'
>
> Then Goody, who had nothing said,
>
> Her bundle from her lap let fall;
>
> And kneeling on the sticks, she pray'd
>
> To God that is the judge of all.

---

[32] DW to Joseph Cottle c.13th March 1798. EY 214

> She pray'd, her wither'd hand uprearing,
>
> While Harry held her by the arm –
>
> 'God! Who art never out of hearing,
>
> O may he never more be warm!'
>
> The cold, cold moon above her head,
>
> Thus on her knees did Goody pray,
>
> Young Harry heard what she had said,
>
> And icy-cold he turned away.[33]

Accepting the curse, Harry takes to his bed. He becomes a chronic invalid. And we are to assume that he dies a victim to his own imagination. If he could cease to associate his condition with Goody's curse, he would be warm. But he cannnot. The idea is compulsive. What could prove more decisively the power of mind, the power of association? But successful and delightful as the poem is, it suffers like 'Strange Fits of Passion' from existing to make a point. Harry's obsession is total. We sympathize with him, shivering in his flannel waistcoats; we respond to his pathetic words 'Poor Harry Gill is very cold'. But we are not for a moment able to see into his mind.

That Wordsworth should go on to write 'The Thorn' is particularly interesting. In place of an allegedly factual account, his source now is a lurid Gothic poem. Superstition still plays its part but he is now asking more complex questions about

---

[33] Cornell LB 61-2

association and mental process. Gottfried Burger's Gothic ballad, translated by William Taylor as *The Lass of Fair Wone*, opens as some may recall with a pond of toads, a ghost and the traditional Gothic blue fire. Then it tells a sad story in rather simple-minded moral terms, beginning that the parson's daughter once was good. Seduced and deserted, she slays her infant with a silver pin and is hanged on the spot providing the ghost and the spooky opening scene. The story, as such, Wordsworth disdains. But his mind fastens on the objects associated in the source with murder – a gibbet, a pond and an infant's grave. Translated into an unGothic natural setting these become an aged thorn tree, a little muddy pond of famous dimensions and a hill of moss that's 'like an infant's grave in size'.

Wordsworth is not writing a murder story but for his own purposes uses his narrator, a credulous and superstitious re-teller of village gossip, to create for the tree, pond and heap of moss associations with infanticide such as have been set up much more crudely in his source:

> This heap of earth o'ergrown with moss,
>
> Which close beside the thorn you see,
>
> So fresh in all its beauteous dyes,
>
> Is like an infant's grave in size
>
> As like as like can be:
>
> But never, never any where,
>
> An infant's grave was half so fair[34].

---

[34] 'The Thorn' 49-55; Cornell LB 78

At the centre of Wordsworth's poem is Martha Ray, who may or may not have had a child which she may have killed but who has certainly been jilted and a habit of sitting on a hilltop in all kinds of weather! Though she is the central figure (character one can hardly say) the poem curiously does not concern her. Wordsworth has imagined himself into the mind of the nameless and faceless narrator who is telling and to some extent inventing her story. At one remove, the poet is imagining himself into his own mind but that remove is an important one. He was later to praise Burns for making narrators out of his own character and situation in society. The narrator of 'The Thorn' is not made out of Wordsworth's character and situation. He is unthinking, has motives which he does not understand and is willing to accept and purvey the most vicious gossip. We are seeing what happens when the *wrong* person obeys 'blindly and mechanically'[35] the impulse to create.

Not all the *Lyrical Ballads* are easy to date. But 'The Mad Mother', whether or not it follows immediately, is a sort of sequel to 'The Thorn', a chance to explore the mind of a woman broadly in Martha Ray's position. 'The Thorn' is a bigger poem, chiefly because of the strange intensity with which the landscape is invested. But 'The Mad Mother' is surely an astonishing achievement of the sympathetic imagination. Jane Austen we are repeatedly told was uneasy about showing men on their own because she didn't know how they would talk. Wordsworth, not content with speaking a whole poem as a woman, has a child at the breast and seems to know very precisely what it is like:

Thy lips I feel them, baby! they

---

[35] Preface to *Lyrical ballads* 1800; OS i 126

> Draw from my heart the pain away.

And if this was not enough, he is able to enter into the nightmare possibility of suckling incubi:

> And fiendish faces one, two, three,
>
> Hung at my breasts, and pulled at me;

Woven through 'The Mad Mother' is the drama of the woman's wavering sanity:

> Where art thou gone, my own dear child?
>
> What wicked looks are those I see?

...and keeping time with it is the quiet menace of potential violence:

> 'Oh love me, love me, little boy! ....
>
> ...And do not dread the waves below,
>
> When o'er the sea-rock's edge we go;
>
> The high crag cannot work me harm
>
> Nor leaping torrents when they howl;

That we are right to hear in the leaping of the torrents the woman's own temptation to jump is confirmed in the lines that follow:

> The babe I carry on my arm
>
> He saves for me my precious soul!

(Suicide was at that time a sin)

Without the child the high crag could indeed do her harm. Not that she is stable as she is. In Wordsworth's strange and powerful intuition only the bodily act of feeding the child can give her full relief, because only in that act is her relation to him entirely maternal. The child is a replacement of his treacherous father but also a reminder of his loss:

> I'll build an Indian Bower; I know
>
> The leaves that make the softest bed:
>
> And if from me thou wilt not go,

The line is surely addressed to the baby as lover

> But still be true 'till I am dead,
>
> My pretty thing! then thou shalt sing,
>
> As merry as the birds in spring.

And then the juxtaposition:

> Thy father cares not for my breast,
>
> 'Tis thine, sweet baby, there to rest;
>
> 'Tis all thine own!

The father's erotic pleasure in the breast is replaced by the child's comforting need but the pain of abandonment can be no more than momentarily assuaged.

Wordsworth's talk in the Preface of 'tracing the maternal passion through many of its more subtle windings'[36], specifically

---

[36] OS i 126

applied to this poem, misses the point so completely that it might almost be designed to mislead. 'Windings' of passion we do indeed see but their subtlety derives from the fact that they are only in part maternal. 'The Mad Mother' could as well be called 'The Absent Father'. The 'windings' are defences, compensations, deflections of pain. For a moment the father even becomes an object of sympathy:

>But he, poor man, is wretched made,

But the 'reflux', to use that inelegant term, is brief. Almost at once we have returning madness, followed by the brilliantly uneasy resolution:

>For I thy own dear mother am.
>
>My love for thee has well been tried:
>
>I've sought thy father far and wide.
>
>I know the poisons of the shade
>
>I know the earth-nuts fit for food;
>
>Then, pretty dear, be not afraid;
>
>We'll find thy father in the wood.

They won't of course but which would she serve him if they did? Poisons or earthnuts?

Wordsworth did not desert Annette. It is not known in what sense he seduced her and she was considerably older than him. To judge from Annette's two surviving letters in 1793 she and William, and Dorothy too, were looking forward to their getting married as soon as the war permitted. Annette's vision of the future sounds a little suffocating but is not so dissimilar from what Wordsworth managed to surround himself with ten years later at Dove Cottage. She speaks in those letters of a time when he will be surrounded by his sister, wife and daughter, who will dedicate themselves to him and who will have a single emotion, one heart, one soul, and will bring these totally to the service of her dear William.

The war did not permit a meeting between Wordsworth and Annette till August 1802 when he was two months away from marrying Mary Hutchinson. No one can know if Annette would have married him after almost ten years of separation. But very probably she would. Nor is it known when Wordsworth decided in spite of Caroline[37] he no longer wished to marry her. No doubt it was a gradual process. I suspect he and Mary Hutchinson came to some sort of agreement – quite a private one – Coleridge for instance didn't know of it – while she was staying at Racedown in the first half of 1797. Written a year later the *Lyrical Ballads* thus belong to a period when feelings of guilt would be very likely. At some point one has to take into account that Wordsworth had written two pieces in the genre of the deserted woman before he ever met Annette – a vignette of the soldier's widow in *An Evening Walk* composed in 1789 and the story of 'The Female Vagrant' probably written in 1791 before being embedded in the *Salisbury Plain* poems and excerpted for *Lyrical Ballads*. Also there is the fact that from the chamois hunter of *Descriptive Sketches* 1792 onwards there are suffering *male* figures to put alongside the women. Though denuded of comfort, the Old Cumberland Beggar perhaps does not suffer but the Discharged Soldier does and so do Simon Lee and the Farmer of 'The Last of the Flock'. Male and female figures are fairly evenly divided even

---

[37] Wordsworth's illegitimate child born to Annette Vallon.

in the Alfoxden period of Spring to early Summer 1798 that produces Volume One of *Lyrical Ballads*. In the 1799-1800 period of Goslar and Grasmere, that produces Volume Two, only 'Ruth', in many ways connected with the Alfoxden Ballads, holds out against male dominance – with 'The Brothers' and 'Michael' being by far the longest narrative poems.

Guilt in Wordsworth is rather like opium in Coleridge. We reach for it to explain an extra intensity perceived in the poetry and then find that we have no critical terms in which to take it into account. But it is not just the degree of sympathy or sympathetic imagination accorded to the women of the ballads that tempts us to think in terms of guilt. There are, as Mary Moorman points out, similarities between lines in 'The Mad Mother' and the phrasing of Annette's letters[38]; the two letters we have were impounded by the customs and not seen by Wordsworth[39]. And the role of the absent father is very disquieting. In Margaret of 'The Ruined Cottage' Wordsworth the previous summer (1797) had portrayed a woman tortured by hope that one day her husband would return. She had not been deserted; it had been poverty and the war that separated them. Now in the spring of 1798, we have a woman maddened by betrayal and Wordsworth is quite unnecessarily good at imagining himself into the shifting obsessional patterns in her mind of loss, pain, need, hate, resentment, revenge, even momentary sympathy. It would after all have been perfectly possible to leave the father out of it and write the poem of maternal 'fluxes and refluxes' that the Preface describes. But he didn't.

---

[38] MM i 385
[39] Mary Moorman observes that though we only have the letters which Wordsworth did not see because withheld by customs there were no doubt others in the same tone.

It is difficult to know what to make of the inaccuracy of Wordsworth's descriptions of the poetry. There is I am sure no conscious attempt to misrepresent. Yet something has prompted the poet to deny the emotional centre of his two most impressive ballads about women. If anything, the Preface is *more* irrelevant in its comments on the 'Forsaken Indian Woman' than in those on 'The Mad Mother'. Unsexing the woman completely, Wordsworth speaks of 'accompanying the last struggles of a human being at the approach of death, cleaving in solitude to life and society, as in the Poem of the Forsaken Indian'[40]. It seems an odd way to introduce the most beautiful of his poems of the mother-child relationship. Wordsworth's emphasis on the woman's clinging to society is surely misplaced and, in so far as she values life, it is in the bond with her child. The implication of the Preface is that Wordsworth doesn't mind which sex he is writing about. He is concerned simply with human beings and the human mind. There is *some* truth in this, but not enough to prevent the statement as made from being a rewriting of the poem. The power, beauty and insight of the poetry depends on this particular forsaken Indian being a forsaken Indian *woman.* It would have been a very different poem had Wordsworth chosen to describe the last thoughts of a male Indian, which as he makes clear in the prefatory note he could very easily have done.[41]

'The Complaint of a Forsaken Indian Woman' is thirty lines

---

[40] OS i 126

[41] 'When a Northern Indian, from sickness, is unable to continue his journey with his companions; he is left behind, covered over with Deer-skins, and is supplied with water, food, and fuel if the situation of the place will afford it. He is informed of the track which his companions intend to pursue, and if he is unable to follow, or overtake them, he perishes alone in the Desart, unless he should have the good fortune to fall in with some other Tribes of Indians.....the females are equally, or still more, exposed to the same fate.' Prefatory note to 'The Complaint of a Forsaken Indian Woman'. Cornell LB 111.

shorter than 'The Mad Mother' to which it is connected by its metre, its ten line stanza being identical but for the absence of internal rhyme in the penultimate line and it is a poem which needs to be considered in its entirety. Again it is a poem entirely of the mind. In the male counterpart poems, 'Last of the Flock', 'Simon Lee', and point-making poems 'We Are Seven', 'Anecdote for Fathers', the poet himself takes part. However impressive they are they exist on the lower emotional plane of the 'episode'. 'The Complaint of a Forsaken Indian Woman', like 'The Mad Mother' is a stream of consciousness, a poetry wholly composed of feelings and associated ideas, wholly dependant on the poet having no self, in Keats' words 'in for [informing] and filling some other body'[42]. There is not the drama this time of the 'fiendish faces one, two, three,'[43] or of the threatened suicide leap or the absent father's dominant presence. Moods alternate as rapidly as before but they are within a calmer register. This is a poem of voices, at times a meditative soliloquy, almost a prayer...'Oh let my body die away'. At times, it is addressed to the companions whose tents the Indian woman will never see again...'Too soon my friends you went away / For I had many things to say'. At times, it is addressed to her poor forsaken child, to the mother's eye more forsaken by being given to another than she is herself in being left to die. Once and most poignantly she addresses the wind. But the difference of address is merely a factor in the larger patterning of voice. It is an art in which Wordsworth excels but nowhere does he perform with greater subtlety. Any part of the poem would serve as an example; take the second and third stanzas as he leads into the cry of maternal pain...'My Child! they gave thee to another'. First is the anguished playfulness as the

---

[42] Keats letter to Woodhouse 27th October 1818; Rollins i 387
[43] 'The Mad Mother' 23

woman identifies herself with the one living thing that has been left to her, her fire. There is an infinite sadness as the mind plods through the logic of impending death, its pauses marked in three out of four lines with the heavy caesura:

> My fire is dead: it knew no pain;
>
> Yet it is dead, and I remain.
>
> All stiff with ice the ashes lie;
>
> And they are dead, and I will die.

then the reflective voice

> When I was well I wished to live
>
> For clothes, for warmth, for food, and fire;

and the too easy acceptance

> ... here contented will I lie;
>
> Alone I cannot fear to die.

that betrays her into the desperation of a continuing life force

> Alas! you might have dragged me on
>
> Another day, a single one!
>
> Too soon despair o'er me prevailed;
>
> Too soon my heartless spirit failed;
>
> When you were gone my limbs were stronger

All this time we have thought of the woman, identified with her, as confronting merely death – terrible enough, but whatever the

Preface may imply, it is not what the poem is about. 'For strong and without pain I lay', the woman reflects, 'Dear friends, when you were gone away'. And instantly the pain returns to claim her; 'My child! they gave thee to another, / A woman who was not thy mother'. In that tender fantasy the lines that follow are as perfect an example of the Wordsworthian sympathetic imagination as one could wish:

>When from my arms my babe they took,
>
>On me how strangely did he look!
>
>Through his whole body something ran,
>
>A most strange something did I see;
>
>- As if he strove to be a man,
>
>That he might pull the sledge for me.

There is a power in the imprecision of these 'somethings'. 'I beheld a something in the sky' says the Ancient Mariner (47-8); 'A sense sublime / Of something far more deeply interfused' ('Tintern Abbey' 96-7). 'Through his whole body something ran / A most strange something did I see'.

Let me draw attention to just one more moment in this extraordinary poem:

>My fire is dead, and snowy white
>
>The water which beside it stood;
>
>The wolf has come to me to-night,
>
>And he has stolen away my food.

The wolf is 'he' not 'it'. This is almost companionship. There is a faint erotic suggestion in the words 'has come to me tonight'. The tones are so natural that one almost passes over the menace. Death in the opening lines of the poem has had the numinous beauty of assimilation into the world of the northern lights, the aurora borealis:

> Before I see another day,
>
> Oh let my body die away!
>
> In sleep I heard the northern gleams;
>
> The stars they were among my dreams;

Now with the wolf we see another aspect of the natural world not wholly unfriendly, just doing its own thing. The fire is dead, the woman is dying, the wolf is very much alive; tonight he steals the woman's food, tomorrow he will feed as he chooses. It cannot be certain that she, like the fire, will feel no pain.

4 KEATSIAN IMAGINATION[1]

This poem was sent by Keats to John Hamilton Reynolds on the 25th March 1818:

>Dear Reynolds, as last night I lay in bed,
>
>There came before my eyes that wonted thread
>
>Of Shapes, and Shadows and Remembrances,
>
>That every other minute vex and please:
>
>Things all disjointed come from North and south,
>
>Two witch's eyes above a cherub's mouth,
>
>Voltaire with casque and shield and Habergeon,
>
>And Alexander with his night-cap on --
>
>Old Socrates a tying his cravat;
>
>And Hazlitt playing with Miss Edgworth's cat;
>
>And Junius Brutus pretty well so, so,
>
>Making the best of 's way towards Soho.
>
>>Few are there who escape these visitings –
>
>Perhaps one or two, whose lives have patent wings;

---

[1] First delivered as a lecture to The Wordsworth Summer Conference 1995

And through whose curtains peeps no hellish nose,

No wild boar tushes, and no Mermaid's toes:

But flowers bursting out with lusty pride;

And young Aeolian Harps personified,

Some, Titian colours touch'd into real life. –

The sacrifice goes on; the pontif knife

Gl[e]ams in the sun, the milk-white heifer lows,

The pipes go shrilly, the libation flows:

A white sail shews above the green-head cliff

Moves round the point, and throws her anchor stiff.

The Mariners join hymn with those on land. –

You know the Enchanted Castle it doth stand

Upon a Rock on the Border of a Lake

Nested in Trees, which all do seem to shake

From some old Magic like Urganda's sword.

O Phoebus that I had thy sacred word

To shew this Castle in fair dreaming wise

Unto my friend, while sick and ill he lies.

   You know it well enough, where it doth seem

A mossy place, a Merlin's Hall, a dream.

You know the clear lake, and the little Isles,

The Mountains blue, and cold near neighbour rills —

All which elsewhere are but half animate

Here do they look alive to love and hate;

To smiles and frowns; they seem a lifted mound

Above some giant, pulsing underground.

   Part of the building was a chosen See

Built by a banish'd santon of Chaldee:

The other part two thousand years from him

Was built by Cuthbert de Saint Aldebrim;

Then there's a little wing, far from the sun,

Built by a Lapland Witch turn'd maudlin nun —

And many other juts of aged stone

Founded with many a mason-devil's groan.

   The doors all look as if they oped themselves,

The windows as if latch'd by fays and elves —

And from them comes a silver flash of light

As from the Westward of a summer's night;

Or like a beauteous woman's large blue eyes

Gone mad through olden songs and Poesies —

   See what is coming from the distance dim!

A golden galley all in silken trim!

Three rows of oars are lightening moment-whiles

Into the verdurous bosoms of those Isles.

Towards the shade under the Castle Wall

It comes in silence – now tis hidden all.

The clarion sounds; and from a postern grate

An echo of sweet music doth create

A fear in the poor herdsman who doth bring

His beasts to trouble the enchanted spring:

He tells of the sweet music and the spot

To all his friends, and they believe him not.

   O that our dreamings all of sleep or wake

Would all their colours from the sunset take:

From something of material sublime,

Rather than shadow our own Soul's daytime

In the dark void of Night. For in the world

We jostle – but my flag is not unfurl'd

On the Admiral staff – and to philosophize

I dare not yet!--Oh never will the prize,

High reason, and the lore of good and ill

Be my award. Things cannot to the will

Be settled, but they tease us out of thought.

Or is it that Imagination brought

Beyond its proper bound, yet still confined, –

Lost in a sort of Purgatory blind,

Cannot refer to any standard law

Of either earth or heaven? – It is a flaw

In happiness to see beyond our bourn –

It forces us in Summer skies to mourn:

It spoils the singing of the Nightingale.

    Dear Reynolds. I have a mysterious tale

And cannot speak it. The first page I read

Upon a Lampit Rock of green sea weed

Among the breakers – 'Twas a quiet Eve;

The rocks were silent – the wide sea did weave

An untumultuous fringe of silver foam

Along the flat brown sand. I was at home,

And should have been most happy – but I saw

Too far into the sea; where every maw

The greater on the less feeds evermore: -

But I saw too distinct into the core

Of an eternal fierce destruction,

And so from Happiness I far was gone.

> Still am I sick of it: and though to day
>
> I've gathered young spring-leaves, and flowers gay
>
> Of Periwinkle and wild strawberry,
>
> Still do I that most fierce destruction see,
>
> The shark at savage prey – the hawk at pounce,
>
> The gentle Robin, like a pard or ounce,
>
> Ravening a worm – Away ye horrid moods,
>
> Moods of one's mind! You know I hate them well,
>
> You know I'd sooner be a clapping bell
>
> To some Kamschatkan missionary church,
>
> Than with these horrid moods be left in lurch –
>
> Do you get health – and Tom the same – I'll dance,
>
> And from detested moods in new Romance
>
> Take refuge – Of bad lines a Centaine dose
>
> Is sure enough – and so 'here follows prose'.[2]

Keats was at Teignmouth working on *Isabella; or, The Pot of Basil* and was looking after his brother Tom who died of tuberculosis eight months later. Reynolds too was ill confined to his house in London with rheumatic fever and, according to Keats, was in 'the worst place in the world for amendment – among the strife of women's tongues in a hot and parch'd room'[3]. In his letters of the period, Keats is trying to keep up Reynolds's spirits by being

---

[2] Letter to Reynolds 25th March 1818; Rollins i 259-63
[3] Letter to George and Tom Keats 21st Feb 1818; Rollins i 236

especially himself; not easy when Tom was coughing blood and their mother had died of tuberculosis in 1810. Until the previous year Keats had been a medical student at Guy's hospital and he knew too much to feel at ease. We see in him already the immense resilience that will enable him (when he himself is dying, his ship lying in quarantine off Naples) to summon up more puns in a sort of desperation in one week than in any year of his life. Unlike Pope's 'Eloisa to Abelard' or the different versions of Coleridge's 'Dejection' addressed to Sarah Hutchinson and Wordsworth, the verse-letter to Reynolds is truly a letter. With Keats that means something between a conversation and a stream of consciousness – but with two guiding principles; the entertainer's pleasure in words and fantasy and the poet's questing for truth and beauty. The prose-letter to Reynolds of the 3rd May is an example of the genre, opening and closing with Tom who 'has spit a leetle blood this afternoon [which] is rather a damper'[4] but taking us hither and thither among matters personal, literary and philosophical and incorporating for us a statement of Keats' practice as a letter writer:

> So you see how I have run away from Wordsworth, and Milton; and shall still run away from what was in my head...... If I scribble long letters I must play my vagaries. I must be too heavy, or too light, for whole pages – I must be quaint and free of [*meaning 'generous with'*] Tropes and figures – I must play my draughts as I please, and for my advantage and your erudition, crown a white with a black, or a black with a white, and move into black or white, far and near as I please.[5]

Things are 'all disjointed', chosen for the pleasure of their incongruity; but not only for that. 'Two witch's eyes above a

---

[4] Rollins i 282
[5] Rollins i 279

cherub's mouth,.../ And Alexander with his night-cap on, / Old Socrates a tying his cravat' – Keats is talking about fantasy, more or less what Coleridge would call Fancy as opposed to Imagination. Editors[6] suggest an allusion to *Art of Poetry* where Horace distinguishes between the effect of incongruity in painting a beautiful woman whose bottom half is a black ugly fish and in poetry that leaves all to be imagined. But Keats is not quoting authority or indulging in literary showing off. He is concerned with the workings of the mind, patterns and pictures thrown up by the unconscious, and with their relation to creativity. To escape such 'visitings', to be one 'through whose curtains peeps no hellish nose' (bed curtains that is) is to be blessed with 'patent wings', to be able calmly to aspire.

But what of that 'nose'? Is it the monstrous nose over which Cyrano de Bergerac was said to have fought a thousand duels? Or the Shandian, Freudian, smutty nose of Sterne? Or did Keats know Gillray's famous cartoon of 1790 'Smelling out a rat', in which the huge disembodied, indeed defaced, nose of Burke intrudes upon Richard Price the revolutionist? It hardly matters. Keats's image of the nose thrusts itself unexpectedly into the poetry to be visualised by each of us separately and differently. What are we to make of those 'Titian colours' of line 19 that are 'touch'd into real life'? And who are the 'some' who respond to them? Syntax has broken down but not necessarily meaning. If the 'flowers bursting out with lusty pride' and 'young Aeolian Harps personified' (a dig at Coleridge?) are visions of harmony as opposed to the nose, tusks and toes then it appears that 'some' should follow on from 'few' and 'one or two' in lines 13-14. To perceive the colours of Titian brought alive is the achievement of, what Wordsworth would term, a 'higher mind'[7], a feat of the imagination. But it is Hazlitt, not Wordsworth, who lies behind

---

[6] Allott 320n.
[7] *Prelude* 1805 xiii 90; FT 514

Keats's enigmatic reference. 'There is gusto', Hazlitt writes in The Round Table of 1817, 'in the colouring of Titian. Not only do his heads seem to think – his bodies seem to feel'. Though Milton is said to have 'gusto' and other poets are mentioned briefly at the end of the Round Table essay, what we see chiefly and what Keats responds to is Hazlitt the painter defining through his art an ideal of imaginative intensity:

> Whenever we look at the hands of Correggio's women or of Raphael's, we always wish to touch them.....Again, Titian's landscapes have a prodigious gusto, both in the colouring and forms. We shall never forget one that we saw many years ago in the Orleans Gallery of Acteon hunting. It had a brown, mellow, autumnal look. The sky was of the colour of stone. The winds seemed to sing through the rustling branches of the trees, and already you might hear the twanging of bows resound through the tangled mazes of the wood.[8]

The picture that Keats has in mind as he moves on in the verse-letter is by Claude, admired by Hazlitt but singled out precisely as lacking in gusto:

> his eye wanted imagination: it did not strongly sympathize with his other faculties. He saw the atmosphere, but he did not feel it.[9]

Landscape with the Father of Psyche sacrificing to Apollo had suggested details for 'Sleep and Poetry' as early as 1816. Now it prompts lines full of a Keatsian 'gusto' which we are in danger of seeing merely as an anticipation of the 'Grecian Urn';

> The sacrifice goes on; the pontif knife

---

[8] Hazlitt 'On Gusto'; Wu(1) ii 80
[9] Ibid p.81

> Gl[e]ams in the sun, the milk-white heifer lows,
>
> The pipes go shrilly, the libation flows.

Gusto, as Keats makes clear in his 27th October 1818 letter to Woodhouse, 'enjoys light and shade….foul or fair'[10]. Here we have the violence that is displaced by the mystery and beauty of the Grecian Urn's 'heifer lowing at the skies / And all her silken flanks with garlands dressed'[11]. In both cases we know what will happen to the sacrificial animal. But in the first we are told that the sacrifice goes on. The knife gleams as it descends, the heifer lows as the throat is cut, in their shrill loss of control the pipes evoke the death throw, the libation is of blood as well as wine. In terms of the verse-letter, Keats has moved us on from disparate images of oddity and horror, things that can suggest, but can't add up to, a single developing image that is an imaginative whole, 'a sort of oneness' [12] as he will later put it. To complete his picture, for it is a picture, there is the numinous white sail, the green cliff, the movement of the boat, the anchoring off shore that enables the mariners to sing across the water in unison with those on land. Little of this is in *The Father of Psyche Sacrificing to Apollo* and Keats's treatment is no less imaginative as he goes on to incorporate in his verse-letter Claude's famous picture, *The Enchanted Castle*:

> You know the Enchanted Castle it doth stand
>
> Upon a Rock on the Border of a Lake
>
> Nested in trees, which all do seem to shake
>
> From some old Magic like Urganda's sword.

---

[10] Letter to Woodhouse 27th October 1818; Rollins i 387, Letter 118
[11] 'Ode on a Grecian Urn' 33-4; Allott 536
[12] *Endymion* 1 796; Allott 155.

'The winds seemed to sing through the rustling branches of the trees'[13], Hazlitt had written of Titian's *Diana and Actaeon*. Whatever powers we may ascribe to Urganda's sword footnotes tell us[14] she came from Southey's *Amadis of Gaul* and who in fact gave the hero a lance; only 'gusto' – the magic of imagination – can shake the pictured trees, just as it is the magic of imagination that enables us to hear the melodies of the Grecian Urn 'For ever piping songs for ever new'[15].

Wordsworth had written in 'Elegiac Stanzas suggested by a Picture of Peele Castle in a Storm':

> Ah! THEN, if mine had been the Painter's hand,
>
> To express what then I saw; and add the gleam,
>
> The light that never was, on sea or land,
>
> The consecration, and the Poet's dream.[16]

Considering how much Wordsworth Keats is quoting at this period, lines 30-32 of the verse letter seem very probably a reminiscence:

> O Phoebus that I had thy sacred word
>
> To shew this Castle in fair dreaming wise
>
> Unto my friend,...

Keats yearns, as Wordsworth yearns, for the power to paint his castle in the gleam of imagination – 'the light that never was on sea or land' – that consecrates, makes holy, and also substantial, the dream within the mind. His appeal for the sacred word is

---

[13] Hazlitt 'On Gusto'; Wu(1) ii 80.
[14] Allott 322n.
[15] l.24
[16] ll.13-16; Cornell Poems in Two Volumes 267

appropriately to Phoebus – or, Apollo, Greek God of poetic inspiration. 'All which elsewhere are but half animate', Keats tells us of the landscape of the Enchanted Castle, 'here do they look alive'; and then he adds 'to love and hate' which doesn't seem to make sense but is by no means as strange as what comes next: 'Here do they look alive to love and hate / To smiles and frowns; they seem a lifted mound / Above some giant, pulsing underground'. Suddenly we could be in the world of *Whistlecraft*, Frere's enchanting tale of mountain giants. One answer might be to relate this subterranean pulsing to Coleridge and that slightly unfortunate line of *Kubla Khan* 'As if this earth in fast thick pants were breathing'. But probably we should be thinking in quite other terms.

In a letter of the 22nd of November 1817 Keats told Reynolds:

> One of the three Books I have with me is Shakespear's Poems: I neer found so many beauties in the sonnets – they seem to be full of fine things said unintentionally – in the intensity of working out conceits – Is this to be borne? Hark ye!
>
> When lofty trees I see barren of leaves
>
> Which erst from heat did canopy the herd
>
> And Summer's green all girded up in sheaves,
>
> Borne on the bier with white and bristly beard. [17]

'Fine things said unintentionally'! As the green of summer gives place to autumn harvesting the image of the dead year emerges in Shakespeare's poetry as the pulsing giant had emerged in

---

[17] Letter to J.H.Reynolds 22nd November 1817 Rollins i 188. Letter 44 quoting Sonnet 12 ll. 5-8

Keats's, not foreseen but generated in the intensity of the creative process. It makes an interesting way of looking at Shakespearean profusion. But more important is what it tells us of Keats himself. On the 31st January he had sent Reynolds a poetical letter. 'God of song / Thou bearest me along / Through sights I scarce can bear'[18]. Keats adds by way of an apology for the impromptu verse a copy of his most recent sonnet 'When I have fears':

>When I have fears that I may cease to be
>
>>Before my pen has glean'd my teeming brain,
>
>Before high piled Books in charactery
>
>>Hold like full garners the full ripen'd grain—
>
>When I behold upon the night's starr'd face
>
>>Huge cloudy symbols of a high romance
>
>And feel that I may never live to trace
>
>>Their shadows with the magic hand of Chance:
>
>And when I feel, fair creature of an hour,
>
>>That I shall never look upon thee more
>
>Never have relish in the fairy power
>
>>Of unreflecting love: then on the Shore
>
>>Of the wide world I stand alone and think
>
>>Till Love and Fame to Nothingness do sink.[19]

---

[18] Letter to Reynolds 31st January 1818; Rollins i 221 Letter 58
[19] Ibid. 222

Borne along by the 'God of song', perceiving in the night sky 'cloudy symbols' of the romance – that is his theme. Keats thinks not of constructing a poem but of tracing 'shadows with the magic hand of Chance'. Woodhouse who transcribed the sonnet comments usefully: 'These lines give some insight into Keats' mode of writing poetry. He has repeatedly said…that he never sits down to write, unless he is full of ideas – and then thoughts come about him in troops…one of his maxims is that if P[oetry] does not come naturally it had better not come at all'.[20]

This presumably would be Keats's defence against Croker's damaging criticism of his method in the *Quarterly Review*. Croker is reviewing *Endymion* and quotes lines 13-21 of Book One;

> Such the sun, the moon,
>
> Trees, old and young, sprouting a shady boon
>
> For simple sheep; and such are daffodils
>
> With the green world they live in; and clear rills
>
> That for themselves a cooling covert make
>
> 'Gainst the hot season; the mid-forest brake,
>
> Rich with a sprinkling of fair musk-rose blooms;
>
> And such too is the grandeur of the dooms
>
> We have imagined for the mighty dead,[21]

Croker comments,

---

[20] *The Keats Circle Letters and Papers 1816-78* ed. H. E. Rollins Two Vols. 1948 I 128.
Also Keats's letter to John Taylor 27th February 1818 'That if Poetry comes not as naturally as the Leaves to a tree it had better not come at all'. Rollins i 238 Letter 65
[21] Allott 121

> He seems to us to write a line at random and then he follows not the thought excited by this line but that suggested by the rhyme with which it concludes...He wanders from one subject to another from the association not of ideas but of sounds. Here it is clear that the word and not the idea, 'moon', produced the simple sheep and their shady 'boon' and that the 'dooms' of the mighty dead would never have intruded themselves but for the 'fair musk-rose blooms'[22].

For Keats the 'dooms' of 'the mighty dead' show the operation of the 'magic hand of Chance'. For Croker they are unfortunate results of searching for rhyme. Some readers will be happy with the *Endymion* 'dooms'; others won't. Most I should think will be a little dismayed by the 'elves' of the verse-letter 49-50:

> The doors all look as if they oped themselves,
>
> The windows as if latch'd by fays and elves –

How a door looks as if it 'oped' itself I'm not quite sure, but the elf is to be found throughout Keats's poetry denuded of any magic it might once have possessed as the standard rhyme for self! One of its appearances is in 'Ode to a Nightingale':

> Forlorn! The very word is like a bell
>
> To toll me back from thee to my sole self!
>
> Adieu! The fancy cannot cheat so well
>
> As she is famed to do, deceiving elf.[23]

If Keats tells us that the rhyme came 'as naturally as the Leaves to a tree' presumably we have to believe him. But the letter to

---

[22] *Quarterly Review* 19 (April 1818) p.204ff
[23] Allott 531-2

Taylor of the 27th February 1818 that includes this famous image offers also the less flamboyant definition:

> I think Poetry should surprise by a fine excess and not by Singularity – it should strike the Reader as a wording of his own highest thoughts, and appear almost a Remembrance. [24]

What could be more just or more beautiful or less in keeping with so much of Keats own writing? In it we have two touchstones for poetry, one dependant on naturalness – a version of Wordsworth's doctrine of spontaneity, but without his safety clauses – the other depending on imaginative rightness. The first is Keats's workaday anything-goes definition, the second is an ideal.

'Mermaid's toes' are unquestionably a rhyme for 'nose'! However, they have a sort of double bluff incongruity. Mermaids are by definition incongruous for having tails! These ones tease us with how to find room for 'toes' as well! They hardly seem a 'Remembrance' but you could argue they were a 'fine excess' rather than mere 'singularity'. Keats is not only lush and sensuous and in quest of truth and beauty but also endlessly facetious and exuberant especially in these letter-poems.

The giant is 'pulsing underground' and there is the strange architectural make-up of the Enchanted Castle; the first part built by a 'santon of Chaldee' (a holy man, usually said to be a Mohammedan which he can't logically be); the second, two thousand years later, by the fanciful Anglo-Saxon 'Cuthbert de Saint Aldebrim'; a third, this time merely 'a little [north facing] wing', built by 'a Lapland witch' turned into a weepy nun! Finally come the 'many other juts' and projections of 'aged stone'

---

[24] Rollins i 238 Letter 65

painfully constructed over the years by different mason-devils, who have, one assumes, (apart from being diabolic) the same relation to the master-builder as the printer's devil (lowest of the low in a printing works: Keats uses the word to Reynolds two weeks later[25]) has to the head of the firm. That is a little bit of linguistic ingenuity! In so far as it can be said to exist (Reynolds is told at line 33 that he knows it 'well enough') the Enchanted Castle is from Claude. But Keats is having fun, enjoying the frivolous thoughts that come to him 'in tropes', products of 'the magic hand of Chance'.

Also, surely, we may see in his imaginary castle with its different sections incongruously insisted upon, a little mockery of Wordsworth's account of *The Recluse*. According to the Preface to *The Excursion* the Recluse was to be seen, not as a castle but as its ecclesiastical equivalent, a gothic cathedral, divided into different major parts – plus by way of additional juts 'the little cells' (Wordsworth writes) 'oratories and sepulchral recesses ordinarily included in those edifices'[26]. The 1814 Preface where Wordsworth, not without self pleasure, spells out his ambitious scheme and his architectural metaphor is quoted by Keats to Reynolds on the 3rd May, just six weeks after the verse letter.

Returning to the Castle door at line 49 and the brief five line paragraph that follows, doors can't look as if they open themselves; windows can't look as if they have been 'latch'd by fays and elves' (this is being pedantic but it may be useful). There is no reason why windows shouldn't produce or reflect a 'silver flash of light' but, if it came from 'the Westward of a summer's night', might it not be pink rather than silver, or even red and black? ('The Clouds that gather round the setting sun / Do take a sober colouring'[27].) Leaving that aside, would windows even in

---

[25] Letter to Reynolds 10th April 1818; Rollins i 269 Letter 77
[26] Wordsworth's Preface to *The Excursion* 1814 O S iii 6

the most enchanted of castles be likely to resemble 'a beauteous woman's large blue eyes'? And if they did how would their appearance be affected by her having gone mad, poor thing, 'through olden songs and Poesies'?

To what extent is Keats's imagination visual? Does he see the things he writes about? The verse letter starts as if he does:

> Dear Reynolds, as last night I lay in bed,
>
> There came *before mine eyes* that wonted thread
>
> Of Shapes and Shadows and Remembrances,
>
> That every other minute vex and please:

The poem opens in reverie drifting into sleep and the poet is still abed when the monstrous 'nose' pokes through his curtains! At line 55 Reynolds is asked to '*See* what is coming from the distance dim'. And at line 67 the theme of night-time imaginings is prolonged with:

> O that our dreamings all of sleep or wake
>
> Would all their colours from the sunset take.

And yet half the time it doesn't seem as if Keats is seeing things at all. Croker pointed to the associationism of sound as a connecting principle in the poetry and is undoubtedly right. There would be no 'leaden-eyed despairs' in stanza three of 'Ode to a Nightingale' if there had not been 'a few sad, last, grey hairs' a few lines back. There would have been no prospect of 'new Love' pining 'beyond tomorrow' (ugly phrase) but for the beautiful line, 'Where but to think is to be full of sorrow'. But rhyme didn't create the 'nose', rhyme didn't create the 'giant pulsing underground'.

---

[27] Wordsworth 'Intimations of Immortality' 196-8; PW iv 285

Though Croker denies it, we have to think that Keats is an associationist of ideas; but a very odd one! The verse-letter is an important poem not least because it tells us of the unpredictability of mental process and shows Keats himself fascinated by the quirks by which he is teased and with which he teases the reader. In this context the Enchanted Castle seems to be proposed to Reynolds as a centrepiece to the poem without ever quite becoming one. The golden galley that appears from nowhere at line 55 is permitted far greater impressiveness:

> See what is coming from the distance dim!
>
> A golden galley all in silken trim! ….

(more anticipation of the *Grecian Urn*; the heifer's 'silken flanks')

> …. Towards the Shade under the Castle Wall
>
> It comes in silence.

The last line and a half seem especially beautiful and especially Wordsdworthian! In the Prologue of *The White Doe of Rylston*, the doe approaches and 'Beside the ridge of a grassy grave / In quietness she lays her down'[28]. Compare 'Towards the shade of the castle wall she comes in silence'. Sailing into the middle of the poem the galley brings with it the mystery of the unknown, just as the voice of the nightingale moving across the landscape at the end of the *Ode* creates a numinous distancing:

> Adieu! adieu! Thy plaintive anthem fades
>
> Past the near meadows, over the still stream,
>
> Up the hill-side…[29]

---

[28] ll. 141-2; Cornell *White Doe* 85
[29] ll. 75-7; Allott 532

Two awkward lines that tell us in their way just as much about the Keatsian imagination:

> Three rows of oars are lightening moment-whiles
>
> Into the verdurous bosoms of those Isles

It is another case in which Keats later rewrote himself. In the magical ending of stanza four of the 'Nightingale', we have just been told about the Queen-Moon 'Clustered around by all her starry fays' and Keats has three lines to finish his stanza. In this situation we could get pleonasm, but not this time. Keats is at his best, his most numinous:

> But here there is no light
>
> Save what from heaven is with the breezes blown
>
> Through verdurous glooms and winding mossy
>
>   ways.

Before there had been oars flashing light into the 'verdurous bosoms' of islands; now there is the still less probable blowing of light through the 'verdurous glooms' of a wood. But the swaying of branches does admit light. The thought that light is actually 'blown' by the wind goes one stage further into the improbable and into the numinous. It has the delicate imaginative quality seen by Lamb in Wordsworth's wish for the Old Cumberland Beggar to have around him, whether heard or not, 'the pleasant melody of woodland birds'. The reader's mind, as Lamb puts it, 'knowingly passes a fiction on herself, first substituting her own feelings for the Beggar's, and, in the same breath, detecting the fallacy will not part with the wish'[30].

---

[30] Lamb's letter to Wordsworth 30th Jan 1801; *The Letters of Charles and Mary Lamb* (Dent 1935) Vol 1 239

The beauty and delicacy enter with the second attempt. Keats's earlier lines of the verse-letter overreach themselves, stretching syntax and language allowing us the pleasure neither of detailed observation nor of wish fulfilment:

> Three rows of oars are lightening moment-whiles
>
> Into the verdurous bosoms of those Isles

Croker who was hard on coinages as well as rhyme would have disliked not just the uneasy compound 'moment-whiles' but the strained concept of 'lightening.....*into* the verdurous bosoms', meaning presumably reflecting light. In this case the problem seems to be not with the imagining but with the over-writing. As readers we are ready to see the trireme with light flashing from her three banks of oars but prevented from doing so as Keats strives too hard for his effect.

The coming of the galley is welcome to us because we are being told a story. The Enchanted Castle has been treated disrespectfully and never given the chance to enchant. Reading backwards from the Odes, as we habitually do, we want it to be a version of the Grecian Urn, at once symbolic in its own right and a source of incident and reflection. But the poetry isn't working that way. A trumpet sounds as the galley docks under the castle wall and both ship and Castle disappear from the poem as Keats offers us a strange and disjointed story of a herdsman who, having brought his cattle to drink at 'the enchanted spring', is frightened at the sound of music echoing from 'a postern grate', tells his friends what he has experienced and is not believed. The herdsman it would seem represents an ordinary world stumbling on the enchanted one. He 'tells of the sweet music and the spot / To all his friends, and they believe him not'. The Castle and its environs we are being reminded are magic. In one sense they exist and in another they don't. As the poetry moves on we see them as 'dreamings', earth-bound in their origins rather than of 'material sublime':

> O that our dreamings all of sleep or wake
>
> Would all their colours from the sunset take:
>
> From something of material sublime,
>
> Rather than shadow our own Soul's daytime
>
> In the dark void of Night.

It is a perpetual theme with Keats; one sees it everywhere not least in the last lines of the 'Nightingale'. Keats's tones have a new wistfulness. There will be no more intrusive noses, no more 'Mermaid's toes'. But the poetry does not at once become simpler. The Longman editor takes the easy way out in her footnote to 68-9:

> 'Echoes Wordsworth's 'Tintern Abbey' (1798) 95-7:
>
> ...a sense sublime
>
> Of something far more deeply interfused,
>
> Whose dwelling is the light of setting suns.'[31]

Keats doesn't echo Wordsworth, he engages with him (as he does with Shakespeare rather than Milton). The footnote is evasive, dodging the issue of how Keats is thinking and how his lines interact with 'Tintern Abbey'.

The verse-letter is the central poem of Keats' great period of enquiry into the nature of Imagination, a period that begins with the famous definitions of the letter to Bailey of the 22nd November 1817 'What the Imagination seizes as Beauty must be

---

[31] Allott 323

Truth....The Imagination may be compared to Adam's dream, he awoke and found it truth'[32] and ends six months later in the letter to Reynolds 3rd May 1818, with comparisons of Wordsworth and Milton and the concept of life as 'a large Mansion of Many Apartments'[33]. No doubt the limits are arbitrary. But it is to this period between the completion of *Endymion* in November and the Scottish walking tour of Summer 1818 that a large majority of Keats's most quoted statements belong.

The letter to Bailey (22nd November 1817) is important, not so much for the neo-Platonist equation of Beauty and Truth (though that will persist in the 'Grecian Urn' and elsewhere) as for the subtlety of Keats's reading of Adam's dream. Adam sleeps during Eve's creation; he is given a heavenly dream of her and wakes to find that she exists. Keats writes in a complex statement that is not very often quoted, 'Adam's dream...seems to be a conviction that Imagination and its empyreal reflection is the same as human Life and its spiritual repetition'[34]. It is the sort of philosophical musing that one expects from Coleridge not Keats. But that is because we have a stereotype of Keats that leaves out a dimension of his thinking. In this case he has been offering a personal view of the after-life, what he terms a 'favourite Speculation of mine that we shall enjoy ourselves here after by having what we called happiness on Earth repeated in a finer tone'[35]. If Imagination has the same relation to its empyreal reflection, its heavenly counterpart, as human life to its spiritual repetition in heaven, we have a definition that closely resembles the higher reaches of the Coleridgean Primary Imagination. It is not precisely 'a repetition in the finite mind of the eternal act of creation'[36], but it is nonetheless a shading of the human through

---

[32] Letter to Bailey 22nd November 1817; Rollins i 184
[33] Letter to Reynolds 3rd May 1818; Rollins i 280
[34] Rollins i 185
[35] ibid
[36] BL Chapter 13, 304

the imaginative pursuit of truth into the divine, or into the spiritual at least.

Keats has at this stage five hundred more lines of *Endymion* to write; a week later he is finished. Though the poem has been designed as a test of his powers of invention, he values Book One and recommends it to Bailey as embodying his favourite speculation. Then he wonders if he has really expressed himself clearly and on the 30th January he sends his publisher Taylor an all-important correction:

> Wherein lies Happiness? In that which becks
>
> Our ready Minds to fellowship divine;
>
> A fellowship with essence, till we shine
>
> Full alchymized and free of space[37]

Originally Keats had written:

> that which becks
>
> Our ready minds to blending pleasurable;
>
> And that delight is the most treasurable
>
> That makes the richest Alchymy[38]

lines that muddle along with no sharpness and make a poor introduction to the famous passage that follows:

> Behold
>
> The clear religion of heaven! Fold
>
> A rose leaf around thy finger's taperness

---

[37] Letter to John Taylor 30th Jan 1818. Rollins i 218
[38] Allott 154n.

> And soothe thy lips; [39]

Keats is concerned with what he defines with Wordsworthian hesitancy as 'a sort of oneness'[40], a loss of self that is to be achieved through intensity of imaginative response:

> Feel we these things? That moment have we stepped
>
> Into a sort of oneness, and our state
>
> Is like a floating spirit's. But there are
>
> Richer entanglements, enthralments far
>
> More self-destroying, leading, by degrees,
>
> To the chief intensity; the crown of these
>
> Is made of love and friendship, and sits high
>
> Upon the forehead of humanity[41].

Between the composition of these lines in April 1817 and the correction sent to Taylor in January, Keats has 'alchymized' the poetry. Imaginative achievement of 'chief intensity' is come to be associated with 'fellowship divine', 'fellowship with essence'. Such thinking follows on from the November letter to Bailey and its portrayal of the mind in its quest for spiritual fulfilment. Keats has experienced, as he tells Taylor, 'a regular stepping of the Imagination towards [a] Truth'[42].

On the 24th March, the day before writing the verse-letter, Keats sends James Rice a letter which is part bawdy:

---

[39] *Endymion* 780-3; Allott 154-5
[40] *Endymion* 796; Allott 155
[41] Ibid. 795-802
[42] Letter to Taylor 30th January 1818; Rollins i 218 Letter 57

> Rantipole Betty she ran down a hill
>
> And kik'ed up her pettic[o]ats fairly
>
> Says I I'll be Jack if you will be Gill –
>
> So she sat on the grass debonnairly[43]

(She did a good deal else in later verses!) The letter is also in part facetious. 'Milton', Keats records, came to stay at Teignmouth and 'rolled himself, for three whole hours, in a certain meadow...where the mark of his nose at equidistances is still shown'.[44] Could it be his nose between the curtains? I think Bloom would like it. And in part the letter is decidedly solemn. Keats is talking about a version of 'negative capability':

> What a happy thing it would be if we could settle our thoughts, make our minds up on any matter in five Minutes and remain content – that is to build a sort of mental Cottage of feelings quiet and pleasant...but Alas! this can never be: for as the material Cottager knows there are such places as France and Italy and the Andes and the Burning Mountains – so the spiritual Cottager has knowledge of the terra semi incognita of things unearthly;...[45]

On the eve of his verse-letter we are presented with Keats the 'spiritual Cottager', tenant of this earth but conscious always of the half-known world of 'things unearthly'.

What relationship does this have with 'Tintern Abbey' and his wish that dreaming might partake of 'material sublime'?

> O that our dreamings all of sleep or wake

---

[43] Letter to James Rice 24th March 1818; Rollins i 256, Letter 72
[44] Ibid. Rollins i 254
[45] Ibid. Rollins i 254-5

> Would all their colours from the sunset take:
>
> From something of material sublime,
>
> Rather than shadow our own Soul's daytime
>
> In the dark void of Night.

The concept of dreams and reveries taking their colours from the sunset is very strange, very Keatsian, very unWordsworthian. Wordsworth will tell us in 'Tintern Abbey' of a pantheist life-force 'whose dwelling is the light of setting suns'[46]. More to the point (according to Bailey, Keats never wearied of repeating the poem) he will speak in 'Intimations' of….

> Clouds that gather round the setting sun
>
> Do take a sober colouring from an eye
>
> That hath kept watch o'er man's mortality;[47]

For Keats the sunset is symbolic of a realm of pure Imagination. It might be inhabited by Wordsworth's 'something far more deeply interfused'[48] but above all it has the 'chief intensity' of the *Endymion* passage. It beckons our ready minds to 'fellowship divine' that is a 'fellowship with essence', not with any personalised version of the traditional God. It may be that the closest Wordsworth gets to this Keatsian sublime is 'Stepping Westward' where imaginative associations of travelling into the sunset are prompted by a casual greeting and the poetry is unusually free of the Wordsworthian 'palpable' design upon us;

> 'twas a sound
>
> Of something without place or bound;

---
[46] Wordsworth 'Tintern Abbey' 97
[47] Wordsworth 'Intimations of Immortality' 199-201
[48] 'Tintern Abbey' 96

> And seemed to give me spiritual right
>
> To travel through that region bright.[49]

But such comparisons serve only to show how essentially Keats is himself. His reference to dreams as 'shadowing' (reflecting) 'our own Soul's daytime / In the dark void of Night', has a plangency that takes us to Belial in *Paradise Lost* Book II:

> who would lose,
>
> Though full of pain, this intellectual being,
>
> Those thoughts that wander through eternity,
>
> To perish rather, swallowed up and lost
>
> In the wide womb of uncreated night,
>
> Devoid of sense and motion?[50]

But the strangeness and the strength of Keats's thinking are his own. Adam had all the luck! Waking from his dream he found it truth. Others wake to find that the intensity of dreaming is compounded merely of elements of day-to-day life, in effect that Fancy has been at work, not Imagination. To Coleridge, Fancy was associative and unvital, working with fixed counters removed from space and time, a mode of memory.

It is hard to get excited about Keats's 'flag' yet to be 'unfurl'd / On the Admiral staff' (even if there is a classical reference to Alcibiades). And the tones of 'to philosophize / I dare not yet', however sincere, are banal to say the least. And

> Oh never will the prize,

---

[49] Wordsworth 'Stepping Westward' 13-16 PW iii 76
[50] PL ii 146-51; Fowler 96

> High reason, and the lore of good and ill
>
> Be my award.

is no less prosaic; but it shows Keats thinking in terms of the Coleridgean higher reason of *Prelude* Book 13, 'reason in her most exalted mood'[51] that is identified with Imagination yet has a Kantean moral dimension. Coleridge deduced the higher reason from *Paradise Lost* and seventeenth century Neo-Platonists as well as from Kant. What Keats's source is remains unclear. He can't have read *The Prelude* and nowhere I think refers to *Biographia*.

The last thirty lines of the verse-letter talk suddenly and impressively of the 'eternal fierce destruction' that goes on within the sea and within the globe as a whole. Keats sickens, as Blake's Urizen sickens, for he sees that life lives upon death. The enigmatic concluding remarks on Imagination which precede that are difficult to be sure about:

> Things cannot to the will
>
> Be settled, but they tease us out of thought.
>
> Or is it that Imagination brought
>
> Beyond its proper bound, yet still confined –
>
> Lost in a sort of Purgatory blind,
>
> Cannot refer to any standard law
>
> Of either earth or heaven?

It is far from clear what 'things cannot to the will be settled'. But if 'they tease us out of thought' it doesn't seem likely that Keats is

---

[51] *Prelude* 1805 xiii 170; FT 520.

saying merely as editors have suggested that life cannot be adjusted to our wishes. 'The Grecian Urn' a year later 'tease(s) us out of thought / As doth eternity'[52]. We can no more grapple with its permanence and its lessons than we can think of timelessness from within our time-bound existence. Unless Keats is using the phrase 'to tease us out of thought' in two completely different ways, the things he has in mind as not subjected to the human will, will have this quality of being too great for our limited perception.

This doesn't answer the question why they can't be 'settled' to our will. It seems the Imagination is confined in a sort of limbo, ineffectual because it is too powerful for earth, too feeble for heaven. It has been assumed, for instance by Miriam Allott, that the 'proper bound' of Imagination is heaven and that it 'cannot adjust itself to laws of everyday reality which belong to earth'[53]. This sounds like saying with Shawcross, Engel and others that for Coleridge the Primary Imagination was Secondary[54]. To Bailey, Keats had written 'imagination and its empyreal [heavenly] reflection' is in the same relation to each other as 'human life and its spiritual repetition'[55]. The 'spiritual Cottager' has his feet on the ground as he aspires to the 'terra semi incognita'[56]. Imagination as one would expect is bounded by the humanity of those to whom it belongs; but they, and it, can be raised to a more than earthly pitch. When this occurs Imagination will be able to conform neither to the earthly laws it has transcended nor to the heavenly ones proper to its empyreal reflection. Purgatory in the circumstances is not a realm of purging but a

---

[52] 'Ode on a Grecian Urn' 44-5. Allott 537
[53] Allott p.324 note to ll.78-82
[54] Discussion of this in *The Infinite I Am; Coleridge and the Ascent of Being* by Jonathan Wordsworth in *Coleridge's Imagination, Essays in Memory of Pete Laver* ed. Richard Gravil, Lucy Newlyn and Nicholas Roe Cambridge 1985
[55] Letter to Benjamin Bailey; 22nd November 1817; Rollins I 185 Letter 43
[56] Letter to James Rice 24th March 1818. Rollins I 255 Letter 72

half-way house. Where Wordsworth or Coleridge would see the Imagination as God-like in its aspiration, Keats sees it in this mood at least as capable of going too far for its own good. It is a 'flaw' in nature 'to see beyond our bourn'.

Imagination in the writing of the verse-letter has been asked to assuage, to amuse, Reynolds in his sickness and keep at bay the realities of Tom spitting blood. Instead it has portrayed Keats with its 'mysterious tale':

> Dear Reynolds. I have a mysterious tale
>
> And cannot speak it. The first page I read
>
> Upon a Lampit Rock of green sea weed
>
> Among the breakers. 'Twas a quiet Eve;
>
> The rocks were silent – the wide sea did weave
>
> An untumultuous fringe of silver foam
>
> Along the flat brown sand.

which is Keats at his very best. The sea ought to be merely beautiful but, because the Imagination insists on looking into it, turns out to parallel the land in its power to disconcert. Keats writes:

> I was at home

in compatible surroundings he means

> And should have been most happy – but I saw
>
> Too far into the sea;...
>
> ...I saw too distinct into the core

Of an eternal fierce destruction

For all his attempts to buy off these thoughts, gathering the 'spring-leaves and flowers gay' and writing the poem itself, Keats is betrayed by 'moods' of his own mind that poke through the bed curtains like the terrible nose. Wordsworth returns not just in the phrase 'moods of my own mind' (it comes from *Poems* 1807) but bringing with him 'the gentle robin...ravening a worm' from 'The Redbreast Chasing a Butterfly'. In a sort of desperation, Keats returns to the fancy and the facetious:

> Away ye horrid moods,
>
> Moods of one's mind! You know I hate them well,
>
> You know I'd sooner be a clapping bell
>
> To some Kamschatkan missionary church,
>
> Than with these horrid moods be left in lurch

There is a terrible sadness, pathos, in all this, recognised in the abrupt transition:

> Do you get health – and Tom the same – I'll dance,
>
> And from detested moods in new Romance
>
> Take refuge

Keats can't stop giving utterance but it must be as the 'clapping bell' or as the writer of 'Romance' pushing aside the 'eternal fierce destruction' into which the Imagination insists upon penetrating. Keats cannot of course stop here. Writing *Isabella; or, the Pot of Basil*, planting the pot with the basil of Romance, won't keep the festering head of violence and sadness in control.

His last great speculation is the concept of 'Soul-making'.

Imagination is put to its final test looking into the sea of time and eternity itself to understand the nature that is red in tooth and claw and to understand human existence in which 'youth grows pale, and spectre thin, and dies'[57]. 'To see beyond our bourn' may be necessary to us to cope with pain and to 'school' the intelligence. Somehow, somewhere there must be a harmony, a 'oneness', that explains it all. Keats is writing to George and Georgiana in America, the date is Feb-May 1819. He refers in passing to *The Eve of St. Agnes* and includes the letter texts of *La Belle Dame Sans Merci* and 'Ode to Psyche'. Before the end of the month he will have written both the 'Nightingale' and the 'Grecian Urn'. This then is Keats at the height of his powers. He begins with a little deliberate pomposity, offers a pithy comment on Christian doctrine of the Atonement and moves on:

> The common cognomen of this world among the misguided and superstitious is 'a vale of tears' from which we are to be redeemed by a certain arbitrary interposition of God and taken to Heaven – What a little circumscribed straightened notion! Call the world if you Please 'The Vale of Soul-Making'. Then you will find out the use of the world. (I am speaking now in the highest terms for human nature admitting it to be immortal which I will here take for granted for the purpose of showing a thought which has struck me concerning it.) …

The parenthesis is important. Keats is not, or not quite, making a statement of faith. One is reminded of the tentative way that Wordsworth will talk about pre-existence in his note to 'Intimations'. He continues:

> I say 'Soul-making', Soul as distinguished from an Intelligence – There may be intelligences or sparks of the

---

[57] 'Ode to a Nightingale' 26; Allott 527

divinity in millions but they are not Souls till they acquire identities, till each one is personally itself. Intelligences are atoms of perception; they know and they see and they are pure, in short they are God – how then are Souls to be made? How then are these sparks which are God to have identity given to them – so as ever to possess a bliss peculiar to each one's individual existence? How, but by the medium of a world like this? This point I sincerely wish to consider because I think it a grander system of salvation than the Christian religion – or rather it is a system of Spirit creation.?[58]

This could in part so easily be Coleridge of 1795. 'Intelligences are atoms of perception; they know and they see and they are pure, in short they are God.' Blake would have accepted the statement without difficulty. Wordsworth surprised himself in a manuscript of 1799 by speaking of 'that one interior life ... In which all beings live with God themselves / Are God'[59]. Coleridge, though he must have prompted Wordsworth's isolated statement, regarded such views as Spinozistic atheism, a failure to distinguish between God and his creation. But he came close to it in his earlier Unitarian days. Keats, though he didn't apparently know *Biographia*, did know Coleridge's 1817 collection of poems *Sybilline Leaves*. There he would have found not Coleridge's Unitarian manifesto-poem 'Religious Musings' of 1794-6, but in its place 'The Destiny of Nations' 1795, with the daring speculation....

> That as one body seems the aggregate
>
> Of Atoms numberless, each organized;
>
> So by a strange and dim similitude

---

[58] Letter to George and Georgiana Feb-May 1819; Rollins ii p.101-2 Letter 159
[59] MS. Drafts and Fragments of the *Prelude;* see Norton p. 496

> Infinite myriads of self-conscious minds
>
> Are one all-conscious Spirit, which informs
>
> With absolute ubiquity of thought
>
> (His one eternal self-affirming Act!)
>
> All his involved Monads[60]

Keats is no Coleridgean but he is from his different position working over similar ground.

The question of individuality that preoccupies him had been faced by Coleridge in a 1795 draft of 'The Eolian Harp' where he extends the image of the wind-harp past the concept of God as the universal soul playing on the instrument of nature, to the level of the varying tunes produced:

> And what if All of animated life
>
> Be but as instruments diversely fram'd
>
> That tremble into thought while thro' them
>
>   breathes
>
> One infinite and intellectual Breeze
>
> Thus God would be the universal Soul
>
> Mechaniz'd Matter as the organic harps,
>
> And each one's Tunes are that, which each calls I.[61]

For Keats, as for Coleridge, the discussion centres on Imagination. Coleridge's reference to God's 'one eternal self affirming act' is

---

[60] Coleridge; 'The Destiny of Nations' 40-7; Mays I 283
[61] STC II 324

inserted in the 1817 text of 'Destiny of Nations' as a direct allusion to *Biographia* Chapter 13 'The primary Imagination I hold to be the living Power and prime Agent of all human perception and as a repetition in the finite mind of the eternal act of creation in the infinite I AM'. Keats meanwhile finds his 'intelligences', 'these sparks which are God', as 'atoms of perception'. The quality in them which is not God-like but actually God is Imagination. And yet the intelligence has to be put to 'school', transformed through hard experience into an independent soul, capable of not so much deserving an after-life as possessing 'a bliss' which is peculiarly suited to its individuality:

> Do you not see how necessary a World of Pains and troubles is to school an Intelligence and make it a soul? A Place where the heart must feel and suffer in a thousand diverse ways!...The heart...is the Mind's Bible, it is the Mind's experience, it is the teat from which the Mind or intelligence sucks its identity. As various as the lives of men are, so various become their souls[62].

This appears to me to be a faint sketch of a system of salvation which does not affront our reason and humanity. Though he uses the term 'salvation', Keats does so having denounced the Christian System it normally implies as a 'little circumscribed straightened notion', a notion that does affront our reason and humanity. He is not like Milton or De Quincey attempting to justify the ways of God to man. Keats accepts the concept of mortality and works with it to create a system that would be tolerable, unaffronting – a salvation not from our being good or being redeemed but from the 'holiness of the heart's affections and the truth of Imagination':

---

[62] Letter to George and Georgiana Keats 21st April 1819; Rollins ii 102-3 Letter 159

> What the Imagination seizes as Beauty must be truth – whether it existed before or not – for I have the same idea of all our Passions as of Love, they are all in their sublime, creative of essential Beauty[63].

Keats's words are impressive and not at all easy to construe. The statement that the passions 'are all in their sublime, creative of essential beauty' is offered as evidence that 'What the imagination seizes as Beauty must be truth'. Two equations emerge; the expected one between truth and beauty and a second between imagination and passion, any passion heightened to a sublime and therefore creative level. These are the circumstances under which one may properly talk of the 'holiness of the heart's affections'.

On the face of it, it is all very Keatsian, very unlike his fellow Romantic poets. Keats's favourite Wordsworthian poem ends with 'Thanks to the human heart by which we live'[64]. From 'The Old Cumberland Beggar', Keats rightly singles out the line 'We have all of us one human heart'[65]. We are told in the Preface to *Lyrical Ballads* that 'Poetry is passion. It is the history or science of feelings'. Though Keats's statements are unWordsworthian in their rhetoric, I suspect that Wordsworth *did* believe that both what the Imagination seizes as beauty must be truth and that human passions, 'in their sublime' (the phrase is important), are 'creative of essential Beauty'. Keats's views of Imagination may *not* be as different from those of the other Romantic poets as we tend to assume. His exuberance, shown in the verse-letter to Reynolds, makes for a special delight in Fancy which others have; Coleridge's 'A Soliloquy of the Full Moon, She being in a mad passion' for instance or Wordsworth's 'Barberry Tree'. And he

---
[63] Letter to Bailey 22nd November 1817; Rollins i 184 Letter 43
[64] 'Intimations of Immortality' 201
[65] At line 153; PW iv 239

values more, or at least more often, the effects of chance, 'fine things said', as they are by Shakespeare, 'unintentionally' in the intensity of working out conceits. Keats does not make a distinction as Coleridge does between a secondary and a primary Imagination, but then neither does anyone else (and Coleridge himself is far less preoccupied by it than twentieth century scholars have been); instead he talks of a human creative activity characterized by moments of special intensity – 'gusto' to use the term he borrows, but had no need to, from Hazlitt – and of 'fellowship with essence' which is a merging of human creativity with the divine.

In all this he relies on the shared Romantic concepts of 'oneness' and 'loss of self':

> Feel we things? That moment have we stepped
>
> Into a sort of oneness, and our state
>
> Is like a floating spirit's.

the 'Tintern Abbey' process in which loss of bodily awareness, a dying away of the merely natural, enables us to become a floating spirit or living soul:

> But there are
>
> Richer entanglements, enthralments far
>
> More self-destroying, leading, by degrees,
>
> To the chief intensity[66]

It is not that the enthralments are self-destroying but that they lead to the destruction of self. As Coleridge puts it, this time in *Religious Musings*, the poem upon which 'Tintern Abbey' draws

---

[66] *Endymion* I 795-7; Allott 155

in its more theological moments:

> Till by exclusive consciousness of God
>
> All self-annihilated it [the soul] shall make
>
> God its Identity, God all in all!
>
> We and our Father one. [67]

Differences of rhetoric conceal positions that are shared. Like Shelley and Blake, Keats detests what he calls 'the pious frauds of religion'[68]. But he is instinctively drawn to 'a sort of oneness' that Blake would call 'fourfold vision'[69], that Coleridge (under the banner of Unitarianism) presents in 'Religious Musings' and 'Frost at Midnight', and Wordsworth in *The Pedlar* and 'Tintern Abbey', that Byron offers somewhat briefly in *Childe Harold* Canto III and Shelley in 'Adonais'. Shelley recognized Keats as imaginatively a part of it all:

> He is made one with Nature: there is heard
>
> His voice in all her music, from the moan
>
> Of thunder, to the song of night's sweet bird;
>
> He is a presence to be felt and known
>
> In darkness and in light
>
> He is a portion of the loveliness
>
> That once he made more lovely[70]

---

[67] 'Religious Musings' 42-45 EHC 110-111
[68] Letter to George and Georgiana Keats 19th March 1819; Rollins ii 80 Letter 159
[69] Blake's Letter to Thomas Butts 22nd Nov 1802; Erdman 720-2

'A sort of oneness', one might say.

---

[70] Shelley's 'Adonais' 370-80

5 DOUBLE BICENTENARY [1]

The title, 'Double Bicentenary', which should be 'Double Scottish Bicentenary', draws attention to the deaths in 1796 of Burns (1759-96) and James Macpherson (1736-96), writer, inventor, forger – it depends how unkind one wishes to be of the epic poems *Fingal* and *Temora*, which purport to be translations from the blind, third century, Celtic poet, Ossian. One way to link Macpherson and Burns might be to bill them as two great success stories. Macpherson was acclaimed not as himself but as Ossian throughout Europe and in America too. Thomas Jefferson described him famously as 'the source of daily and exalted pleasure...the greatest poet that has ever existed'[2]. And Burns, twenty five years later, had thirty eight pages of subscribers for the 1787 Edinburgh edition and further editions in Dublin, Belfast, London, Philadelphia and New York. Only Byron among the later Romantics could claim anything of a kind and that not at the outset of his career.

But success is not interesting in itself. What did that success mean? What did the buyers of Macpherson and Burns think they were reading? What were the conditions which made them so eager to spend their money? At that stage one finds oneself

---

[1] First delivered as a lecture to The Wordsworth Summer Conference 1996
[2] Letter to Charles Macpherson in *The Papers of Thomas Jefferson* Princeton 1950; Vol 1 96

discussing a craving among late eighteenth century readers of poetry that takes one close to the origins of Romanticism. 'Craving' seems a strong word but 'primitivism' can't be seen merely in literary or aesthetic terms; it is a need. Romanticism is the full flowering, to use a florid but appropriately organic metaphor, of the quest for origins and abiding human values that is implied in eighteenth century primitivism. It asserted the permanent, the simple and the sublime. It is to be heard in Gray's 'Bard'[3], in Collins's 'Ode on the Popular Superstitions of the Highlands' [4], in Chatterton's fake medieval poems and above all in the bogusness of Macpherson and the genuineness of Burns.

Wordsworth says he opens the book 'at random'[5]. It is reasonable to do so since we find much the same on every page.

> Now Fingal arose in his might, and thrice he reared his voice. Cromla answered around, and the sons of the desert stood still. They bent their red faces to earth, ashamed at the presence of Fingal. He came like a cloud of rain in the days of the sun, when slow it rolls on the hill, and fields expect the shower. Swaran beheld the terrible king of Morven, and stopped in the midst of his course. Dark he leaned on his spear, rolling his red eyes around. Silent and tall he seemed as an oak on the banks of Lubar, which had its branches blasted of old by the lightning of heaven. It bends over the stream, and the grey moss whistles in the wind; so stood the king. Then slowly he retired to the rising heath of Lena. His thousands pour around the hero, and the darkness of battle gathers on the hill.

---

[3] 'The Bard. A Pindaric Ode' 1768, Thomas Gray.
[4] Written 1749-50, published 1788
[5] 'Essay, Supplementary to the Preface' OS iii 77

> Fingal, like a beam from heaven, shone in the midst of his people. His heroes gather around him, and he sends forth the voice of his power. 'Raise my standards on high. Spread them on Lena's wind, like the flames of an hundred hills. Let them sound on the winds of Erin, and remind us of the fight. Ye sons of the roaring streams, that pour from a thousand hills, be near the king of Morven: attend to the words of his power. Gaul, strongest arm of death! O Oscar, of the future fights; Connal, son of the blue steel of Sora; Dermid of the dark-brown hair and Ossian king of many songs, be near your father's arm'. [6]

Hazlitt writes of Ossian (who we should sometimes remind ourselves didn't exist) 'He is a feeling and a name that can never be destroyed in the minds of his readers'[7]. Hazlitt knows that Ossian is a fake but, like so many of Macpherson's readers, modern scholars among them, he pushes the knowledge into the back of his mind, preferring to believe that if *Fingal* and *Temora* are not literally translations of third century epic they contain early materials and are nearly so:

> As Homer is the first vigour and lustihed, Ossian is the decay and old age of poetry. He lives only in the recollection and regret of the past...The cold moonlight sheds its faint lustre on his head; the fox peeps out of the ruined tower; the thistle waves its beard to the wandering gale; and the strings of his harp seem, as the hand of age, as the tale of other times, passes over them, to sigh and rustle like the dry reeds in the winter's wind!

---

[6] *Fingal* Bk IV. *Ossian's Fingal 1792*; Facsimile edition pub.1996 by Woodstock Books 56-7
[7] Hazlitt; *Lectures on the English Poets:* Lecture 1; 'On Poetry in General'. Wu (1) ii. 180

Hazlitt, who never writes better than when he falls into the idiom of the poets he admires, brings this passage of evocation to an end with a strange act of contortion:

> If it were indeed possible to shew that this writer was nothing, it would only be another instance of mutability, another blank made, another void left in the heart, another confirmation of that feeling which makes him so often complain, 'Roll on, ye dark brown years, ye bring no joy on your wing to Ossian'.[8]

If Ossian proved not to have existed, Hazlitt is saying, his loss would confirm to readers the feeling of mutability of a void left in the heart of which Ossian, though he didn't exist, so often and powerfully complained. For a moment Hazlitt concedes that the poetry is faked by a modern, not passed down by the old blind seer of the 'dark brown years'. But imaginatively he can't accept the betrayal; whatever the banal facts of the case, Ossian will remain 'a feeling and a name that can never be destroyed'. Hazlitt's presumably unconscious quotation or echo from 'Tintern Abbey' ('a feeling and a love, / That had no need of a remoter charm, / By thought supplied') associates Ossian with the absolute emotional rightness of nature unthinkingly loved ('the sounding cataract / Haunted me like a passion').

> As regards Ossian though, Wordsworth was on the other side:

> All hail, Macpherson! hail to thee, Sire of Ossian! The Phantom was begotten by the snug embrace of an impudent Highlander upon a cloud of tradition – it travelled southward, where it was greeted with

---

[8] ibid

acclamation, and the thin Consistence took its course through Europe, upon the breath of popular applause…..Open this far-famed Book! I have done so at random, and the beginning of the 'Epic Poem *Temora*', in eight Books, presents itself. 'The blue waves of Ullin roll in light. The green hills are covered with day. Trees shake their dusky heads in the breeze. Grey torrents pour their noisy streams. Two green hills with aged oaks surround a narrow plain. The blue course of a stream is there. On its banks stood Cairbar of Atha. His spear supports the king; the red eyes of his fear are sad. Cormac rises on his soul with all his ghastly wounds'. Precious memorandums,

Wordsworth continues sarcastically,

from the pocket-book of the blind Ossian![9]

He is not usually so satirical or indeed so funny. The begetting of Ossian by a kilted 'Highlander, upon a cloud of tradition' is marvellously pictorial! But it also makes its point about the nature of the poetry. Wordsworth does not come upon Ossian by chance in his 1815 *Essay Supplementary to the Preface*. He has been discussing Bishop Percy whose *Reliques of Ancient English Poetry* are 'collected, new-modelled, and in many instances (if such a contradiction in terms may be used) composed by the Editor'[10]. All this Wordsworth approves of. In contrast to Hazlitt he is thinking very clearly. Macpherson is objectionable to him not because he recreates early poetry, or even because he lies about it, but because the poetry he makes is spurious in itself;

Having had the good fortune to be born and

---

[9] Wordsworth's 'Essay, Supplementary to the Preface'. OS iii 77.
[10] ibid 75

> reared in a mountainous country, from my very childhood I have felt the falsehood that pervades the volumes imposed upon the world under the name of Ossian. From what I saw with my own eyes, I knew that the imagery was spurious. In nature every thing is distinct, yet nothing defined into absolute independent singleness. In Macpherson's work, it is exactly the reverse; every thing (that is not stolen) is in this manner defined, insulated, dislocated, deadened – yet nothing distinct. It will always be so when words are substituted for things.[11]

linking the passage with a very important Wordsworthian discussion of words and things[12]. It is easy to read past this excellent piece of criticism. It sounds rather rhetorical and we are not used to Macpherson's work being looked at in such detail. Wordsworth's accusation is that he has no eye. In the passage quoted from *Temora* each of the characteristically short Ossian sentences has its natural feature and its separate colour…'blue waves', 'green hills', 'trees…dusky heads', 'grey torrents', 'green trees' plus the 'blue course of a stream' and 'the red eyes of his (the King's) fear'. The final detail is more impressive but still, I would suggest, a manipulation of words as opposed to something vividly seen. All the details, as Wordsworth says, are 'insulated, dislocated, deadened', 'nothing distinct' because nothing comes distinctively to life. It is a 'do-it-yourself' kit for a picture to be entitled 'Romantic landscape with King and attendant warrior'! We are to add the imaginative depth that is lacking ourselves and give to the verse the emotion that it craves.

Why then was the impact of Ossian so great on Hazlitt,

---

[11] ibid 77
[12] BOV Ch. 7, 211-212.

Goethe, Jefferson, Madame de Stael and many others? There seem to be two answers. First, that for individual readers the very absence of significant detail in the poetry contributed to the generation of mood – a non-specific, pervasive, tender melancholy. Hazlitt responded to 'the feeling of cheerless desolation, of the loss of the pith and sap of existence'[13] – like Goethe as young Werther as he reads a passage of *Fingal* to Charlotte in the last fatal meeting before he commits suicide. Secondly, there was the seeming fact of Ossian's antiquity. Suddenly a past was revealed that nobody had ever known about which had an important bearing on the readers' present lives. Primitivists took *Fingal* as support for a return to earlier standards (which never existed) of simplicity and genuineness. Scots took it as a national epic. At a time when their liberties and traditions had been suppressed after the 1745 rebellion, Highlanders might be forbidden to bear arms, play bagpipes or wear the tartan but this new past was a source of pride which could not be taken away.

    The Reverend Hugh Blair, Minister of the Church of Scotland and recently appointed Professor of Rhetoric and Belles Lettres at Edinburgh University, was both a primitivist and a Scot. His dissertation on Ossian, printed with the poetry in all but the very earliest editions, authenticated Macpherson's fake and was for a time almost as famous as the poems it accompanied. Writing to Blair on April 6th 1765, David Hume, philosopher and historian, described Blair's dissertation as incomparably the best piece of criticism in the English language. Though it is important, Blair saw what he wanted to see and what MacPherson wanted him to see:

---

[13] Wu (1) ii. 180; see note 7.

> Besides this merit, which ancient poems have with philosophical observers of human nature, they have another with persons of taste. They promise some of the highest beauties of poetical writing. Irregular and unpolished we may expect the productions of uncultivated ages to be; but abounding, at the same time, with that enthusiasm, that vehemence and fire, which are the soul of poetry. For many circumstances of those times which we call barbarous are favourable to the poetic spirit. That state, in which human nature shoots wild and free, though unfit for other improvements, certainly encourages the high exertions of fancy and passion.[14]

'fancy' in this context being the imagination – the distinction is not yet being made.

Blair, whose *Lectures on Rhetoric and Belles Lettres* would become a dominant influence on poetry and criticism in the 1790's and form the basis of the 1800 Preface to *Lyrical Ballads*, has already in 1763 arrived at his views on spontaneity and the origins of figurative language:

> In the infancy of societies men live scattered and dispersed, in the midst of solitary rural scenes, where the beauties of nature are their chief entertainment...Their passions have nothing to restrain them: their imagination has nothing to check it. They display themselves to one another without disguise: and converse and act in the uncovered simplicity of nature. As their feelings are strong, so their language, of itself, assumes a poetical turn. Prone

---

[14] Hugh Blair: 'A Critical Dissertation on the Poems of Ossian' reprinted in *The Poems of Ossian and Related Works* ed. Howard Gaskill; Edinburgh University press 1996, p.345

to exaggerate, they describe every thing in the strongest colours; which of course renders their speech picturesque and figurative[15].

Forty years ahead of time, the Preface to *Lyrical Ballads* is there, waiting to be written. All that is required is to see primitivism in terms of the countryside instead of the past, which is where Burns comes in. But I leave him on one side for the moment.

Blair was not alone in his views. Twenty five years before the death of Dr. Johnson times were on the change. *Fingal* is devised and acclaimed because Macpherson knows what his contemporaries will find acceptable. In Walter Scott's memorable phrase from 1805, he is 'kneading' his ingredients 'into a cake of the right leaven for the sentimental and refined critics, whom it was his object to fascinate'[16]. It is Hume who gives us the most telling account of Ossian's early reception:

> I live in a place where I have the pleasure of frequently hearing justice done to your dissertation, but I never heard it mentioned in a company where some one person or other did not express his doubts with regard to the authenticity of the poems which are its subject, and I often hear them totally rejected, with disdain and indignation, as a palpable and most impudent forgery. This opinion has indeed become very prevalent among men of letters in London.

That is as early as 1763! Hume at this stage is drawn to Ossian. As a Scot and friend of Blair he hopes that authenticity may be established. But he sees the difficulties very clearly. Good as the

---

[15] Ibid.
[16] *The Edinburgh Review* 1805 p.445

poetry may be, it will not be read if it turns out to be a forgery. Macpherson's absurd pride and caprice have not been a help. His refusal to satisfy anybody who doubts his veracity has tended to confirm the general scepticism. Internal evidence that Blair has found seems insufficient or can be interpreted in different ways. Hume is disquieted by the unbarbarian, almost chilvalric, manners of third century Celtic warriors and by 'the preservation of such long and connected poems by oral tradition alone during a course of fourteen centuries'. Hume's letter concludes:

> My present purpose is, to apply to you, in the name of all men of letters of this, and I may say of all other countries, to establish this capital point, and to give us proofs that these poems are, I do not say so ancient as the age of Severus, but that they were not forged within these five years by James Macpherson. These proofs must not be arguments but testimonies...It will not be sufficient that a Highland gentleman or clergyman say or write to you that he has heard such poems; nobody questions that there are traditional poems in that part of the country where the names of Ossian and Fingal and Oscar and Gaul are mentioned in every stanza. The only doubt is whether these poems have any farther resemblance to the poems published by Macpherson. [17]

Extraordinarily he is applying in the name of *all* men of letters in *all* other countries.

---

[17] *Life and Correspondence of David Hume;* From the papers bequeathed by his nephew to the Royal Society of Edinburgh and Other Original Sources; ed. John Burton. Edinburgh 1846 Vol.1 466. The Letter is also cited in *Report of the Committee of the Highland Society of Scotland to enquire into the nature and authenticity of the Poems of Ossian: Drawn Up, according to the Directions of the Committee,* by Henry MacKenzie Esq. (Edinburgh: Constable; London: Hurst, Rees and Orme 1805)

The improbability of fourteen hundred years' oral transmission was not a matter that greatly concerned Blair though he had done his best to explain it away. In pointing to the Celtic warrior's incongruous sensibility however, Hume was questioning what, according to the dissertation, was the core of Ossian's, not Macpherson's, achievement. It was this aspect that drew Blair to the poetry:

> We find tenderness and even delicacy of sentiment greatly predominant over fierceness and barbarity. Our hearts are melted with the softest feelings...[18]
>
> Ossian himself appears to have been endowed by nature with an exquisite sensibility of heart prone to that tender melancholy which is often an attendant on great genius...[19]
>
> The two great characteristics of Ossian's poetry are tenderness and sublimity. He moves perpetually in the high region of the grand and the pathetic. One key note is struck at the beginning, and supported to the end[20].

The results of Blair's attempt to comply with Hume's request are to be seen in the Appendix to his dissertation. He goes about this work somewhat grumpily:

> ...in England, it seems, an opinion has prevailed with some, that an imposture has been carried on;...in the case of...old traditionary poems of our own country, of poems asserted to be known in the original to many thousand inhabitants...such extreme scepticism is altogether out of place.[21]

---

[18] Hugh Blair; op. cit. 349
[19] Ibid. 352
[20] Ibid. 356

But grumpy or not he goes ahead, listing a large number of Scottish gentlemen and clergymen prepared to vouch that they knew the poetry before they heard of Macpherson. In doing so he fell, as Hume predicted, into the trap of assuming that a knowledge of traditional material worked up by Macpherson proved that he was, as he claimed, translating epics by the blind third century poet Ossian.

Making his personal assessment on his journey to the Western Islands with Boswell in 1773, Dr. Johnson fell into no such traps. Among those he questioned was a clergyman whose name was on Blair's list:

> I asked a very learned minister in Skye who had used all arts to make me believe the genuineness of the book whether at last he believed in it himself but he would not answer. He wished me to be deceived for the honour of his country, but would not directly and formally deceive me. Yet has this man's testimony been publicly produced as of one that held *Fingal* to be the work of Ossian? [Johnson is at his best]. I suppose my opinion of the poems of Ossian is already discovered; I believe they never existed in any other form than that which we have seen...[The Scots have good reason] to plead for their easy reception of an improbable fiction. They are seduced by their fondness for their supposed ancestors.

And then we have a wonderful Johnson statement:

> A Scotchman must be a very sturdy moralist who does not love Scotland better than truth! [22]

---

[21] Ibid. 402
[22] Dr Johnson; *A Journey to the Western Islands of Scotland* ed. Mary Lascelles;

So Blair, who has all the correct instincts about poetry – and will be the critic who ushers in the Romantic movement – can't tell primitivism when he sees it but backs a shameless imitation. While Johnson the critic of the past age, and famously wrong about so many things, gets it right!

It was left to the Highland Society of Scotland at the beginning of the new century to compile once and for all the evidence as to Macpherson's source material and Ossian's existence. Appropriately they used Hume's 1763 letter to Blair as their starting point. Reviewing their findings in July 1805 for the *Edinburgh,* Scott has also in front of him Malcolm Laing's edition of Macpherson with its compulsive tracking down of literary echoes, borrowings and plagiarisms. For a long while, Scott reveals, he too had cherished the pleasing belief that much of Macpherson's translation, perhaps more than half, was authorised by an authentic original. That is no longer a possible view but he leans over backwards to be fair:

> It would be in the highest degree unjust to disallow a certain extent of foundation to the fabric erected by Macpherson…..Upon the other hand it is believed that no patron of Celtic poetry however zealous will now venture to assume the high ground originally taken by Macpherson[23].

The 'certain extent of foundation' consists not of any trace of the Ossian epics that Macpherson claimed to have translated but of a working into *Fingal* and the first book of *Temora* (but not the other seven) of all the surviving Highland poetry that MacPherson could lay his hands on, none of it within a thousand years of being as old as Ossian was claimed to be. Intended or not, the effect had

---

Yale 1971 pp.118-9
[23] *The Edinburgh Review* 1805 p.431

been to create a host of witnesses who felt honestly and often passionately that they had evidence of Ossian's authenticity:

> So artfully has Macpherson availed himself of every scrap of poetical tradition which then floated in the Highlands that it becomes very difficult and almost impossible for the natives to read them without recognizing events and even phrases with which they were familiar in infancy[24].

Scott was not a Gaelic speaker but the Highland Committee had published translations of the poetry they reproduced. In his review he goes through them one by one, concluding:

> ...we have thus briefly noticed almost all the originals which can now be produced for the poems of Ossian. It is remarkable that they all have reference to Macpherson's first publication in which doubtless he thought it necessary to preserve a certain degree of caution and to give as much authenticity to his poems as he could consistently with his plan of kneading them into a cake of the right leaven for the sentimental and refined critics whom it was his object to fascinate'.[25]

Macpherson, Scott assumes, has worked in the Highland ingredients of his cake 'simply because it was his obvious interest to do so, if he meant to carry on his intended imposture with the least prospect of success'.

Macpherson's 'imposture' does not matter much so long as one keeps it clearly in view. There is nothing wrong in saying this fake is good poetry in its own right and of immense literary and

---

[24] Ibid. 436
[25] Ibid. 445

historical importance. But the moment the author's dishonesty is fudged or forgotten we lose sight of the fact that Ossian was valued across the known world for its antiquity. Had it not been thought to be authentic it would have had few readers then and fewer now.

Between them, The Highland Committee, Laing's edition and Scott's review made it impossible for any but the most secluded to accept Macpherson on his own terms. Byron for instance commented in his note to *Oscar of Alva* 1806 'I fear that Laing's late edition has completely overthrown every hope that Macpherson's *Ossian* might prove the translation of a series of poems complete in themselves'. Wordsworth seems in this process to have responded with unusual indignation. Like others he had no doubt been to some extent deceived. The claim to have felt the falsehood of Macpherson's volumes from childhood has to be weighed against the presence of Ossian in his schoolboy poem *The Vale of Esthwaite*[26] and the pleasure with which he and Dorothy had written of Ossian during and after their Scottish tour of 1803[27]. But something more is needed to explain the poet's

---

[26] 'Wordsworth would know that in Ossianic lore, as gleaned from the pages of Macpherson, the spirits of the departed find their habitation in mist and cloud: hence the attendant ghosts that he introduces...into this mist-filled setting; and the other kind of spirit he perceives in this setting, a spirit of nature is a benign version of the Ossianic spirit of the battered mountain that he was to envisage in Storm Fragments I and II.' Cornell: *Early Poems and Fragments 1785-1797* ed. Landon and Curtis; Cornell 1997, 547

[27] 'I must say, however, that we hardly ever saw a pleasing place in Scotland, which had not something of wildness in its aspect of one sort or another. It came from many causes here: the sea, or sea-loch, of which we only saw as it were a glimpse crossing the vale at the foot of it, the high mountains on the opposite shore, the unenclosed hills on each side of the vale, with black cattle feeding on them, the simplicity of the scattered huts, the half-sheltered, half-exposed situation of the village, the imperfect culture of the fields, the distance from any city or large town, and the very names of Morven and Appin, particularly at such a time, when old Ossian's old friends, sunbeams and mists, as like ghosts as any in the mid-afternoon could be, were keeping company with them.'

unaccustomed vehemence in 1815. It appears he is agitated chiefly by the comparison he himself has set up between Ossian and Bishop Percy. Percy, he has frankly pointed out, tampers with, sometimes actually writes, the ancient poetry he purports to edit. But, for Wordsworth, his is the genuine voice nonetheless, the voice whose tones are to be heard in *Lyrical Ballads* and the new Romantic poetry of simplicity and emotional directness. Macpherson is Percy's vastly more successful spurious counterpart who, in England at least, has inspired no major writer – except perhaps Blake whom Wordsworth could not know about – and no major work even among minor ones. Looked at in terms of Blair who has paradoxically supported the wrong man, it was a case of Percy's *bona fide* primitivism (one did largely know what was original among his ballads) versus Macpherson, the pseudo-primitive. Posterity has tended to be on Percy's and Wordsworth's side, seeing the evolution of Romantic poetry in terms of the ballad revival rather than Ossian's larger gestures.

But Hazlitt's words 'he is a feeling and a name that can never be destroyed' stay in the mind. The wistful plangency that is Macpherson's, not Ossian's, contribution to poetry has proved to have lasting qualities. Scott ended his beautifully judicious essay in 1805 pleading for a new way of valuing Macpherson that should face the strange facts of his achievement. As a result of the Highland Committee's enquiries, not one poem of the celebrated Ossian had been recovered. And Scott adds:

> ....while we are compelled to renounce the pleasing idea that 'Fingal lived, and that Ossian sung', our national vanity may be equally flattered by the fact that a remote, and almost barbarous corner of Scotland, produced, in the

---

Recollections of a Tour in Scotland 1803 JDW i 320

eighteenth century, a bard capable of not only making an enthusiastic impression on every mind susceptible of poetical beauty, but of giving a new tone to poetry throughout all Europe.[28]

Matthew Arnold sixty years later was able to make distinctly larger claims. For him Ossian is an embodiment of 'the poetical Celtic nature in us' that gives passion to English Literature and mitigates our heavy German inheritance; Macpherson's 'Ossian' carried, in the last century, this vein 'like a flood of lava through Europe'.[29] The 'thin Consistence' that had drifted southwards in Wordsworth's metaphor 'begotten... upon a cloud of tradition' in the Highlander's 'snug embrace' has taken on volcanic energy – a flood of lava! Arnold declines to criticize Macpherson's Ossian and proceeds to out-Hazlitt Hazlitt in his determination to hold on to what he feels to be precious whatever the odds may be:

> Make the part of what is forged, modern, tawdry, spurious in the book as large as you please; strip Scotland if you like of every feather of borrowed plumes which on the strength of Macpherson's *Ossian* she may have stolen....there will still be left in the book a residue with the very soul of the Celtic genius in it and which has the proud distinction of having brought this soul...into contact with the nations of modern Europe and enriched all our poetry for it.[30]

It is a reformulation of the old opposition 'Celtic genius' standing for the 'Romantic', the more ordered German inheritance of

---

[28] Scott; *The Edinburgh Review* 1805 462
[29] 'On the Study of Celtic Literature' in *Lectures and Essays in Criticism*, Matthew Arnold ed. R.H.Saper, University of Michigan press 1962, 370
[30] ibid

English poetry replacing in this Victorian context the neo-classical.

So where in all this does Burns stand? The obvious answer is that he was the genuine article, a poet of integrity where Macpherson was a trickster and Ossian a fake. But far more important, it is Burns who brings primitivism up to date, gives it the new sense of direction and forward-looking energy that we tend to think of as Wordsworthian. Up-to-dateness can in a sense be claimed for Ossian too. Part of the original Scottish appeal of *Fingal* and *Temora* was that Macpherson gave to his fellow countrymen, routed at Culloden in 1746 and harshly repressed ever since, a source of national pride. Ossian had been heroic in defeat, his melancholy had a dignity that could be heard across the intervening fifteen hundred years. Countless Scots, so the story went, had sung his work, transmitting it through the generations down to the moment when Macpherson's translation could make it available in print, make Scotland's past and Scotland's poetry known across the world. Outside Scotland, Ossian has the up-to-dateness of the product uniquely well-designed and manufactured for its period. Like Goethe's *Sorrows of the Young Werther*, which quotes it so lavishly, it expresses perfectly the mood and the need of a moment. It was not impossible for readers later (Arnold and Yeats among them) to respond to the mood. But Macpherson's writing as such opens up no new possibilities. Ossian could be imitated but there was no life, no blood, scarcely when it came down to it any imagination, to Macpherson's prose-poetry. It has a wistfulness, a plangency, but page after page it played the same tricks which is why Wordsworth and Byron, though they were moved by it in their juvenilia, never touched it as adults.

Burns by contrast did open up new possibilities. By an odd

chance he was acclaimed first by the very group of sentimental and refined Edinburgh critics, Blair and Henry MacKenzie among them, whom Macpherson had first successfully taken in and who had closed ranks to defend him when Ossian's authenticity was disputed by Johnson and Hume's sceptical London acquaintancies. Burns' *Kilmarnock Poems* were published in July 1786 when the poet was on the run from the family of Jean Armour who bore him their first pair of twins in September. The poet had booked a passage to Jamaica! Success came just in time; but the date was significant too from the point of view of literary history. It was just three years since Blair had published his *Lectures* revealing as he did so that he had been giving them for twenty four years at Edinburgh University. In their primitivist positions they thus go back to the first appearance of Ossian and Blair's own writing of the *Dissertation*. Lecture thirty five, 'On the Origin and Progress of Poetry' is especially important:

> Poetry however in its ancient original condition was perhaps more vigorous than in its modern state. It included then the whole burst of the human mind, the whole exertion of its imaginative faculties. It spoke then the language of passion and no other for to passion it owed its birth. Prompted and inspired by objects which to him seemed great by events that interested his country or his friends the early bard arose and sang. He sang indeed in wild and disorderly strains but they were the native effusions of his heart; they were the ardent conceptions of admiration or resentment, of sorrow or friendship which he poured forth. It is no wonder therefore that in the rude and artless strain of the first poetry of all nations we should often find somewhat that captivates and transports the mind.

Then the passage which is so important to the Preface to *Lyrical Ballads*:

> In after ages when poetry became a regular art studied for reputation and for gain authors began to affect what they did not feel. Composing coolly in their closets they endeavoured to imitate passion rather than to express it. They tried to force their imagination into raptures or to supply the defect of native warmth by those artificial ornaments which might give composition a splendid appearance.

Clearly the 'bard' whom Blair has in mind is Ossian. But in his attack on modern writers 'composing coolly in their closets' his emphasis on poetry as song, the native, or natural, effusions of the heart, he has set the scene for a modern poet of spontaneity.

In the words of *The Edinburgh Review* for October 1786, Burns's Kilmarnock volume is 'a striking example of native genius bursting through the obscurity of poverty and the obstructions of labouring life'. To some extent Burns plays up to this image in his Preface:

> Unacquainted with the necessary requisites for commencing Poetry by rule, [the author] sings the sentiments and manners he felt and saw in himself and his rustic compeers around him in his and their native language.[31]

Much is going on in this single sentence. Burns's native language is Scots, but he is writing in extremely correct English prose. The reference to 'himself and his rustic compeers' permits

---

[31] Robert Burns *Poems Chiefly in the Scottish Dialect* (Kilmarnock 1786) iii.

condescension and invokes the patronage accorded to working class poets: Stephen Duck, the 'thresher poet', James Woodford, the 'shoemaker poet' and many others. But to sneer at those who commence poetry by rule shows something close to arrogance. Burns was quite widely read and knew what he was up to.

As the example of 'native genius bursting through the obscurity of poverty and the obstructions of labouring life', we could turn to Wordsworth's creation of the inspired poet in *The Ruined Cottage* of March 1798 'His eye flashing poetic fire he would repeat the songs of Burns', just as Burns outside the poem is Wordsworth's own ideal at this highly important moment in his life. The manuscript of *The Ruined Cottage* that Dorothy produces at this stage has a very significant epigraph:

> Give me a spark of nature's fire
>
> 'Tis the best learning I desire.
>
> My muse though homely in attire
>
> May touch the heart [32]

The lines are quoted from Burns's *Epistle to J. Lepraik, An Old Scotch Bard*, and contain just about all that Burns in 1786 or Wordsworth twelve years later wished to say about poetry. The one word that both poets might have wished to change is 'though'. In effect, both mean 'My muse *because* homely in attire / May touch the heart.' Burns in the *Epistle* is at his most exuberant. Having a crack at 'your critic folk' who 'cock their nose' not to mention his views on the 'jargon of your schools' and those who 'think to climb Parnassus / By dint o' Greek'! Wordsworth for his part has just completed the full-length *The Ruined Cottage*

---

[32] Cornell *The Ruined Cottage and The Pedlar* Ithaca New York 1979

inserting the character study of the Pedlar (him with 'the flashing poetic fire') who tells Margaret's story and making the poem ready to be a section of *The Recluse*. For his central story he has perfected a way of writing that is indeed 'homely in attire', pared down blank verse dealing in elemental, understated emotions experienced by a country woman of the lowest social class, or very nearly. That Wordsworth has Burns in mind as he writes is confirmed by a further reference that is in inverted commas in *The Ruined Cottage* manuscript. This is the Pedlar speaking:

> My best companions now the driving winds,
>
> And now the 'trotting brooks' and whispering
>
> > trees,
>
> And now the music of my own sad steps[33]

As in the lines to J. Lapraik, Wordsworth is quoting from memory a passage of Burns that is especially important to him and quoting it slightly wrong. Burns had written (and I will anglicise as indeed Wordsworth does):

> Oh nature all thy shows and forms
>
> To feeling pensive hearts have charms!
>
> Whether the summer kindly warms,
>
> > With life and light,
>
> Or winter howls in gusty storms,
>
> > The long dark night!

---

[33] *Ruined Cottage* 294-6; MOH 42

> The muse no poet ever found her,
>
> Till he himself had learned to wander
>
> Adown some trotting burn's meander[34]

(note 'burn' for brook). Wordsworth wandering beside a stream or river comes to seem so natural but Byron chooses it for parody;

> Young Juan wandered by the glassy brooks
>
> Thinking unutterable things [35]

But this special closeness to nature, like the spontaneity, the language of the heart, the homeliness of attire, is a part of the inspired primitivism of Burns before we meet it in Wordsworth.

This was an area it should be said in which Wordsworth did pay his debts. He writes at the grave of Burns in 1803:

> ...He was gone,
>
> Whose light I hailed when first it shone,
>
> And showed my youth

---

[34]   O NATURE! A' thy shews and forms
To feeling, pensive hearts hae charms!
Whether the Summer kindly warms,
    Wi' life an' light,
Or Winter howls, in gusty storms,
    The lang, dark night!

The Muse, nae Poet ever fand her,
Till by himself he learn'd to wander,
Adown some trottin burn's meander,
    An' no think lang;
O sweet, to stray an' pensive ponder
    A heart-felt sang!
from Burns's 'To W. Simpson Ochiltree'

[35] Byron. *Don Juan* Canto 1 713-4

> How Verse may build a princely throne
>
> On humble truth[36].

It was true that Wordsworth had hailed the light of Burns when first it shone. A letter from Dorothy in December 1787 shows that at the age of seventeen he has read the poetry and 'admired many of the pieces very much'[37]. Dorothy at almost sixteen likes especially the *To a Mountain Daisy* and *To a Louse*[38]. Building a 'throne / On humble truth', however, did not come easily or early to Wordsworth. As we see from 'Tintern Abbey' it took time for him to feel the shows and forms of nature, to hear 'the still sad music of humanity'. Wordsworth encounters Burns and reads him with pleasure and probably has memorised much at seventeen. But he comes to rely upon him ten years later. [There is an echo in 'He was gone whose light I hailed'; it is a self-quotation. Thinking of Burns as having shown the way to a poetry of humble truth, Wordsworth in 1803 echoes *The Ruined Cottage*, 'he was gone whose hand / At the first nippings of October frost'[39].]

The timing of this reliance on Burns is significant. Just at the moment when Coleridge is broadening Wordsworth into the great philosophic poet of 'Tintern Abbey' and the *Prelude*, Burns gives to him the poetry of everyday life, the poetry of ordinariness lit by a 'spark of nature's fire'. Who should be in the background of it all but Macpherson's old supporter Blair. In January 1798, Coleridge took *Lectures on Rhetoric and Belles Lettres* out of the Bristol library. This book, with a little help from Joanna Baillie, herself a Blair follower, was to be the chief source of the 1798

---

[36] Wordsworth; 'At the grave of Burns' 32-6; PW iii 66
[37] DW to Jane Pollard 7th December 1787. EY 13
[38] Ibid.
[39] *The Ruined Cottage* 477-8 in MOH 47

'Advertisement'[40] and, of course, also very important in the 1800 Preface and the 1802 Appendix on Poetic Diction and was with Wordsworth and Coleridge at Alfoxden as they planned the scheme of *The Recluse*, as they revised and lengthened 'The Ancient Mariner' and *The Ruined Cottage* and as they composed the *Lyrical Ballads* and 'Christabel'.

Blair's definitions of verse and poetry are in the background;

> The most just and comprehensive definition which I think can be given to poetry is that it is the language of passion or of enlivened imagination formed most commonly into regular numbers...The truth is, verse and prose, on some occasions, run into one another like light and shade. It is hardly possible to determine the exact limit where eloquence ends and poetry begins; or is there any occasion for being very precise about the boundaries, as long as the nature of each is understood.[41]

But Blair remains an antiquarian primitivist. He thinks still in terms of Ossian, of an ancient bard who arises and sings spontaneously the native effusions of his heart. He can update this by thinking of American Indians who were still in the savage state that is favourable to the poetry of the heart but always he sees the greatest poetry as having preceded civilisation and the artificiality of men composing 'coolly in their closets' forcing their imagination into 'raptures'. So this greatest formative document that underlies Romantic literary thinking is a voice that comes down from 1760 with all the preoccupations of that moment. Because he thought always of origins, Blair never makes the

---

[40] i.e. to *Lyrical Ballads* 1798
[41] From Lecture xxxviii para 3 of *Lectures on Rhetoric and Belles Lettres* by Hugh Blair in Three Volumes London Fifth Edition 1793 85-6

Romantic stride forward that was available to him of seeing what Wordsworth terms in the Preface 'low and rustic life' of the present day as having the all-important closeness to nature, simplicity, plainness, truth to the heart.

That step is made by Wordsworth and Coleridge – others including Baillie, Taylor and Enfield had anticipated it as change was in the air – as Wordsworth in late February or early March 1798 (with 'Goody Blake and Harry Gill', first of the *Lyrical Ballads*, just days away) writes of the Pedlar of *The Ruined Cottage*:

> From his native hills
>
> He wandered far. Much did he see of men
>
> Their manners, enjoyments and pursuits,
>
> Their passions and their feelings, chiefly those
>
> Essential and eternal in the heart
>
> Which 'mid the simpler forms of rural life
>
> Exist more simple in their elements
>
> And speak a plainer language. [42]

Looking at a graveyard, Wordsworth can say 'Andrew's whole fireside is there'[43]. Looking at these lines, we can say Wordsworth's whole poetic creed is there. It is the new vital primitivism which (though the second generation of Romantics won't accept it straight) will carry forward to be at the centre of Romanticism and which comes from Burns.

---

[42] *The Pedlar* 239-45; MOH 180
[43] 'To a Sexton' l.12; PW ii 134

Hazlitt had identified so deeply with the melancholy of Ossian that he could not bear to think it a fake. We may end – not with the indignant Wordsworth who speaks magnificently of 'clouds of tradition' amid the 'snug embrace' of an 'impudent Highlander' – but with the Wordsworth who quietly buries Ossian because he is a beautiful idea; the landscape needs him:

> Does then the bard sleep here indeed
>
> Or is it but a groundless creed? What matters it?
>
> I blame them not whose fancy in this lonely spot
>
> Was moved and in this way expressed
>
> Their notion of its perfect rest[44].

Burns far more than is normally understood enabled Wordsworth to build his 'princely throne / On humble truth'[45]. Ossian, the myth of Ossian that is, contributes to the no less important side of Wordsworth that values above all the 'strong creative power of human passion'[46].

---

[44] Wordsworth; 'Glen Almain' 15-20.

[45]   I mourned with thousands, but as one
      More deeply grieved, for he was gone
      Whose light I hailed when first it shone,
      And showed my youth
      How verse may build a princely throne
      On humble truth. 'At the Grave of Burns' Wordsworth 1803
            (seven years after Burns's death)

[46]   The Poets , in their elegies and songs,
      Lamenting the departed, call the groves,
      They call upon the hills and streams to mourn,
      And senseless rocks; nor idly, for they speak,
      In these their invocations, with a voice
      Obedient to the strong creative power
      Of human passion. *The Excursion* 1 507-513; Cornell Ex 62

6 THE DOORS OF PERCEPTION[1]

If the doors of perception were cleansed every thing would appear to man as it is: infinite[2].

Blake's words in *The Marriage of Heaven and Hell* 1790 seem simple enough. They are a starting point for a meditation on the nature of Romanticism, 'every thing would appear to man as it is: infinite.' There is a defiance in 'as it is'. Blake later accused Wordsworth of being a Platonist and not a Christian but this statement of his is pure Platonism. Two worlds are implied, two modes of existence; the world of the infinite from which we are blocked by our limited sensual perception and the lower world which we inhabit and which we treat as if it were all that existed. Many shared Blake's Platonism in 1790 but what makes Blake's statement exceptional is the implication that we could remove the barrier, become part of the higher world of the spirit to which in a sense we belong. His words offer the first great definition of Romantic Imagination, the human faculty which Wordsworth in 1805 would celebrate in the *Prelude* which 'in truth / Is but another name for absolute strength / And clearest insight'[3]. It is

---

[1] First delivered as a lecture to The Wordsworth Summer Conference 1997
[2] *The Marriage of Heaven and Hell* Plate 14. Erdman 39
[3]   This love more intellectual cannot be
    Without imagination, which in truth
    Is but another name for absolute strength
    And clearest insight, amplitude of mind

Platonism again which Coleridge will claim in *Biographia Literaria* enables us 'to lose and find all self in God'[4], and which Shelley will see as the 'interpenetration of a diviner nature through our own'[5], a rather Coleridgean definition again.

I am interested by what the great writers of the period seem to have in common, despite their differences of age, education, class and temperament. Blake, Coleridge Wordsworth and Shelley will feature; Keats and Byron rather less so. I used to think the term 'Romanticism' had no meaning. But in 1987 I had three months to write the catalogue for the Wordsworth Trust's American exhibition *William Wordsworth and the Age of English Romanticism*[6] and I could no longer get by without asking questions and making definitions. In building up the exhibition we had reasonably taken for granted that there were connections between Romanticism and the French Revolution, between poetry and painting. These had to be examined more closely. Convenient as it was to explain the Romantic impulse in terms of

---

And reason in her most exalted mood.
Prelude 1805 XIII 166-70; FT 520

[4] 'We begin with the I KNOW MYSELF, in order to end with the absolute I AM. We proceed from the SELF, in order to lose and find all self in GOD'. Chap 12 Thesis IX; BL 283.

[5] 'Poetry is the record of the best and happiest moments of the happiest and best minds. We are aware of evanescent visitations of thought and feeling sometimes associated with place or person, sometimes regarding our own mind alone, and always arising unforeseen and departing unbidden, but elevating and delightful beyond all expression - so that even in the desire and the regret they leave, there cannot but be pleasure, participating as it does in the nature of its object. It is, as it were, the interpenetration of a diviner nature through our own; but its footsteps are like those of a wind over a sea, which the coming calm erases, and whose traces remain only as on the wrinkled sand which paves it'. *Defence of Poetry* from *Shelley's Critical Prose* p.31 ed Bruce R. McElderry, Jr. 1967 University of Nebraska Press

[6] The exhibition was accompanied by the volume *William Wordsworth and the Age of English Romanticism* by Jonathan Wordsworth, Michael C. Jaye and Robert Woof: 1987; Rutgers University Press and The Wordsworth Trust.

political events, the great assertions of independence in America and France were themselves symptomatic of something larger going on. As for poetry and painting, we had pictures borrowed from the National Collections of England and America, but we still had to answer the question in what sense the painted landscapes of Constable's childhood by the placid River Stour were akin to the mountainous Cumbrian ones of Wordsworth's poetry. Did Turner and Shelley, or Turner and Byron, have things in common that could be written about intelligibly? The question returned to most often was not so much 'How could an age of Romanticism come about?' as 'What could it consist of?' In what sense did it ever happen? Who at this time (aside from a handful of poets and painters) would have been involved in it or known it was going on – as opposed, for instance, to being involved in the Industrial Revolution which was surely paying a lot more people a lot more wages! No-one ever called themselves 'Romantics'. No-one ever thought there was a movement that brought Wordsworth and Byron together let alone find room for the eccentricities of Blake.

William Wordsworth and the Age of English Romanticism was seen in 1987-8 by two hundred thousand people at the New York Public Library, the Indiana University Art Museum and the Chicago Historical Society; and by two million more in the form of poster panels which can be seen in the Trust museum[7] and which, thanks to the National Endowment for the Humanities[8], travelled in every state in the Union. Years later people who saw the exhibition were still moved by it. I have been told that there was something special about it, that its theme of Romanticism took people back to their roots. Partly, they meant that it took them

---

[7] The Museum at the premises of the Wordsworth Trust in Grasmere.
[8] '....a federal agency established by Congress' (see Acknowledgements in *William Wordsworth and the Age of Romanticism*).

back to a shared heritage, the period before British and American culture diverged. But it was more personal than that, one might say more spiritual. Many who walked up the grand steps of The New York Public Library and into the marble-pillared exhibition room found themselves unexpectedly thinking about childhood, about nature (none too evident on Fifth Avenue), about values that easily get forgotten in city life. Since 1988 I have been trying through the volumes of the *Revolution and Romanticism* series and the volumes of essays which they have generated[9] to understand what did go on in the Romantic period. What, for example, were the other ten important books that readers of *Lyrical Ballads* bought or read or saw reviewed in 1798? How much have we created the period through hindsight on the basis of the half dozen poets who now seem most significant? But I come back often to the larger questions of the nature of Romanticism, questions that perhaps we cannot answer but are right to go on asking. I have even come to think that there is a sense in which we may have some of the answers.

The bigger the question the less an answer can be formulated. But formulation isn't everything. We know because we know, intuitively, imaginatively, not because we have thought the answer through. As Romantics, or lovers of Romantic poetry, or participants in the Wordsworth Summer Conference we have a sense of what Romanticism means. We do not need Keats to tell us that 'Beauty is truth, truth beauty'. We may not wish to be hit on the head as we are in the famous concluding lines of 'Ode on a Grecian Urn' with the words 'that is all / Ye know on earth, and all ye need to know'[10]. But even here we might pause before

---

[9] *Revolution and Romanticism,* an extensive series of contemporary facsimiles published by Woodstock Books, each prefaced with an introductory essay by JFW.

dismissing or ridiculing what the poet has said. How different is it from Blake's statement in *The Marriage of Heaven and Hell*? 'If the doors of perception were cleansed', beauty and truth 'would appear' as they are, identical in the higher world of Platonic absolutes. And, of course, as Keats was aware, there is another world in which 'Truth' and 'Beauty' are one, the world of our reading of great poetry. For those who read it sensitively, poetry is the world of the imagination, the world of our wish for something bigger, purer, more true. It is a world that Coleridge evokes in *Biographia* and Shelley more beautifully still in *The Defence of Poetry*:

> '.....poetry defeats the curse which binds us to be subjected to the accident of surrounding impressions. And whether it spreads its own figured curtain or withdraws life's dark veil from before the scene of things, it equally creates for us a being within our being. It makes us the inhabitants of a world to which the familiar world is a chaos. It reproduces the common universe of which we are portions and percipients, and it purges from our inward sight the film of familiarity which obscures from us the wonder of our being'.[11]

Coleridgeans may notice that Shelley has read *Biographia*! We are reminded by the 'figured curtain' and the 'dark veil' that Shelley is the truest Platonist of them all, a reader and translator of Plato who came to his works via Bishop Berkeley and found in them (the *Symposium* and the *Republic* especially) a way of thinking that conformed to his deepest instincts, though not of course to his early sceptical training through Hume, Holbach and Godwin.

---

[10] 'Ode on a Grecian Urn' 49-50; Allott 537
[11] *A Defence of Poetry* op.cit. 32

Whether or not we believe in what Blake termed the 'infinite' we have an impulse to do so which is enhanced by our response to poetry. Shelley expresses in exalted language, which we should not ourselves have used, something that makes sense to us. Wordsworth carries an extraordinary variety of readers with him, most of whom no longer had the faith that his first audience took for granted when he writes in 'Tintern Abbey' of:

> that serene and blessed mood,
>
> In which the affections gently lead us on,

All of us

> Until, the breath of this corporeal frame
>
> And even the motion of our human blood
>
> Almost suspended, we are laid asleep
>
> In body and become a living soul. (41-47)

'If the doors of perception were cleansed', if 'we were laid asleep / In body', 'every thing would appear as it is: infinite', we should respond to the power of an ultimate harmony, oneness, and, in doing so, 'see into the life of things'[12]. To believe this is an act of faith. To enter into it as most of us do imaginatively is an act of sympathy, a feeling *with*. In either case we have passed however briefly into a realm in which Truth and Beauty are names for an absolute that has in its nature to be one. Broadly speaking all the Romantics are Platonists, even Byron in the Wordsworthian Third Canto of *Childe Harold* 'I live not in myself but that I become /

---

[12] While with an eye made quiet by the power
     Of harmony, and the deep power of joy,
     We see into the life of things. 'Tintern Abbey' 48-50. Cornell LB 117

Portion of that around me'[13].

But Platonism comes in many forms. In Blake's *Marriage*, we have just been told under the heading of 'A Memorable Fancy' of a supper party given by Blake for Isaiah and Ezekiel[14]. Memorable Fancies in *The Marriage* parody the *Memorable Relations* narratives of the mystic Emanuel Swedenborg with whom Blake carries on a love/hate relationship. But parody is being put to Blake's own purposes. The prophets find themselves cross-examined on the nature of their apprehension of God:

> The prophets Isaiah and Ezekiel dined with me, and I asked them how they dared so roundly to assert that God spake to them; and whether they did not think at the time that they would be misunderstood, and so be the cause of imposition?

It is a fair question; could the prophets really be sure that God was speaking to them? If not shouldn't they be worried about deceiving people? Isaiah's reply is defensive but has an air of straightforwardness:

> I saw no God, nor heard any, in a finite organical perception; but my senses discover'd the infinite in

---

[13] I live not in myself, but I become
Portion of that around me; and to me,
High mountains are a feeling, but the hum
Of human cities torture: I can see
Nothing to loathe in nature, save to be
A link reluctant in a fleshly chain,
Classed among creatures, when the soul can flee,
And with the sky, the peak, the heaving plain
Of ocean, or the stars, mingle, and not in vain.
Childe Harold's Pilgrimage Canto 3 Stanza 72; *The Complete Poetical Works of Byron* ed. Jerome J. McGann 1980 O.U.P. Vol ii 103-4

[14] Plates 12-13. Erdman 38-9

everything, and as I was then perswaded, and remained confirmed; that the voice of honest indignation is the voice of God, I cared not for consequences but wrote.

God cannot be seen in a 'finite organical perception', with one's ordinary limited senses. But the 'doors' of Isaiah's perception are unobstructed, either cleansed or clean from the first. He perceives the infinite, sees everything as it truly is. Feeling in himself the voice of 'honest indignation' he takes it for the voice of God and writes – much, it would seem, what Blake does himself. At this point, Blake, not as author but as Isaiah's host, asks the big question that underlies any discussion of Romantic Imagination or of faith. 'Does a firm perswasion that a thing is so, make it so?' Isaiah's answer this time is elegant but slippery. It is the reply that we should get if we summoned Blake from the dead as he himself summoned the prophets:

> Does a firm perswasion that a thing is so, make it so?
>
> He replied. All poets believe that it does, and in ages of imagination the firm perswasion removed mountains, but many are not capable of a firm perswasion of anything'.

We can seldom be sure how to read Blake, but in the struggle to follow his intentions, tone often has things to tell us. Here it is gently ironical. All poets believe that imagination moves mountains; does Blake himself? Well, maybe. 'But many are not capable of a firm perswasion of anything'. The question is brilliantly deflected. Blake does have firm persuasions, no-one has firmer. But moving on from the Memorable Fancy of Isaiah and Ezekiel to Plate 14 of *The Marriage* and his key statements on 'the doors of perception' we have been disconcerted, warned against taking all at face value:

> The ancient tradition that the world will be consumed in fire at the end of six thousand years is true, as I have heard from Hell.
>
> For the cherub with his flaming sword is hereby commanded to leave his guard at the tree of life, and when he does, the whole creation will be consumed, and appear infinite and holy whereas it now appears finite and corrupt.
>
> This will come to pass by an improvement of sensual enjoyment.
>
> But first the notion that man has a body distinct from his soul is to be expunged; this I shall do by printing in the infernal method, by corrosives, which in Hell are salutary and medicinal, melting apparent surfaces away, and displaying the infinite which was hid.
>
> If the doors of perception were cleansed, everything would appear to man as it is: infinite.
>
> For man has closed himself up, till he sees all things thro' narrow chinks of his cavern.[15]

Much is happening in this passage. It contains the moment about which we are able to feel most clear, Blake's own works as an engraver, using acid to bite into copper plate and melt apparent surfaces away, which become a metaphor for revelation, the truth that is to be revealed.

---

[15] Plate 14. Erdman 39

However, that man has no body distinct from his soul, takes a little explaining. Blake is attacking the dualism of orthodox Christianity not from the materialist point of view (seen for instance in Priestley) that man is entirely physical, but from the opposite end. Did he but know it he is a spiritual being. Why does he not know it? Because he has closed himself up and sees everything through the narrow chinks of the cavern of his skull. The moral implication is clear. Man should be able to see, should be able to perceive the 'infinite' but has accepted limitation. Blake as prophet, empowered by 'honest indignation', proposes to do something about it with the satire implied in the use of corrosives that are 'salutary and medicinal' and in a more peremptory mood by commanding a reversal of man's expulsion from Paradise. The 'cherub' who is necessarily placed in Genesis to stand guard over the Tree of Knowledge[16], of which the human pair have already eaten, is to leave his post; at this point the world of our material existence will burn up and be reassimilated into the realm of pure spirit, the 'infinite'.

That Blake should be in a position to order the end of the world is a little surprising. But the tradition that Creation was designed to end after six thousand years to be followed by the Millenium, the thousand years of Christ's Second Coming, was widely accepted, for instance by Cowper and Coleridge. That Hell should be able to tell Blake of the prediction's accuracy reflects a basic upside-downness in *The Marriage* that follows from his mischievous reading of *Paradise Lost*. Heaven and its angels in the context of this parody are pale, restrictive. Hell is powerful, imaginative, exuberant, full of energy.

More difficult to be certain about is Blake's assertion that

---

[16] KJV *Genesis* Chap. 3

'Creation will be consumed' and 'appear infinite and holy' as the result of 'an improvement of sensual enjoyment'. It may be that at first we are supposed to be shocked by the idea that man will achieve the infinite by having greater sensual pleasure. But with consideration, the concept of improved sensual enjoyment leads directly to the cleansing of 'doors' of imagination and may mean something not very different. The 'infinite', in each case, is to become apparent as the result of an intensifying of the senses, thought of by Blake as a return to an earlier, unfallen state in which the senses were expansive, 'all-flexible'[17].

This playful but deeply serious early Blake moves this discussion on the nature of Romanticism forward in four possible directions; the Millenium, the Infinite, the senses and Romantic Imagination. Romanticism is by its nature anarchic and whether its themes and practitioners will remain content beneath such headings is far from certain. Everything connects, interlocks, interacts. The Millenium matters because it underlies the hopefulness which is so large a part of Romanticism. Ludicrous as it now seems, the ancient tradition (to which Blake now refers) of the world being consumed by fire after six thousand years was accepted Christian belief of the day. Archbishop Ussher's arithmetic printed in English and American bibles till half way through the twentieth century put Creation at 4004 B.C. giving the earth a lifespan ending in 1996! It is all a little difficult to take seriously. Scientists were fully aware of the evidence of the fossil record. Erasmus Darwin conjectured in 1794 in *Zoonomia*, sixty five years before his grandson's *Origin of Species*[18], that the earth

---

[17] Earth was not: nor globes of attraction
  The will of the Immortal expanded
  Or contracted his all flexible senses.
                  Urizen Chapter II 37-8; Plate 3, Erdman 71
[18] 1859

was millions of ages old and that life derived from the ocean evolving from a single living filament. The surgeon, John Hunter, meanwhile had been painted by Joshua Reynolds with an engraving of six skulls on his desk ranging from lower primates through the apes to man. Yet we find the ageing Coleridge, as late as 1815, huffing and puffing indignantly at the absurd notion put forward by Darwin and others at 'Man's having progressed from an Ouran Outang state – so contrary to all history, to all Religion, nay to all Possibility'.[19]

Millenarian thinking was not always comfortable. Calvinists believed that a large proportion of the human race was predestined to hell. But the concept of a fore-ordained course of history was a source of optimism and confidence in a God who had things under control. William Cowper was a depressive whose letters show a terrifying sense of being damned. But he still managed in *The Task* Bk. V1 to present the Millenium as 'the time of rest', 'the promised Sabbath'. 'The groans of nature in this nether world', he writes:

...have an end.

Foretold by prophets, and by poets sung

Whose fire was kindled at the prophets' lamp,

The time of rest, the promised Sabbath comes.

Six thousand years of sorrow have well-nigh

Fulfilled their tardy and disastrous course

Over a sinful world. [20]

---

[19] Letter from Coleridge to Wordsworth 30th May 1815. Griggs iv 574-5
[20] *The Task* vi 729-736; WC ii 255.

It is a kind of thinking which is most common in periods when events seem to fulfil a divine plan. It had been strong in the 1640's and 50's, Archbishop Ussher's period, when Puritan success in the Civil War led to thoughts of the rule of the Saints on earth and an imminent end of the world. And it reached new heights as the American and French Revolutions of 1776 and 1789 roused hopes of a worldwide political liberty and religious toleration. 'Few persons', Southey wrote in 1823, 'but those who have lived in it, can conceive or comprehend what the memory of the French Revolution was, nor would a visionary world seem to open upon those who were just entering it. Old things seemed passing away, and nothing was dreamt of but the regeneration of the human race.'[21]

The exuberance and somewhat complicated political allusions of *The Marriage of Heaven and Hell* derive from it being written in the year following the French Revolution. Wordsworth's abiding faith in humanity and belief in future human happiness come from the year that he spent in France 1791-2 as a committed follower of the Revolution. The following lines are well-known: 'Bliss was it in that dawn to be alive, / But to be young was very heaven!'[22] and the earlier one "twas a time when Europe was rejoiced, / France standing on the top of golden hours, / And human nature seeming born again'[23]. Hazlitt wrote:

> For my part, I set out in life with the French Revolution, and that event had considerable influence on my early feelings, as on those of others. Youth was then doubly such. It was a dawn of a new era, a new impulse had been

---

[21] *The Correspondence of Robert Southey and Caroline Bowles* ed. Edward Dowden (Dublin 1881), 52: Letter of 24th Feb.1824.
[22] *Prelude* 1805 X 692-3. FT 440
[23] Ibid. VI 352-5. FT 226

given to men's minds, and the sun of Liberty rose upon the sun of Life, and both were proud to run their race together. [24].

Coleridge was more complicated, as always. Both the thinkers whose work formed the basis of his Unitarian Christianity, David Hartley (*Observations on Man* 1749, reissued 1791) and Joseph Priestley, were Millenarians. Hartley puts forward a system that will lead to the future happiness of the human race and Priestley who is his disciple and editor and who thinks him literally the greatest human being since Jesus Christ sees the French Revolution as the fulfilment of Old Testament prophecies about the years leading up to the end of the world. Coleridge himself in his apocalyptic 'Religious Musings' of 1794-6, the most important poem he wrote (except for the first version of 'Dejection') if you want to know what he really thinks conflates the French Revolution and the Second Coming of Christ, uniting as he commonly did religion and politics. Like Blake he had learned his trade from the Book of Revelation:

> The hour is nigh
>
> And lo! the Great, the Rich, the Mighty Men,
>
> The Kings and the Chief Captains of the World
>
> With all that fix'd on high like stars of Heaven
>
> Shot baleful influence, shall be cast to earth,
>
> Vile and down-trodden, as the untimely fruit
>
> Shook from the fig-tree by a sudden storm.[25]

---

[24] William Hazlitt, 'On the Feeling of Immortality in Youth'. Wu(1) ix 137
[25] 'Religious Musings' 1794-6 308-314; STC I 186

This is grand early Coleridge. But there is a gentler Coleridge in 'Religious Musings', one who promises future happiness for mankind as the 'vast family of love', a cosmic version of Pantisocracy, the commune he had planned with Southey to found on the banks of the Susquehanna:

> Return pure FAITH! return meek PIETY!
>
> The kingdoms of the world are yours: each heart
>
> Self-govern'd, the vast family of Love
>
> Rais'd from the common earth by common toil
>
> Enjoy the equal produce.[26]

It is a radical political agenda based on the sharing of love in hearts that are appropriately 'self-govern'd', not subject to authority. The blessed future that rushes on the poet's view, however, is on the grand apocalyptic scale. Coleridge loves the big gesture:

> For in his own and in his Father's might
>
> The SAVIOUR comes! While as the THOUSAND YEARS
>
> Lead up their mystic dance, the DESERT shouts!
>
> Old OCEAN claps his hands! The mighty Dead
>
> Rise to new life.........[27]

This is Coleridge but a few years before 'The Ancient Mariner'.

---

[26] Ibid. 339-343; p.188
[27] Ibid 358-362

The footnote to this last passage in 1797 reads:

> The Millenium:- in which I suppose that Man will continue to enjoy the highest glory, of which his human nature is capable. – That all who in past ages have endeavoured to ameliorate the state of man, will rise and enjoy the fruits and flowers, the imperceptible seeds of which they had sown in their former Life: and that the wicked will during the same period, be suffering the remedies adapted to their several bad habits. I suppose,[Coleridge concludes after sorting the wicked away rather satisfactorily to Hell] that this period will be followed by the passing away of this Earth and by our entering the state of pure intellect; when all Creation shall rest from its labours.

For 'pure intellect' read pure spirit (in Blake's terms, the 'infinite') which was the second of the headings that I suggested. To Coleridge's fellow Unitarian, Lamb, 'Religious Musings' is 'the noblest poem in the language next after the Paradise Lost' to which he adds 'and even that was not made the vehicle of such grand truths'.[28] As with Blake, we are to take it all quite seriously. Man has the capacity to lead a spiritual existence, is destined to do so. Blake was a lapsed Swedenborgian who disliked being associated with any religious grouping. Coleridge was a paid-up Unitarian who nearly became a minister in January 1798 in between writing and revising 'The Ancient Mariner'.

Among the relatively few contemporary influences on each was Thomas Taylor. Taylor was the Romantic period's professional Platonist who made sure that his contemporaries as well as

---

[28] *Letters of Charles Lamb* ed. E.V.Lucas 3 vols 1935 Dent and Sons Ltd; Vol. I 93; Letter Lamb to STC begun 5th Feb, sent 6th Feb 1797

feeling in different degrees attracted to the dogma were in a position to read the original sources. As well as Plato himself, Taylor translated Aristotle, Plotinus, Proclus, Iamblichus and others. Not content with this, he upset his Christian contemporaries by proclaiming himself a pagan and managed to live in Regency London much like a fourth century Alexandrian Greek! He was profoundly eccentric. In Taylor's view, Platonism was 'coeval with the universe'[29] itself, as old as human consciousness. One is reminded of Shelley's claim in the *Defence*, 'poetry is connate with the origin of man'[30], born at the same time. 'However its [i.e. Platonism's] continuity may be broken', says Taylor, 'by opposing systems, it will make its reappearance at different periods of time as long as the sun himself shall continue to illuminate the world'[31]. Taylor's assumption is that Platonism will always return because there will always be human beings who at some level intuit the oneness of existence. At times he seems very close to the first generation Romantic poets. Blake probably knew him personally; Coleridge reckoned his work among the 'darling studies'[32] of his youth (but later dismissed him as a bigot). Wordsworth owned one of his Plato translations very possibly bought in 1794. When Taylor speaks for instance of the 'sanctuary of the soul' where she is 'enabled to contemplate with her eyes closed to corporeal vision'[33] he seems so close to 'Tintern Abbey' that one wonders about direct influence. But probably we should be thinking rather in terms of affinity, the zeitgeist. Platonism was in the air.

---

[29] *The Eleusinian and Bacchic Mysteries; A Dissertation* trans. Thomas Taylor ed. Alexander Wilder, fourth edition (New York 1891); 29-30
[30] Shelley; *Defence of Poetry* op. cit. 4
[31] *The Eleusinian and Bacchic Mysteries* see n.29
[32] Coleridge; Letter to John Thelwall 19th Nov 1796; Griggs I 260
[33] *An Essay on the Beautiful*, Plotinus; trans Thomas Taylor. Woodstock Books 1997 p.9

An extraordinary range of people at this period turned out to be thinking in terms of the infinite. Goethe writes, in *The Sorrows of Werter* (1774, first published in English 1779) 'the vivifying heat that animates all nature was everywhere displayed before my eyes, it filled and warmed my heart, I was lost in the idea of infinity'[34]. Madame Roland before her execution in September 1793, addresses with extraordinary courage and clarity the 'Supreme Being, Soul of Universe, thou in whose existence I believe because I must needs emanate from something better than that which I see around me. I am about to be reunited with thy essence'[35] (this is somebody who is about to be guillotined). According to Godwin's 1798 *Memoirs*, Mary Wollstonecraft, whom we tend to think of as a rationalist and city-dweller, 'found an inexpressible delight in the beauties of nature and the splendid reveries of the imagination. But nature itself she thought would be no better than a vast blank if the mind of the observer did not supply it with an animating soul. When she walked amidst the wonders of nature she was accustomed to converse with her God'[36]. All are directly alluding to Plato's 'Anima Mundi' (or 'World Soul') and all have very probably read the early sources.

There were many places however where readers could gain an insight into Platonism. It is to be found in Cudworth and other seventeenth century Neo-Platonists, in Shaftesbury's *Characteristics of Man, Manners and Opinions* 1711, in Bishop Berkeley's *Siris* 1744 and among the poets, in both Pope and Thomson (Pope, notice!). Pope though a Roman Catholic offers in

---

[34] *The Sorrows of Werter*; Chiswick, Press of C Whittingham 1823 p. 51 Letter xxx.
[35] Madame Roland's *Prayer*.
[36] *Memoirs of Wollstonecraft*; William Godwin. Reprinted in Woodstock Books 1990 p.27

his *Essay on Man* a Platonist view of the infinite that is as thoroughgoing as anything in Blake, Coleridge, Wordsworth or Shelley:

> All are but parts of one stupendous whole,
>
> Whose body Nature is, and God the soul;
>
> That, chang'd thro' all, and yet in all the same,
>
> Great in the earth, as in th'aethereal frame;
>
> Warms in the sun, refreshes in the breeze,
>
> Glows in the stars, and blossoms in the trees,
>
> Lives thro' all life, extends thro' all extent;
>
> Spreads undivided, operates unspent![37]

The passage was in Wordsworth's mind when he wrote the great lines on the Simplon Pass (odd place to find Pope!).[38]

Thomson meanwhile celebrates the divine life-force of 'Spring' in terms that anticipate Romantic Platonism to an amazing degree:

> What is this mighty breath? Ye Curious, say,
>
> That, in a powerful language, felt not heard,

---

[37] 'An Essay on Man': Epistle 1 267-274; *The Poems of Alexander Pope* ed. John Butt Methuen 1963 p 514

[38] The unfettered clouds and region of the heavens,
Tumult and peace, the darkness and the light,
Were all like workings of one mind, the features
Of the same face, blossoms upon one tree,
Characters of the great Apocalypse,
The types and symbols of eternity,
Of first, and last, and midst, and without end. *Prelude* 1805 VI. 566-572; FT 242

> Instructs the fowls of heaven; and through their breast
>
> These arts of love diffuses? What, but God?
>
> Inspiring God! Who, boundless spirit all
>
> And unremitting energy, pervades,
>
> Adjusts, sustains, and agitates the whole.[39]

God, as 'mighty breath' as in Coleridge's 'The Eolian Harp', Wordsworth's Glad Preamble to the *Prelude*, Shelley's 'Ode to the West Wind'; God as powerful 'language' as in Coleridge's 'Frost at Midnight', Wordsworth's 'The Pedlar', Shelley's *Defence of Poetry*; God as 'boundless spirit all' is to be found everywhere in Romantic poetry; and God, most interestingly, as 'unremitting energy'. Thomson it seems has anticipated the new scientific dimension of Romantic Platonism. *Spring* would surely have been in Coleridge's mind when in 1795 he addressed God as;

> Glory to Thee, Father of Earth and Heaven!
>
> All-conscious PRESENCE of the Universe!
>
> Nature's vast Ever-acting ENERGY!
>
> In will, in deed, IMPULSE of All to All![40]

Coleridge's 'ever-acting energy' and Thomson's 'unremitting energy' sound suspiciously alike, virtually identical in sense and rhythm.

---

[39] James Thomson, *The Seasons* ed. James Sambrook 1981 O.U.P. 'Spring' 849-855.
[40] 'The Destiny of Nations: A Vision'; STC I 298

But Coleridge's phrase had stronger and more concise associations in 1795 than Thomson's could have had in 1730. 'To the genius truly modern', Thomas Taylor comments in his translation of Plotinus's *Essay on the Beautiful* (second edition, 1792, right in our period) 'the crucible and the air pump are alone the standards of truth'[41]. The allusion, as all would know, was to Joseph Priestley, regarded by Coleridge as 'Saint and Sage'[42] because he was the founder of modern Unitarianism but famous too as the experimental scientist who changed the basis of chemistry by discovering oxygen with his air pump. It is referred to in Anna Laetitia Barbauld's 'The Mouse's Petition' in which the mouse is imprisoned for experiment with the air pump by Priestley and also in Joseph Wright's picture[43] in the Tate Gallery. Taylor's advice to his Platonic readers was that as 'there is no portion of matter that may not be the subject of experiments without end' they should betake themselves to 'the regions of mind...where everything is permanent and beautiful eternal and divine'[44]. It was a rear guard action of Platonism at its most pure, fighting its natural enemy, materialism, but it was materialism in a new and insidious form. To Platonists, matter is illusion; 'If the doors of [our] perception were cleansed' (if we could turn round in our Platonic cave and see reality in place of the shadows) 'everything would appear to man as it is, infinite', immaterial, ideal. To the materialist on the other hand matter is all that exists. The two positions are logically incompatible. But now Priestley, as

---

[41] *An Essay on the Beautiful*; Plotinus. op cit. p.xiii

[42] 'Lo! PRIESTLEY there, Patriot, and Saint, and Sage'; 'Religious Musings' 372; STC 1 189

[43] 'An Experiment on a Bird in the air pump'.

[44] 'since then there is no portion of matter which may not be the subject of experiments without end, let us betake ourselves to the regions of the mind, where all things are bounded in intellectual measure; where everything is permanent and beautiful, eternal and divine'. Taylor's introduction to *An Essay on the Beautiful*; op cit p.ix.

theologian and experimental scientist, had created of all things a materialist Platonism. 'The Divine Being and his energy', he writes in *Matter and Spirit* 1777, 'are absolutely necessary to that of every other being. His power is the very life and soul of everything that exists and strictly speaking without him we are, as well as can do, nothing'. We have our existence in God as material beings powered by his energy.

In terms of Keats's 1819 letter to George and Georgiana we are 'sparks of divinity'. 'Intelligences are atoms', he writes,'....they know and they see and they are pure, in short they are God'[45]. But Keats, though his image of 'sparks' sounds electrical and scientific, has his own version of the Christian body-soul dualism. He sees the sparks as 'schooled' by suffering. 'As various as the lives of men are, so various become their souls and thus does God make individual beings, Souls,...of the sparks of his own essence'[46]. Given that sparks are 'atoms of perception', and that they have presumably through their perception the capacity to become souls, portions of the infinite, we have another variant of Blake's cleansing of 'the doors'. Keats, like De Quincey, in his life-long quest, is concerned to understand the purposes of suffering. Effectively he is saying as De Quincey does in *Savannah la Mar* 'less than these fierce plough-shares' would not suffice for the agriculture of God[47]. Suffering is education; without it the intelligence would not be schooled to understand the nature of the infinite. Such thinking is alien to Priestley whose materialism and determinism restrict his conception of human potential. Man is not in his nature immortal. According to Priestley, man has no

---

[45] Letter to George and Georgiana; Feb-May 1819. Rollins ii 103
[46] ibid
[47] *Savannah-la-Mar*; quoted from *De Quincey's Works* (16 vols) Vol 16 p. 35; pub. A and C Black, Edinburgh 1884 (reprint).

soul and is granted no means of attaining to a perception of the infinite. At God's pleasure, however, he may rise from the dead, as Jesus the carpenter's son rose from the dead, not as spirit but as body carrying with him his mental powers which are bodily too. That is the pure materialist position.

Blake's position was the opposite of Priestley's. Priestley may have been in his mind when he wrote in Plate IV of The Marriage 'Man has no body distinct from his soul for that called body is a portion of soul discerned by the five senses the chief inlets of soul in this age'. For Blake there is no body distinct from the soul. For Priestley there is no soul distinct from the body. What other Christian sects and churches regarded as spirit is a function of the body, part of the working of the material brain as described in Hartley's *Observations on Man* of which Priestley had edited a version in 1775.

Where to place Coleridge in all this is a problem. He is a disciple of Hartley and Priestley who should be a materialist but often seems not to be. Scholars with a philosophical training accuse him of failing to perceive contradictions, merging incompatible systems. But how can he, as he seems to do from early in 1796, reconcile Hartley and Priestley with the Platonist idealism of Berkeley? One answer may be that worshipping a God who is both active energy and world soul, he didn't feel there to be a difficulty. I think that probably is the answer. Another however might be that when put to it he could, and did, reconcile the incompatible positions. Discussing Necessitarianism in a 1794 letter to Southey he writes:

> I go farther than Hartley and believe in the corporeality of *thought*, namely that it is motion.'[48]

'Thought', standing for Berkeley's vision of the universe as an idea in the mind of God, becomes 'corporeal', a fact of the material world in the form of 'motion'. Coleridge does not as far as I know make the point elsewhere in his letters and published writings. But it must have been part of his conversation with Wordsworth three years later at Alfoxden. 'Motion', in this unusual philosophical sense, is not recorded in the Oxford English Dictionary but of course turns up as part of Wordsworth's definition of the divine presence that 'disturbs' him 'with the joy/ Of elevated thoughts' in 'Tintern Abbey'[49]. With his sense sublime of 'something far more deeply interfused', Wordsworth manages to sound quite imprecise. But he is thinking philosophically when he describes the 'presence' as 'a motion and a spirit that impels / All thinking things, all objects of all thought, / And rolls through all things'[50]. Coleridge is doubly or in fact triply present. His Priestleian description of God, quoted a little while back, as 'In will, in deed, IMPULSE of All to All', offers us Wordsworth's verb 'impels' and suggests his quadruple repetition of 'all'. But the use of motion is more significant. It is surely offered as a material fact – opposed to spirit – a force that 'impels' as opposed to the spirit that 'rolls through'. And Coleridge offers us a footnote on 'rolling through'. At the end of 'Religious Musings' we hear of spirits of

...plastic [*that, creative*] power, that interfus'd

like Wordsworth's 'presence' in 'Tintern Abbey'

Roll thro' the grosser and material mass

In organizing surge!'[51].

---

[48] 11th December 1794; Griggs i 137
[49] 'Tintern Abbey' 94-5.
[50] Ibid. see 96-102.
[51] Coleridge; 'Religious Musings' STC I 190

'Holies of God', Coleridge calls the 'Contemplant Spirits' and conjectures that they may be 'Monads' (particles) 'of the infinite mind'[52]. Spirit 'rolls' in 'organizing surge' through matter, giving it form and life. 'Thought', no less divine, though in the corporeal form of 'motion', 'impels' the thinking human world and the objects it has in mind – 'all thinking things' (nobody but Wordsworth would describe a human being as a thinking thing!) 'all objects of all thought'.

Wordsworth in all probability did not much care about such precision when he'd been away from Coleridge for any length of time. But 'Tintern Abbey' was the climax of their year together at Alfoxden. He was clearly writing with Coleridge's lines in mind and it seems a little affronting to assume he didn't understand them. By and large the two of them at this date thought alike. Wordsworth was more intuitive, less interested by theology. He borrowed Coleridge's formulations if they sounded right and suited his purposes. It was a pattern that continues into the 1799 and 1805 *Preludes* though by then there had been considerable divergence. One area in which it is possible that they disagreed instinctively is the part played by the senses in perception of a larger and more important kind. Wordsworth typically described a staged experience in which heightened emotional response to Nature often irrelevant at the time ('collateral' to use his favourite word) later gives rise to imaginative contemplation leading in turn to oneness with the infinite. Coleridge is more anxious about the senses. He too longs 'to behold and know something great something one and indivisible'[53]. But sensual awareness, which for Wordsworth (or Wollstonecraft) is a necessary first stage in the process, is for Coleridge a barrier. Those who have been

---

[52] Ibid.
[53] Letter to Thelwall 14th Oct 1797. Griggs i 349.

educated, he tells Poole in October 1797 – a month before writing 'Kubla Khan' and the first 'Ancient Mariner', 'through the constant testimony of their senses... contemplate nothing but parts – and all parts are necessarily little – and the Universe to them is but a mass of *little things*'[54].

Blake has in an extreme form Coleridge's fear of smallness and division. But he is prepared to envision the possibility of an 'improvement of sensual enjoyment'. It is doubtful if Coleridge ever would; or, if he did, he would regard it as something from which he himself was shut out. Blake's association of perception and enjoyment is, if we think about it, shared however by Wordsworth. In 'Tintern Abbey' we are to '*see into the life of things*' with 'an eye that has been made quiet' not only by the 'power of harmony' but by 'the deep power of joy'. Later in the poem (this is sensual enjoyment, this 'joy') Wordsworth himself feels (the senses again) a 'presence that disturbs' him 'with the joy of elevated thoughts'. 'Joy' in the first case is that of sharing in the 'One Life'; 'In all things he saw One Life and felt that it was joy'[55]. In the second it is the 'joy of elevated thoughts' that sets man apart in his God-like capacity to perceive his relation to the deity.

It is time I brought this meditation to a close. But there may be scope for a few thoughts under my final heading of 'Romantic Imagination'. I brought together at the beginning four definitions; the Blakean perception that if one's senses were in tune, 'every thing would appear to man as it is: infinite'; Wordsworth's claim that Imagination is but another name for 'absolute strength and clearest insight'; Coleridge's concept of

---

[54] Letter to Thomas Poole 16th October 1797 Griggs i 354.
[55] *The Pedlar* 218; MOH 179

losing and finding 'all self in God'; and Shelley's 'interpenetration of a diviner nature though our own'. For good measure we have also Goethe or Werter's losing himself in the idea of infinity in response to a 'vivifying' and animating 'heat' in Nature, Roland's sense of reunion with the 'soul of the universe' of whose essence she is an emanation and Wollstonecraft's conversing with her God as a result of herself supplying Nature with an 'animating soul'. We could add if we chose, Keats's famous enigmatic words 'The Imagination may be compared to Adam's dream, he awoke and found it truth'[56].

I have suggested that all these great writers and thinkers were Platonists all questing for confirmation of the oneness of existence, that can be defined as 'beauty' or 'truth' or 'love' – Wordsworth sometimes called it 'knowledge'. It doesn't matter which one chooses because all are synonyms for the infinite, the absolute, the world of Platonic higher reality. Romanticism is the intuitive belief in the existence of such a world. And Imagination is the divine quality in man that enables him at moments to glimpse what that world might be like. The two crucial concepts are loss of self and the principle of creative perception. The first is seen in Blake's cleansing of the doors, leaving behind the world of our present limited senses. It is seen also in 'Tintern Abbey' when the poet has to be 'laid asleep in body' in order to become a living soul and thus able to 'see into the life of things'. And in 'Religious Musings' again Coleridge tells us:

'Tis the sublime of man,

Our noontide Majesty [*our highest achievements*]

to know ourselves

---

[56] Keats; Letter to Benjamin Bailey. 22nd Nov 1817; Rollins I 185.

> Parts and proportions of one wond'rous whole![57]

and then offers a horrifying picture of the alternative, man as a 'sordid solitary thing'; and this of course is the Ancient Mariner:

> A sordid solitary thing,
>
> Mid countless brethren with a lonely heart
>
> Thro' courts and cities the smooth Savage roams
>
> Feeling himself, his own low Self the whole;
>
> When he by sacred sympathy might make
>
> The whole ONE SELF! SELF, that no alien knows!
>
> SELF, far diffus'd as Fancy's wing can travel!
>
> SELF, spreading still! Oblivious of its own,
>
> Yet all of all possessing![58]

Imagination is the losing and finding of self in an act of 'sacred sympathy', giving.

But no single definition will do. We need to take into account Wollstonecraft's position. 'She found', Godwin writes in his wonderful *Memoirs of the author of a Vindication of the Rights of Woman*:

> an inexpressible delight in the beauties of nature and in the splendid reveries of the imagination. And nature herself she thought would be no better than a vast blank if the mind of the observer did not supply it with an

---

[57] 'Religious Musings'; STC I 180
[58] Ibid 181

animating soul. When she walked among the wonders of nature she was accustomed to converse with her God[59].

It is a remarkable partly because of its date, January 1798, before either Wordsworth or Coleridge has published anything similar; and partly because Godwin as a sceptic (he claimed to be an atheist) is trying so hard to be accurate. Though supplied by Wollstonecraft to fill a void, the 'animating soul' does exist, does animate. It is fact not projection. As a result of the creative reveries of imagination, Wollstonecraft is enabled to 'converse with her God'. As in the major Wordsworth/Coleridge definitions of Imagination from the 1799 *Prelude* to *Biographia,* Imagination is at once perceptive and creative. Godwin doesn't believe in the God with whom Wollstonecracft converses. For him the 'splendid reveries of the imagination' are pleasurable self-delusion. The animating soul is projected.

One major aspect of Romanticism, surely, is pathos. Romantic poetry offers a world, so vividly evoked by Shelley, in which poetry 'purges from our inward sight the film of familiarity which obscures from us the wonder of our being'. Thus far we can most of us go. But what is our response when asked to go a step further? Believe with Wordsworth that there *is* a life in things, or with Blake that 'everything would appear...as it is: infinite'? The larger the gestures of Romanticism the less we can believe in them and the more we would like to do so. It is akin to our response to the sadness of heroic loss. Quite where the pathos lies I am not sure. Maybe not so much with the writer who did believe as with ourselves wishing with Hardy that 'it might be so'[60].

---

[59] Op cit, chapter iii
[60] Thomas Hardy. 'The Oxen',

Finally, a passage of prose/poetry from Shelley's *On Love*, which encompasses it all;

> ...in solitude or in that deserted state when we are surrounded by human beings and yet they sympathise not with us, we love the flowers and the grass and the waters and the sky. In the motion of the very leaves of spring in the blue air there is then found a secret correspondence with our heart. There is eloquence in the tongueless wind and a melody in the flowing brooks and the rustling of the reeds beside them which by their inconceivable relation to something within the soul awaken the spirits to a dance of breathless rapture and bring tears of mysterious tenderness to the eyes like...the voice of one beloved singing to you alone.

7 TWO STRANGERS AND A PAIR OF WILD EYES[1]

Hazlitt writes in the best of all his essays, 'My First Acquaintance with Poets':

> It was in January, 1798, that I rose one morning before day-light, to walk ten miles in the mud and wet to hear this celebrated person preach. Never, the longest day I have to live, shall I have such another walk as this cold, raw, comfortless one in the winter of the year 1798....When I got there, the organ was playing the 100th psalm[2] and, when it was done, Mr Coleridge rose and gave out his text 'And he went up into the mountain to pray, HIMSELF, ALONE'[3]. As he gave out this text, his voice 'rose like a stream of rich distilled perfumes'[4] and when he came to the two last words which he pronounced loud, deep, and distinct, it seemed to me who was then young, as if the sounds had echoed from the bottom of the human heart, and as if that prayer might have floated in solemn silence through the universe[5].

---

[1] First delivered as a lecture to The Wordsworth Summer Conference 2000
[2] 'Make a joyful noise unto the Lord, all ye lands'; KJV Psalm 100
[3] 'And when he had sent the multitudes away, he went up into a mountain apart to pray: and when the evening was come, he was there alone'; KJV Matthew 14:23.
[4] Milton; *Comus* 556
[5] 'My First Acquaintance with Poets', Hazliitt; Wu (1) ix 96

'Frost at Midnight' was written by that 'celebrated person', the twenty five year old Coleridge, a month after he descended from the pulpit that January day in 1798:

> .....the living spirit in our frame
>
> That loves not to behold a lifeless thing,
>
> Transfuses into all its own delights
>
> Its own volition, sometimes with deep faith,
>
> And sometimes with fantastic playfulness.[6]

It is a strange, unexpected statement. Coleridge, when the nineteen year old Hazlitt went to hear him at Wem in Cheshire, had been applying for a vacant post as Unitarian Minister. Back in Somerset he was writing poetry, 'Frost at Midnight' to be precise, not because he didn't get the job but because the Wedgwood brothers had presented him with an annuity and he no longer needed the money to feed his family. He was free to pursue his vocation as a poet. It is difficult not to make it sound as if there was an opposition between Unitarianism and poetry. But there wasn't. Poetry is for Coleridge the medium through which he understands and makes available to others his faith in 'the one Life within us and abroad'[7]. He thinks habitually as he does towards the end of 'Frost at Midnight' in pantheist terms of the 'Great universal teacher' who 'from eternity doth teach / Himself in all, and all things in himself'[8]. That he should regard the life

---

[6] 'Frost at Midnight' 1798 21-25; Wu(2) 624
Note on texts: The most convenient way to access the cited texts is in Wu (2) at pp. 20-1 for Cowper's 'The Winter Evening' and at pp.624-9 for parallel early and later 'Frost at Midnight' texts. All line refs. to these two poems are to Wu (2).
[7] 'The Eolian Harp' 26; STC II 323

'within' as conferring 'its own delights' and conferring them sometimes at least in a spirit of 'fantastic playfulness' raises interesting questions. It also takes us back to Cowper and his reflections on 'The Winter Evening' published thirteen years earlier in his ruminative poem *The Task*. The passage concerned is famous as Coleridge's source but neither Cowper's lines nor their relation to 'Frost at Midnight' have been particularly well understood.

Cowper is not writing a separate poem like Coleridge; but he is nonetheless crafting this sixty six line sequence of *The Task* with especial care. It has a beginning, middle and end, offering in its understated climax 'Earth receives gladly the thickening mantle' (239) a harmony and reconciliation that are precious and appropriate but – on a Coleridgean level, one might say on the level of Romantic as opposed to Augustan art - less than fully satisfying.

Note Cowper's creation of himself and his surroundings. Wordsworth praised Burns for making out 'of his own character and situation in society...a poetic self...for the purpose of recommending his opinions...inspiriting his incidents' and exploring his values and emotions[9], which is precisely what Cowper is doing here. We are in Book Four of a long personal poem and know a good deal by this time about the writer who in one way or another is often his own subject. Yet the sequence opens in conscious redefinition of this 'poetic self':

---

[8] 'Frost at Midnight' 62-3

[9] Wordsworth wrote, 'Not less successfully does Burns avail himself of his own character and situation in society, to construct out of them a poetic self – introduced as a dramatic personage – for the purpose of inspiriting his incidents, diversifying his pictures, recommending his opinions, and giving point to his sentiments.' 'Letter to a Friend of Robert Burns' OS iii 125

> Just when our drawing-rooms begin to blaze
>
> With lights by clear reflection multiplied
>
> From many a mirror (in which he of Gath,
>
> Goliath, might have seen his giant bulk
>
> Whole without stooping, tow'ring crest and all),
>
> My pleasures too begin.   (267-272)

Candles have been brought in; the drawing rooms that the poet shares with his late Georgian audience are high and well lit with seven or eight feet mirrors between the tall windows and elegantly placed (their purpose being to set off the panelling). None of which accounts for the presence of Goliath, 'he of Gath', whom the shepherd boy David slew with a smooth pebble from the brook. In order to tell us how tall the mirrors are, Cowper has brought a giant into the drawing room and into the drawing rooms of our minds. There he stands, his plumed helmet making him taller still, looking incongruously at himself in the mirror. It may even be that we see him, 'tow'ring crest and all', with 'his giant bulk' outlined in different mirrors ('many a mirror') around the room. What is he doing here? Long ago David, whose slingshot from a distance had been so devastating, borrowed his sword and cut off that head, 'tow'ring crest and all'[10]. But it's safely on again now, or his giant bulk couldn't be seen 'whole without stooping'! What is the relevance of that to Cowper? It doesn't exist unless it comes to mind. Let a giant into your drawing room - let a giant into your readers' drawing rooms - and you can't expect to control the situation! Cowper's pleasures have

---

[10] The story of how David slew Goliath and cut off his head is told in KJV 1 Samuel 17

already begun. It was he who let the giant in.

Bear it in mind with the following:

> ....the living spirit in our frame
>
> That loves not to behold a lifeless thing
>
> Transfuses into all its own delights
>
> Its own volition, sometimes with deep faith,
>
> And sometimes with fantastic playfulness.

'Deep faith' belongs to the world of the 'something far more deeply *inter*fused'[11]. For the moment we have quite enough to do with the living spirit that '*trans*fuses into all its own delights'....a tale of two fusings, 'trans' now, 'inter' later.

The 'my' (of 'My pleasures too begin') is self-assertive. The drawing rooms have their pleasures, beginning to blaze with lights. 'He of Gath' has his, thinking what a fine giant he is in front of the mirror! And now if I let him, Cowper will tell us of his own;

> But me perhaps
>
> The glowing hearth may satisfy awhile
>
> With faint illumination that uplifts
>
> The shadow to the ceiling, there by fits
>
> Dancing uncouthly to the quiv'ring flame.
>
> Not undelightful is an hour to me

---

[11] Wordsworth: 'Tintern Abbey' 96

> So spent in parlour twilight; such a gloom
>
> Suits well the thoughtful or unthinking mind
>
> (272-9)

Coleridge, in 'Frost at Midnight', has been left to a solitude which 'suits / Abstruser musings' (5-6). ''Tis calm indeed!' he comments, 'so calm, that it disturbs / And vexes meditation with its strange / And extreme silentness' (8-10). The little word 'suits' reveals how the larger pattern of Coleridge's thinking has once again been prompted by Cowper:

> such a gloom
>
> *Suits* well the thoughtful or unthinking mind
>
> The mind contemplative, with some new theme
>
> Pregnant, or indisposed alike to all.
>
> Laugh ye, who boast your more mercurial pow'rs
>
> That never feel a stupor, know no pause
>
> Nor need one. I am conscious, and confess
>
> Fearless, a soul that does not always think.
>
> Me oft has fancy ludicrous and wild
>
> Soothed with a waking dream of houses, tow'rs,
>
> Trees, churches, and strange visages expressed
>
> In the red cinders, while with poring eye
>
> I gazed, myself creating what I saw.

> Nor less amused have I quiescent watched
>
> The sooty films that play upon the bars –
>
> Pendulous, and foreboding in the view
>
> Of superstition, prophesying still,
>
> Though still deceived, some stranger's near
>
> > approach.
>
> 'Tis thus the understanding takes repose
>
> In indolent vacuity of thought,
>
> And sleeps and is refreshed.   (278-298)

So schooled have we been not to seem lazy that even when alone and in our own surroundings we take on protective colouring. Coleridge takes the point and allows his associations to carry him back to Christ's Hospital and the former self who sat in class his 'eye / Fixed with mock study on my swimming book' (42-3), a workbook out of focus as he daydreams. Returning to Cowper:

> Meanwhile the face
>
> Conceals the mood lethargic with a mask
>
> Of deep deliberation, as the man
>
> Were tasked to his full strength, absorbed and lost.
>
> Thus oft reclined at ease, I lose an hour
>
> At evening, till at length the freezing blast
>
> That sweeps the bolted shutter summons home

> The recollected powers and, snapping short
>
> The glassy threads with which the fancy weaves
>
> Her brittle toils, restores me to myself.
>
> How calm is my recess, and how the frost
>
> Raging abroad, and the rough wind, endear
>
> The silence and the warmth enjoyed within.
>
> (298-310)

A new tone makes itself felt in the poetry and a new scene as Cowper's eye moves outwards and he begins to fashion his conclusion:

> I saw the woods and fields at close of day
>
> A variegated show; the meadows green
>
> Though faded, and the lands, where lately waved
>
> The golden harvest, of a mellow brown,
>
> Upturned so lately by the forceful share.
>
> I saw far off the weedy fallows smile
>
> With verdure not uprofitable, grazed
>
> By flocks fast-feeding, and selecting each
>
> His fav'rite herb; while all the leafless groves
>
> That skirt th'horizon wore a sable hue
>
> Scarce noticed in the kindred dusk of eve.

> Tomorrow brings a change, a total change
>
> Which even now – though silently performed…
>
> (311-323)

Here then is Coleridge's starting point, as revealed not just by the transformation of nature but by the unexpected emphasis on performance ('the Frost performs its secret ministry').

> And slowly, and by most unfelt – the face
>
> Of universal nature undergoes.
>
> Fast falls a fleecy show'r. The downy flakes,
>
> Descending, and with never-ceasing lapse
>
> Softly alighting upon all below,
>
> Assimilate all objects. Earth receives
>
> Gladly the thick'ning mantle, and the green
>
> And tender blade that feared the chilling blast,
>
> Escapes unhurt beneath so warm a veil.   (322-332)

Cowper is acutely self-conscious. He watches himself and he watches himself being watched. He makes serious points about the nature and workings of the mind; parlour twilight with its numinous gloom and a fire casting shadows on the ceiling do indeed suit the 'thoughtful or unthinking mind'. But then he pushes the implications on into comedy. There is no need to take account of the jeers of his critics…'Laugh ye, who boast your more mercurial pow'rs / That never feel a stupor, know no pause / Nor need one. I am conscious and confess / Fearless, a soul that does not always think'. At first sight it seems ridiculous to put oneself in such a position, lay open one's vulnerability. But there is power in doing so, perhaps more power than folly. Cowper sounds defensive but is on the attack. And what sort of souls do *they* have pray, these folks who never daydream? We are led on into the workings of 'fancy, ludicrous and wild' – Coleridge's 'fantastic playfulness' – by a writer in evident control:

> Me oft has fancy ludicrous and wild
>
> Soothed with a waking dream of houses, tow'rs,
>
> Trees, churches, and strange visages expressed
>
> In the red cinders, while with poring eye
>
> I gazed, myself creating what I saw.   (286-290)

Here perhaps are the lines that particularly drew Coleridge to Cowper's sequence. But I will come back to that. 'Houses, tow'rs, trees, churches' seem all benignly pictorial; only 'tow'rs' carries even a hint of possible disquiet. But what of the 'strange visages' that unsettle the pattern and with it our response? Like Goliath, the faces have an obstinate presence in the poetry; they don't go away. Does Cowper's waking dream maybe have room for the Freudian uncanny? Is it less than wholly soothing? More important to us at least is the value that appears to be set on the words 'myself creating what I saw'. Cowper has created a good deal by this stage, a giant, an uncouth flame-dance on the ceiling, some obstreperous critics with mercurial powers, a poetic self eager to put himself in foolish positions and now the cinder-red houses, towers, trees and visages. And often his creations seem to have been associated with pleasure. There can be no doubt that, in Coleridge's terms, Cowper has been 'transfusing into all [his] own delights'. But we haven't expected such clear implication that fantasy is enjoyed *as* fantasy.

Enter the stranger! – on one level, as Cowper says, a 'sooty film' of carbon flaps in the draught between the bars of an iron grate – on another, an omen, a little piece of magic. It is time that Coleridge joined us. It is he, after all, who converts the stranger into a 'companionable form' with which he can hold commune;

> The frost performs its secret ministry
>
> Unhelped by any wind. The owlet's cry
>
> Came loud - and hark, again! loud as before.
>
> The inmates of my cottage, all at rest,
>
> Have left me to that solitude, which suits
>
> Abstruser musing, save that at my side
>
> My cradled infant slumbers peacefully.
>
> 'Tis calm indeed! so calm, that it disturbs
>
> And vexes meditation with its strange
>
> And extreme silentness. Sea, hill, and wood,
>
> This populous village! Sea, and hill, and wood
>
> With all the numberless goings on of life
>
> Inaudible as dreams.   (1-13)

With Cowper in mind we are aware at once that Coleridge begins at the end, opening with the transformation of nature that Cowper will reach in his conclusion. Introduced at once, the miracle of the frost is a continuous, unheard, unseen process to which the poet needn't again allude but which is known to be going on all the time. We are aware too of likenesses between the two poets in their philosophical seclusion - and of the one great difference, the presence of Coleridge's cradled infant, a living being who is loved and observed and listened to but who never overrides his father's need to transfuse into the inanimate the spirit of life;

> The thin blue flame
>
> Lies on my low-burnt fire, and quivers not;
>
> Only that film, which fluttered on the grate...
>
> Still flutters there, the sole unquiet thing,
>
> Methinks its motion in this hush of nature
>
> Gives it dim sympathies with me who live,
>
> Making it a companionable form,
>
> With which I can hold commune. Idle thought!
>
> But still the living spirit in our frame
>
> That loves not to behold a lifeless thing
>
> Transfuses into all its own delights
>
> Its own volition - sometimes with deep faith
>
> And sometimes with fantastic playfulness.
>
> (13-25)

the early text again in its original context.

If 'Frost at Midnight' were a musical work it would be called 'Variations on a theme by Cowper'! Later artists frequently pay homage to an earlier work, structure themselves on a series of allusions that the viewer is expected to recognise and take into account. Poets do this, of course. When working in the mock-heroic, Belinda's dressing room in 'The Rape of the Lock' famously depends on Pope's readers to recall the arming of Achilles. But then the mock-heroic, however dignified it may be on occasion, is a form of parody and parody necessarily works off a pre-existing text. What makes 'Frost at Midnight' so unusual is that it is *not* parodic. It takes Cowper's lines in full seriousness. It does not steal them or borrow from them or imitate them. It recreates them as a wholly new poem. Coleridge beside his cottage fire is a version of Cowper in his drawing room. If we do not know this though, 'Frost at Midnight' stands perfectly well on its own but a dimension of the poetry is lost. In passing, Romantic poetry is full of frequently detailed references (especially to Milton). But not even the allusions of Wordsworth in 'Nutting' to Satan's landing in Paradise[12], set up anything like as complex a relationship as the Cowper/Coleridge one between old poem and new. Transfusing 'into all [his] own delights', Cowper animates 'the quiv'ring flame' that throws uncouth shadows on the ceiling, 'the red cinders' that turn before his eyes into buildings, trees, faces and the stranger on the grate. Of these the least developed is the last. Cowper takes 'the sooty films that play upon the bars / pendulous' as excuse for a little fine writing in the manner of Milton…'prophesying still, / Though still deceived, some stranger's near approach'. It is associated as much with delusion as with pleasurable fantasy and closed off finally with a certain abruptness: "Tis thus the understanding takes repose / In indolent

---

[12] cf. BOV pp. 48-50

vacuity of thought / And sleeps and is refreshed'.

Coleridge is not to be silenced. For him it is 'the stranger' and the presence of superstition so important both to him and to Wordsworth in this *Lyrical Ballads* Spring that stirs the mind to creativity. There are no 'red cinders' to be pored over in his 'low-burnt fire'; 'the thin blue flame' is there, not for its persisting signs of life but for its stillness, emphasised by his playing off of long beats ('thin blue flame', 'low burnt fire') against the onomatopoeic 'quiver not' ('quiver' being picked up at once in the similar movement of 'flutter' in 'Only that film, which flutter'd on the grate / Still flutters there, the sole unquiet thing'). Fluttering on the grate, 'the stranger' has a sort of after-life when the fire of life itself has gone out. The temptation to hear a quiet pun on 'sole' is strong. There is no mention at this moment and no implication of 'fantastic playfulness'. Coleridge's landscape is full of significant association, calling out for us to take seriously his apparently unserious train of thought:

> Methinks, its motion in this hush of nature
>
> Gives it dim sympathies with me, who live,
>
> Making it a companionable form
>
> With which I can hold commune.   (17-19)

Sympathies are 'dim' not because they are vague but because they are numinous, as in so many 'border' moments, without apparent source or origin. To 'hold commune' is not merely to talk or enter into a dialogue. In their slightly ponderous way, the words hint at a spiritual dimension. Coleridge's opposition of 'motion' and the 'silent hush' of nature is especially interesting. Not only will Wordsworth in 'Tintern Abbey', five months later, speak of a pantheist 'motion and a spirit that impels / All thinking things, all objects of all thought' (100-1) but Coleridge has himself earlier claimed in a letter to believe in the 'corporeality of thought – namely that it is motion'[13]. 'Thought' is a material fact because it is 'motion'. On the other hand, 'motion' is the divine essence, impelling thinking things, human beings, to think move and live.

So where does Coleridge stand in 'Frost at Midnight'? It is hard to know. First we have self-reproof, idle thought, about as credible as a rebuke from Sarah at the end of 'The Eolian Harp'. Then the counterturn 'but still the living spirit in our frame' – we are back with the early text. I wonder how often Coleridge referred to this in that lost sermon of 1798. 'The living spirit', we recall, 'transfuses' not merely 'its own delights' but 'its own volition'. Wishing to 'hold commune' with the stirring 'stranger', Coleridge imputes to it the wish to commune with *him*. This clearly is not 'deep faith' but to judge from the language used we may have to regard it as rather more than 'fantastic playfulness'. Coleridge, in his final text of 'Frost at Midnight'[14], takes up a moral position that is disapproving. We hear nothing of 'the living spirit in our frame', nothing of the human tendency to transfuse delights and wishes. Even the thought of holding 'commune' has gone, replaced by an uneasy companionship;

> Methinks its motion in this hush of nature
>
> Gives it dim sympathies with me who live,
>
> Making it a companionable form

---

[13] ' I am a compleat Necessitarian – and understand the subject as well as Hartley himself – but I go farther than Hartley and believe the corporeality of thought – namely that it is motion.' Coleridge's letter to Robert Southey 11th Dec 1794; Griggs i 137.
[14] 1829 STC I 453-5 and Wu (2) 625-9

(and here is the difference)

> Whose puny flaps and freaks the idling spirit
>
> By its own moods interprets, every where
>
> Echo or mirror seeking of itself,
>
> And makes a toy of Thought.

The poetry is tighter but at considerable expense. Where the 'living spirit' was instinctively generous, now it is egotistical. The 'stranger' is now 'puny' and freakish, the human watcher is idle, unserious, self-deprecating. Cowper it is true had associated the processes of fancy with losing an hour and being abstracted from himself. It takes a 'freezing blast' rattling the shutters to summon home his not so much 'recollected' as re-collected powers. The 'glassy threads with which the fancy weaves / Her brittle toys' (306-7) must be snapped short before he can be restored to himself. It may well be that we have in the woven threads the origin of Coleridge's 'curious toys / Of the self-watching subtilizing mind' of 1798 making a 'toy of Thought' in the later passage.

But Cowper's pleasure in creating what he sees precludes open and shut morality. Coleridge, even in the early text, is more anxious. Also he is moving on to make larger claims for the powers of mind – effectively to distinguish as none had before between Fancy (which he deprecates at all stages) and Imagination.

> Ah me! amused by no such curious toys
>
> Of the self-watching subtilizing mind,
>
> How often in my early schoolboy days,

> With most believing superstitious wish
>
> Presageful have I gazed upon the bars
>
> To watch the *stranger* there!

Superstition, associated by most of us with ignorance and falsehood, is here associated with presage, foresight, even poverty because it belongs to a child. It has, like the cottage girl of 'We Are Seven', through a refusal to accept the adult definition of death, a kind of imaginative rightness in its wrongness. It is the child's imaginative credentials that become the subject of Coleridge's thoughts as, for the moment, he leaves aside the 'stranger' to introduce the city schoolboy's dreamings of his two hundred mile away Devonshire birthplace:

> …..and oft belike
>
> With unclosed lids, already had I dreamt
>
> Of my sweet birthplace, and the old church-tower
>
> Whose bells, the poor man's only music, rang
>
> From morn to evening all the hot fair-day,
>
> So sweetly that they stirred and haunted me
>
> With a wild pleasure, falling on mine ear
>
> Most like articulate sounds of things to come!
>
> So gazed I till the soothing things I dreamt
>
> Lulled me to sleep, and sleep prolonged my
>
> > dreams!

His eyes open as Cowper's eyes are open as he stares into the cinders; the child Coleridge dreams of Ottery St. Mary[15] and the tower of his father's (now his brother's) church and the magical day of the fair when the bells rang from morn to evening (as Mulciber in *Paradise Lost* had fallen 'from morn to noon, from noon to dewy eve'[16]).

There is a new dimension in the poetry, that of memory and time. Association which for Cowper had been arbitrary – 'houses, tow'rs, / Trees, churches and strange visages' – has become personal. Night carries his dreams on into day, the school day. Loneliness creates from the superstition of the 'stranger' a faith such as Cowper could not have envisaged:

> And so I brooded all the following morn,
>
> Awed by the stern preceptor's face, mine eye
>
> Fixed with mock study on my swimming book;
>
> Save if the door half-opened, and I snatched
>
> A hasty glance, and still my heart leaped up,
>
> For still I hoped to see the *stranger's* face –
>
> Townsman, or aunt, or sister more beloved,
>
> My playmate when we both were clothed alike!

The poet sees the 'stranger' on his grate in Nether Stowey[17] and welcomes its companionship in a spirit of 'fantastic playfulness'. The child who was father to this man had seen one on the bars at

---

[15] Coleridge's birthplace.
[16] Milton *Paradise Lost* I 740-44; Fowler 87
[17] Home to Coleridge 1797-9

Christ's Hospital as a presage to be relied upon. Someone would certainly come, perhaps even the loved sister who had looked after Coleridge when he too wore skirts as boys did at the time till the age of eight or so when they were put into breeches. Memory provides the adult not just with assurances from the past but with hopes for a future. Beside him lies the child in whom alone the future can be vested, the child who is to make all well by living the life his father was not permitted to live;

> Dear babe, that sleepest cradled by my side,
>
> Whose gentle breathings heard in this dead calm
>
> Fill up the interspersed vacancies
>
> And momentary pauses of the thought;
>
> My babe so beautiful, it fills my heart
>
> With tender gladness thus to look at thee,
>
> And think that thou shalt learn far other lore
>
> And in far other scenes! For I was reared
>
> In the great city, pent mid cloisters dim,
>
> And saw nought lovely but the sky and stars.
>
> But *thou*, my babe, shalt wander like a breeze
>
> By lakes and sandy shores, beneath the crags
>
> Of ancient mountain, and beneath the clouds
>
> Which image in their bulk both lakes and shores
>
> And mountain crags

The perspectives of Coleridge's poem are expanding. He has moved into a realm that is beyond the scope of Cowper's Augustan vision. Yet the pattern the two poets are following continues to be similar. Cowper's eye too moves outward at this point in preparation for a conclusion which will place his seeing 'into the life of things' within a larger harmony. But where Coleridge moves in time, indeed beyond time, Cowper thinks less ambitiously in terms of place and space, his refuge and the outside world. Back to Cowper:

> How calm is my recess, and how the frost
>
> Raging abroad, and the rough wind, endear
>
> The silence and the warmth enjoyed within.
>
>   I saw the woods and fields at close of day,
>
> A variegated show; the meadows green
>
> Though faded, and the lands where lately waved
>
> The golden harvest, of a mellow brown,
>
> Upturned so lately by the forceful share.
>
> I saw far off the weedy fallows smile
>
> With verdure not unprofitable, grazed
>
> By flocks fast feeding and selecting each
>
> His fav'rite herb; while all the leafless groves
>
> That skirt th'horizon wore a sable hue
>
> Scarce noticed in the kindred dusk of eve.

(308-321)

The drawing room with its candles and fire and mirrors and giant of the imagination has been exchanged for a variegated show of external nature, a show that we expect to be of high winds and raging frosts but turns out to be of Nature domesticated, Nature pleased. All is in order. The meadow is faded by the summer sun but still with the green of pastureland; the 'golden harvest', a memory now, is prompted by the 'mellow brown' of fields already ploughed for the season to come; the 'weedy fallows', fields left unploughed in accordance with crop rotation, are smiling as their profusion of different plant species permit the feeding animals (in Cowper's fantasy – could it be in his observation?) the luxury of choosing their menu ('selecting each his fav'rite herb'). That the poet is 'transfusing' into all his own enjoyments could scarcely be more clear. Does he, perhaps, *need* to do so as Coleridge more obviously *needs* to believe that his infant son, free to be the child of nature, may know intuitively the 'eternal language' of God?

The Task never shows us the Cowper, whom we know from the mental breakdowns and the letters, who believed himself to be unregenerate, damned from eternity. But beneath the surface of the poetry and the country gentleman poet the terrified Calvinist is there. Coleridge uses poetry to explore his feelings, needs, despairs. Cowper never does, or never dares. His God is unforgiving, maybe he is approachable in hymns (Cowper is among the greatest of English hymn writers) but not with one's personal hopes and fears. Coleridge by comparison is lucky. Not that the author of 'The Ancient Mariner' and 'Pains of Sleep' couldn't feel himself to be damned but because Unitarian determinism is optimistic and of course because the two-fold child, Hartley (the infant who slumbers peacefully in the cottage parlour in Somerset and the spirit-child of his father's musing who wafts across the landscape of a sort of notional Lake District) is at once a creature and a definition of the Imagination:

> But *thou*, my babe, shalt wander like a breeze
>
> By lakes and sandy shores, beneath the crags
>
> Of ancient mountain, and beneath the clouds
>
> Which image in their bulk both lakes and shores
>
> And mountain crags, so shalt thou see and hear
>
> The lovely shapes and sounds intelligible
>
> Of that eternal language which thy God
>
> Utters, who from eternity doth teach
>
> Himself in all, and all things in himself.
>
> Great universal teacher! He shall mould
>
> Thy spirit, and by giving make it ask.

Coleridge as he writes these lines has not formulated the definitions of Imagination and Fancy published in *Biographia* nineteen years later (1817) but he has come close! Perhaps he understands things better before he allows the definitions to harden. There can be no sharp distinction between Fancy and Imagination. As Wordsworth recognised, the two were merged. And Fancy, if it brings giants into the drawing room and sees visages in cinders, is far from being the merely mechanical process defined by the Coleridge of 1817. Wordsworth is surely right to point out that Fancy's links and juxtapositions have as much to do with feeling as with memory. Turning to Imagination, the problem is not with the Godlike Primary but with the idea that there could possibly be a single Secondary form. Defined in *Biographia Literaria* at the end of Chapter Thirteen as 'prime agent of all human perception', the Primary Imagination confuses scholars by being 'primary' in two senses of the word. It is at once the basic imaginative function that enables us to make a coherent pattern from sense experience and the highest imaginative act enabling the chosen few to perceive and share in the presence of God. Preoccupied in *Biographia* with the role of the poet or creative artist, Coleridge defined the Secondary Imagination as an 'echo' of the Primary 'coexisting with the conscious will' and therefore less impressive. Logically there must be many other secondary forms of imagination including for instance the numinous imagination of the child who hears in the church bells 'articulate sounds of things to come'; and including too the imaginative faith of the Christ's Hospital schoolboy waiting for the 'stranger' hoping it may be the 'sister more beloved'. *Biographia* offers its definitions in a sequence of diminishing importance; Primary Imagination, Secondary Imagination and Fancy. 'Frost at Midnight' offers them mounting to a climax, through from 'fantastic playfulness' to 'deep faith'...as Coleridge 'transfuses' into the quite ordinary child at his side the most extravagant 'volition' of them all - nothing short of a realisation through oneness with Nature of the truths of his Unitarian creed.

Cowper's progression offers no such exalted moments but has nonetheless its surprises in store:

> Tomorrow brings a change, a total change
>
> Which even now – though silently performed,

> And slowly, and by most unfelt – the face
>
> Of universal nature undergoes.
>
> Fast falls a fleecy show'r. The downy flakes
>
> Descending, and with never-ceasing lapse
>
> Softly alighting on all below,
>
> Assimilate all objects. Earth receives
>
> Gladly the thick'ning mantle, and the green
>
> And tender blade that feared the chilling blast
>
> Escapes unhurt beneath so warm a veil.   (322-332)

The landscape at nightfall had been a variegated show. Now the following morning we have a 'change, a total change' that is 'silently performed'. Apart from providing Coleridge with his opening line and central motif, Cowper has through his theatrical imagery of show and performance implied the existence of a Director, a controlling presence behind the scenes. His poetry is full of a quiet reassurance; somebody cares. Coleridge goes further in his concept of a 'ministry'. Neither makes explicit, as Wordsworth will do with reference to the mist on Mount Snowdon, the analogy between Nature's transforming powers (snow, frost, mist) and those of the human imagination[18]. But both Cowper and Coleridge have shown us in their poetry the mind creating what it sees and at the same time valuing its own creation. Cowper in his tranquil and beautiful conclusion (no-one has more perfectly evoked the 'never-ceasing lapse' and silent alighting of snowflakes) delicately turns the arrival of the snow

---

[18] Wordsworth; *Prelude* 1805 xiii 29-84; FT 512-14

into a blessing as the green and tender blade of grass hides childlike under a blanket that will save it from the cutting edge of the wind. The living spirit in the poet's frame is for the last time in this passage transfusing 'into all its own delights / It's own volition'. Cowper offers no 'Great Universal Teacher'; the 'shapes and sounds' of Nature are not for him an 'eternal language' but there is a tenderness about the poetry, a sharing at the personal level, which is felt to go no less deep. We may be a little surprised as Coleridge too ends with the actual, the personal. He is shaping his poem and writers do draw back in conclusion from their grandest statements. But this perhaps is more a giving than a drawing-back, a giving back to Hartley of his humanity:

>Therefore all seasons shall be sweet to thee,
>
>Whether the summer clothe the general earth
>
>With greenness, or the redbreasts sit and sing
>
>Betwixt the tufts of snow on the bare branch
>
>Of mossy apple tree, while all the thatch
>
>Smokes in the sun-thaw; whether the eave-drops
>
>>fall
>
>Heard only in the trances of the blast,
>
>Or whether the secret ministry of cold
>
>Shall hang them up in silent icicles,
>
>Quietly shining to the quiet moon

Coleridge has six lines to go which he may have been right in his final text to cut but which were important to him when he wrote them in 1798:

> Like those, my babe, which ere tomorrow's warmth
>
> Have capped their sharp keen points with
>
>   pendulous drops,
>
> Will catch thine eye, and with their novelty
>
> Suspend thy little soul; then make thee shout
>
> And stretch and flutter from thy mother's arms,
>
> As thou would'st fly for very eagerness.

Coleridge has taken on an almost priest-like role as he addresses his sleeping child. His words come across to us as something between a blessing and a prayer; 'Great Universal Teacher! He shall mould / Thy spirit, and by giving make it ask. / Therefore all seasons shall be sweet to thee'. Moulding Hartley's spirit, giving to it the gift of imaginative sharing in the 'One Life', God, who proclaims 'Himself in all, and all things in himself', will cause it to 'ask', to be aware of its own need, effectively to pray. For this reason all seasons, the warm and the cold, will be 'sweet'.

The best gloss on this passage is Wordsworth's recollection of it in 'Tintern Abbey':

> Therefore am I still
>
> A lover of the meadows and the woods
>
> And mountains; and of all that we behold
>
> From this green earth; of all the mighty world

> Of eye, and ear, – both what they half-create
>
> And what perceive... (102-7)

'Therefore all seasons shall be sweet to thee', 'Therefore am I still / A lover of the meadows'; in each case we have just had a grand affirmation of the divine presence in Nature. And in each case the poet is concerned to emphasize that sharing in the natural world at a more day-to-day level is directly related to spiritual awareness. But he, the poet, does so at a moment when the poetry is about to become more personal; for Wordsworth in the address to Dorothy as the 'dear, dear sister' whose 'wild eyes'[19] are his inspiration, his link with the past and guarantee of a future; for Coleridge as he brings the spirit-child (last seen wafting like a breeze across a mental landscape) to rest in the domestic surroundings of a Somersetshire cottage garden amid apple trees and robin redbreasts and thatch that smokes as the last night's frost thaws and evaporates. Especially beautiful in Coleridge's giving-back is the interplay between the fall of the eave-drops (drops coming down the thatch and falling from the edge) 'heard only in the trances of the blast' and the child's gentle breathings heard earlier in the dead calm of Nature filling up the 'interspersed vacancies / And momentary pauses of [his father's] thought'.

A final thought about endings. Tying back to his opening line

---

[19] Nor perchance,
If I were not thus taught, should I the more
Suffer my genial spirits to decay:
For thou art with me here upon the banks
Of this fair river; thou my dearest Friend,
My dear, dear Friend: and in thy voice I catch
The language of my former heart, and read
My former pleasures in the shooting lights
Of thy wild eyes.   'Tintern Abbey' 111-119;

Coleridge offers us the 'secret ministry of cold' - more absolute than the later reading's 'ministry of frost' and less straightforward in its echo - hanging up the eave-drops 'in silent icicles / Quietly shining to the quiet moon'. The later text ends here achieving one of the most perfect of all concluding lines; the homage of the icicles to the moon and the moon's quiet acceptance beautifully evoke 'the living spirit in our frame / That loves not to behold a lifeless thing'. But Coleridge is not just playing the proud father as he continues (in the earlier version):

> Like those, my babe, which ere tomorrow's warmth
>
> Have capped their sharp keen points with
>
> pendulous drops
>
> Will catch thine eye, and with their novelty
>
> Suspend thy little soul; then make thee shout
>
> And stretch and flutter from thy mother's arms,
>
> As thou would'st fly for very eagerness.

Two allusions tell us that Coleridge, whether consciously or not, is thinking of the 'strangers' of my title; one allusion to *The Task*, one to 'Frost at Midnight'. 'Pendulous drops' that catch the eye of the child on the icicle's tips recall directly the 'sooty films' catching the quiescent Cowper's eye as they 'play' 'pendulous' 'upon the bars'. Stretching and fluttering from his mother's arms, Hartley recalls, surely deliberately, the film which fluttered on the grate and 'Still flutters there the sole unquiet thing'. Hartley's excitement at the icicle-drops, the trace-like suspension of his little soul, depends on a life-force which is *not* conferred, *not* the result of his father's 'abstruser' midnight 'musings'. He knows intuitively the 'eternal language which [his] God / Utters'. Neither the 'shades of the prison house'[20] nor the 'cloisters' of a city school have closed upon him. He is himself.

---

[20] Shades of the prison house begin to close
              Upon the growing boy,
       But he beholds the light and whence it flows,
              He sees it in his joy;
       The youth who daily farther from the east
              Must travel, still is nature's priest,
                  And by the vision splendid
                  Is on his way attended:
                       Wordsworth; 'Intimations of Immortality' 67-72

8 BLAKE AND THE IMAGINATION[1]

How know you this said I small Sir?[2]

Almost everyone who is concerned with the Romantic Imagination heads for Coleridge and the definitions of *Biographia Literaria* 1817, 'The Imagination then I consider either as Primary or Secondary' and so on[3]. If they look further it will be to Wordsworth and the *Prelude,* Shelley and 'Mont Blanc', Keats and Adam's Dream[4]; Blake is ignored or gets at best a few passing references. Living in isolation from fellow writers, publishing his strange views in illuminated books that hardly sold at all, he seems an irrelevance. Yet before Coleridge or any of the rest he had a sustaining theory of the Imagination that was, or became, the basis of his entire complex system of thought and myth. I want to consider here the extraordinary likeness between Blake's thinking and that of Coleridge and the others, a likeness not to be explained merely by these very different writers having read the same Neo-Platonist sources, though in some cases they had.

Blake is difficult. If we are honest we have to admit that half the time we don't understand him, or don't fully understand. The problem is that he is not just poet and painter but prophet too in

---
[1] First delivered as a lecture to The Wordsworth Summer Conference 2002
[2] see note 7.
[3] BL Chapter 13 304
[4] Letter to Benjamin Bailey 22nd Nov 1817; Rollins i 185 Letter 43

the tradition of Isaiah, John of Patmos, author of Revelations, and mystics Jacob Boehme and Emanuel Swedenborg. He is a myth of his own and, if we dare to say so, is by most standards crazy. This is not a fashionable statement among Blakean scholars!

This discussion is restricted to five passages of his writing. The first from *The Marriage of Heaven and Hell* (1790), tells how Blake had Isaiah and Ezekiel to supper to find out how Imagination appeared from their side of the fence. The second, from Blake's *Europe* (1794), gives me my title; he meets and captures a Fairy, 'a small sir', who knows a thing or two about the fallen world: however small he may be he is himself an 'Eternal', an Immortal (in Blake you belong either to the fallen world, man's world, or to the world of Eternity, infinity – there are no middle states). My third and fourth passages come from *Milton*, shortest and most attractive of Blake's prophetic books, offering cosmic Blakean 'spots of time' and a rather different way of thinking about the loss of self. Fifth and last is an early passage from Blake's great epic *Jerusalem* drafted around 1810-15; it is not whimsical, as are the first and second passages, but again showing the poet in a mood that allows of the personal alongside the grand and unapproachable. Taken as a sequence, the passages allow us a little closer to the poet than we normally get and offer something like a connective view of Blakean Imagination in the context of other Romantic views. We never learn incidentally where 'the small sir' got his information!

First Blake's dinner party. Everything depends on tone, as in much of Blake. He is both passionate in his beliefs and very funny and can be outrightly whimsical:

> The Prophets Isaiah and Ezekiel dined with me, and I asked them how they dared so roundly to assert that

God spake to them; and whether they did not think at the time that they would be misunderstood and so be the cause of imposition.

Isaiah answer'd, I saw no God, nor heard any, in a finite organical perception; but my senses discover'd the infinite in everything, and as I was then perswaded, and remain confirm'd, that the voice of honest indignation is the voice of God, I cared not for consequences but wrote.

Then I asked: does a firm perswasion that a thing is so, make it so?

He replied. All poets believe that it does, and in ages of imagination this firm perswasion removed mountains; but many are not capable of a firm perswasion of anything.'[5]

Lacking 'a firm perswasion of anything', some of us may choose not to believe that Isaiah and Ezekiel left their places among the long dead to dine with Blake one evening in 1790. It must be admitted though that the dialogue has an authentic ring. 'Does a firm perswasion that a thing is so, make it so?' Answer, 'All poets believe that it does.' We are being teased and Swedenborg is being parodied but at the same time Blake's most strongly-felt beliefs are being held up to the light. He himself surely *is* persuaded that 'the voice of honest indignation is the voice of God'. It is the assumption upon which his work as a satirist proceeds. And he surely does feel that he ought to be able to move mountains or walk on water. This is possibly self-mockery

---

[5] *The Marriage of Heaven and Hell* Plate 12, A Memorable Fancy. Erdman 38-9. All quotations from Blake are taken from *The Complete Poetry and Prose of William Blake* Newly revised Edition edited by David V. Erdman with Commentary by Harold Bloom Anchor Books 1988 abbreviated Erdman

but the questions asked are serious. Can Blake, or can we, in what is patently not an age of Imagination, perform the imaginative act that is an act of faith? Are we, Blake's readers, truly seeing and hearing God in moments when our senses discover the infinite in everything? 'If the doors of perception were cleansed', Blake writes a page or two later in *The Marriage*, 'every thing would appear to man as it is: infinite.'[6] The 'as it is' is almost cocky; he accuses us of having no faith. 'For man has closed himself up, till he sees all things thro' narrow chinks of his cavern.'[7] Man is responsible; he ought to be able to perceive the infinite; it is he who has closed himself off, condemned himself to live in the cavern of his skull, seeing through chinks of his ears, eyes, nose, mouth that represent the fallen senses, the gates of our wilfully limited perception. Isaiah and Ezekiel have cleansed senses or ones that were clean from the first. We by contrast have to await a cleansing that may never happen. Blake's 'if' and the conditional 'were', 'if the doors of perception were cleansed', don't sound promising.

Unpredictably between the four years of my first passage and the second there has been a positive change. The Fairy's view of man's fallen state (in *Europe* 1794) is quite optimistic! (this despite the fact that the book *Urizen*, with its portrayal of Creation as disastrous and the future of mankind as utterly bleak, belongs also to 1794, as do the uncompromising *Songs Of Experience*). When Blake first sees the 'small sir', he (the Fairy) is singing a song of mockery about human limitation, using once again the metaphor of the cavern of the skull. We expect him to say that man is wilfully and more or less completely shut off from the Eternal. But he doesn't. 'Five windows', he tells us, 'light the

---

[6] Plate 14; Erdman 39
[7] Ibid.

cavern'd man'. From being a peerer through chinks, man has gone on to being looked after, almost pandered to, with 'five windows':

> Five windows light the cavern'd Man: thro' one he breathes the air;
>
> Thro' one, hears music of the spheres; thro' one, the eternal vine
>
> Flourishes, that he may receive the grapes; thro' one can look
>
> And see small portions of the eternal world that ever groweth;
>
> Thro' one, himself pass out what time he please, but he will not;
>
> For stolen joys are sweet, and bread eaten in secret pleasant.
>
> So sang a Fairy mocking as he sat on a streak'd Tulip,
>
> Thinking none saw him: when he ceas'd I started from the trees!
>
> And caught him in my hat as boys knock down a butterfly.
>
> How know you this said I small Sir? where did you learn this song?
>
> Seeing himself in my possession thus he answered me:

My master, I am yours. command me, for I must obey.

Then tell me, what is the material world, and is it dead?

He laughing answer'd: I will write a book on leaves of flowers,

If you will feed me on love-thoughts, and give me now and then

A cup of sparkling poetic fancies; o when I am tipsie,

I'll sing to you to this soft lute; and shew you all alive

The world, when every particle of dust breathes forth its joy.

I took him home in my warm bosom: as we went along

Wild flowers I gathered; & he shew'd me each eternal flower:

He laugh'd aloud to see them whimper because they were pluck'd.

They hover'd round me like a cloud of incense: when I came

Into my parlour and sat down, and took my pen to write:

My Fairy sat upon the table, and dictated EUROPE.[8]

The poet's opening question 'How know you this...small sir?' implies surely that he accepts what has been said as accurate. It is known not asserted. In addition to being a mocker and little enough to be knocked down with a hat, the Fairy has 'knowledge', meaning knowledge of Eternity, in effect vision. By way of local colour he is given an appetite for love-thoughts and poetic fancies and has enough of the traditional mischief–making fairy about him to enjoy the 'whimper' of plucked flowers. But he commands respect; he is a supernatural being and in this role will dictate Blake's new poem. It is on this authority that we have it that 'every particle of dust breathes forth its joy'. In its positive form, 'What is the material world and is it alive?' (versus 'is it dead?'), the poet's second question to the Fairy is vital to Romanticism. One associates it however less with Blake than the others.

Coleridge comes to be preoccupied with it in 1794-5 as he devises his Unitarian theology within months of Blake's wholly unnoticed printing of *Europe*. It will be at the centre of 'The Ancient Mariner' 1797-8. Wordsworth in the spring of 1798 gives it as his 'faith' that 'every flower / Enjoys the air it breathes'[9], and writes of his alter-ego, the Pedlar, 'in all things / He saw one life and felt that it was joy'[10]. Shelley in the next generation is drawn to the concept of an active universe and even Byron and Keats will find themselves turning over the possibilities. Perhaps the reason why Blake is less concerned than his Romantic contemporaries with this way of thinking is that as a prophet he is not worried by the two great Coleridgean anxieties; namely, in what form is God present in the universe and how do we know that the life we see

---

[8] *Europe* Plate iii.1-24; Erdman 60.
[9] 'Lines Written in Early Spring' 11-12; Cornell LB 76
[10] 'The Pedlar' 217-8; MOH 179

in nature is not a projection of our own?

Taking our cue from the reappearance of the image of the cave, we expect the Fairy's song to be an uncompromising restatement of the *Marriage* of man closed off with no way back to the infinite world of which he was once a part, no means of cleansing doors. The Fairy turns out however, despite his mocking, to be cheerful. Man, in his new well-appointed cavern (a decidedly superior piece of real estate!) is illuminated by windows that seem designed to encourage a relationship with the Infinite. There is an emphasis on self-willed limitation as fallen man. Fallen, hopeless man breathes through the first of the windows, hears the sacred music of the spheres through the second and receives the fruit of the eternal vine through the third. He is privileged to share in at least some of the products and attributes of Eternity and must surely exist on a more imaginative level than is envisaged for his counterpart in the *Marriage*. The Fairy's comment on window four can be read in different ways. Man can see only small portions of the Eternal world expanding beyond his vision; but it is surely remarkable that he can see into the Infinite at all. It is window five that brings in the implication of humanity's preference for the fallen; 'thro' one, himself pass out what time he please, but he will not; / For stolen joys are sweet, and bread eaten in secret pleasant'. The senses we recall are referred to in the *Marriage* a little paradoxically as 'chief inlets of Soul in this age'[11]. What would be the chief inlets of soul in an age of Imagination we are not told. But presumably we are talking of 'cleansed', and therefore more imaginative and efficient, 'doors of perception'. Assuming the inlets to be uncleansed doors, very little could have been let in. Four years later the mood of the Fairy's song makes everything seem more possible. The question

---

[11] *The Marriage of Heaven and Hell* Plate 4 ; Erdman 34

raised is the relation of the senses to the Imagination. It is all very well to say that if the senses could be spiritualised they would become the entry to a fully imaginative world. But what part in practice did Blake see them playing?

The Wordsworth of 'Tintern Abbey' is 'well pleased' to see 'In nature and the language of the sense ... the nurse, / The guide, the guardian of my heart, and soul / Of all my moral being'[12]. Blake is not pleased by any such thing. 'Natural Objects', he writes in the margin of Wordsworth's Poems of 1815, 'always did and now do Weaken deaden and obliterate Imagination in Me'. He continues 'Wordsworth must know that what he Writes Valuable is Not to be found in Nature'[13]. Blake is surely right; Wordsworth does know that what he writes of value is not to be found in natural objects as such. He relies however on the language of the sense as 'nurse', 'guide' and 'guardian' and to help him store up material to be worked upon by the mind, which is, as he says, his 'haunt, and the main region of [his] song'[14]. Significantly 'Tintern Abbey', the poem that explicitly celebrates the language of the sense, offers us the copybook mystical experience in which 'see[ing] into the life of things' comes as a result of a dying away of sensual awareness:

> that serene and blessed mood,
>
> In which the affections gently lead us on, –
>
> Until, the breath of this corporeal frame
>
> And even the motion of our human blood

---

[12] 'Tintern Abbey' 107-12; Cornell LB 119
[13] *Annotations to Wordsworth's Poems*, Blake. Erdman 665
[14] Preface to *The Excursion* l.41

> Almost suspended, we are laid asleep
>
> In body, and become a living soul: (41-6)

The metaphor is of death into which the affections (which I see as emotions dependant on sense experience) 'gently lead us on'. In all this we may notice at least an apparent difference between Blake's point of view in which the senses are heightened, cleansed into an Eternal vision, and Wordsworth's more common mystical position that it is when 'the light of sense *goes out*'[15] that the invisible world is revealed.

There is a parallel that not all will see between Blake's position and the working of Coleridge's Primary Imagination. The Primary is the faculty which makes sense of things. At its basic level it enables us to turn the disconnected evidence produced by

---

[15] Imagination – lifting up itself
Before the eye and progress of my song
Like an unfathered vapour, here that power,
In all the might of its endowments, came
Athwart me! I was lost as in a cloud,
Halted without a struggle to break through;
And now, recovering, to my soul I say
'I recognize thy glory.' In such strength
Of usurpation, in such visitings
Of awful promise, when the light of sense
Goes out in flashes that have shown to us
The invisible world, does greatness make abode,
There harbours whether we be young or old.
Our destiny, our nature, and our home,
Is with infinitude, and only there –
With hope it is, hope that can never die,
Effort, and expectation, and desire,
And something evermore about to be.
The mind beneath such banners militant
Thinks not of spoils or trophies, nor of aught
That may attest its prowess, blest in thoughts
That are their own perfection and reward –
Strong in itself, and in the access of joy
Which hides it like the overflowing Nile. *Prelude* 1805 vi 525-548; FT 240

the senses into the world of our common experience. At its highest it enables the individual to be aware of and a part of the existence of God. There is a natural progression from the lower state to the higher. The more sense you make (it is very difficult to avoid the pun) the closer you come to God or to an understanding of his role in your existence. *Observations on Man* 1749 was usefully reissued in 1792 by Coleridge's hero David Hartley. Hartley sees both pleasure and pain as conducting to wisdom over a period of years and that wisdom is a knowledge of God. Achievement of the eternal in the early Blake of *The Marriage* and *Europe* is something that man ought to be capable of. It is folly that prevents his walking out of the fifth window to assume his proper place in Eternity. He likes his fallen lot, his 'stolen joys'. Not surprisingly, things in the great prophetic books are more complex.

Written on the south coast at Felpham in 1802-3 *Milton* is a poem of strange, powerful, unique moments that hold the poem together. First the moment that collapses time and space;

> Every Time less than a pulsation of the artery
>
> Is equal in its period and value to Six Thousand Years;
>
> For in this Period the Poet's Work is Done; and all the Great
>
> Events of Time start forth and are conceivd in such a Period,
>
> Within a Moment: a Pulsation of the Artery.[16]

---

[16] *Milton*; plate 28 ll.62-3 and plate 29, ll.1-3 Erdman 127

> ....For every Space larger than a red Globule of Mans blood
>
> Is visionary.....
>
> And every Space smaller than a Globule of Mans blood opens
>
> Into Eternity of which this vegetable Earth is but a shadow:[17]

It is a difficult passage. According to the arithmetic of Archbishop Ussher (1581-1656) (and here we are on sure ground accepted by Anglican and other Christian denominations) earth had been created in 4004 B.C. and was to last six thousand years[18]. The 'pulsation of [an] artery is [therefore] equal in its period and value' (interesting words) to the entire lifespan of Creation. Though there can be no possible connection I am reminded of De Quincey's musings in *Savannah La Mar* on the impossibility or at least the inconceivability of present time:

> Put into a Roman clepsydra [measuring glass] one hundred drops of water; let these run out as the sands in an hourglass; every drop measuring an hundredth part of a second, so that each shall represent but the three hundred and sixty thousandth part of an hour. Now, count the drops as they race along; and, when the fiftieth of the hundred is passing, behold! forty nine are not because already they have perished; and fifty are not because they are yet to come. You see, therefore, how narrow, how

---

[17] ibid plate 29, ll.19-22 Erdman 127
[18] See BOV 342-3.

incalculably narrow, is the true and actual present. Of that time which we call the present, hardly a hundredth part but belongs either to a past that has fled or to a future which is still on the wing. It has perished or it is not born. It was, or it is not.

Yet even this approximation to the truth is *infinitely* false. For again subdivide that solitary drop, which only was found to represent the present into a lower series of similar fractions, and the actual present which you arrest, measures now but the thirty sixth millionth of an hour, and so by infinite declension the true and very present, in which only we live and enjoy, will vanish into a mote of a mote, distinguishable only by heavenly vision.....The time which is contracts into a mathematic point and even that point perishes a thousand times before we can utter its birth.[19]

For Blake the events of Earth's history (and with them the work of the poet) are over and done with in the 'pulsation of [an] artery' that constitutes present time by contrast with Eternity. In De Quincey the same comparison is made but by a mathematical logic that denies the present and with it the suffering of which, for him, life has consisted; that is it denies it the possibility of a discernible existence. Beyond a certain point we cannot discern. I hardly need mention Blake's seeing eternity in a grain of sand[20].

---

[19] *Savannah la Mar*; De Quincey's Works, Author's Edition; Vol xvi p. 34; A and C Black, Edinburgh 1871.
[20]   To see a World in a Grain of Sand
      And a Heaven in a Wild Flower,
       Hold Infinity in the palm of your hand
      And Eternity in an hour.   Blake: 'Auguries of Innocence' 1-4 Erdman 490.

No less powerful and idiosyncratic is the second of the moments, the one that Satan's 'Watch Fiends' cannot find:

> There is a Moment in each Day that Satan cannot find
>
> Nor can his Watch Fiends find it, but the Industrious find
>
> This Moment and it multiply and when it once is found
>
> It renovates every Moment of the Day if rightly placed.[21]

Within each day (we are incidentally located outside time, so day is a metaphor) there is a moment that belongs to Eternity, a moment of such Imaginative intensity that the state police of rationalism are baffled by it. But it is far from clear how we are to understand the 'industrious' who because they are imaginative can not only find but 'multiply' and manipulate the moment. If they were human workers there would be little to explain but the industry seems strange amongst immortals. Commenting on the passage, Harold Bloom hits on a comparison that probably occurs to most of us. 'The whole of this sequence', he writes, 'finds a clear parallel in Wordsworth's 'spots of time' in *The Prelude*, for like Wordsworth Blake is concerned with renovation, and a renovation initially dependent on mundane experience.'[22] Well yes and no but more no. One poet talks of Satan's 'Watch Fiends', the other of a cottage woman with a pitcher on her head[23]. The sense in which Blake is 'dependant on', or even prepared to

---

[21] *Milton;* plate 35 ll 42-5; Erdman 136
[22] Erdman, see Bloom's Commentary at 925
[23] *Prelude* 1805 xi 278-315; FT 480

acknowledge, mundane experience is very limited. The parallel is attractive for slightly spurious reasons; because the phrase 'spot of time' sounds as if it ought to apply and because by chance the two poets both make use of the word 'renovate'. In the case of Wordsworth, it is his third attempt at an adjective in the 'spots of time' passage – the first two being 'fructifying' and 'vivifying' and the third 'renovating'[24]. It is chance in any case. The big difference is that, though both poets are talking about Imagination, Wordsworth is talking about the mind and Blake about the Cosmos. Wordsworth's claims are odd enough. The mind is he says 'nourished and invisibly repaired'[25] by childhood imaginative experience refracted by the adult Imagination. Blakes's claims are a great deal odder.

My last reference to *Milton* is the less abstract moment of fulfilment (referred to four times but never described) when the lark rises. This time we are permitted, up to a point anyway, to bring our own experience to the poetry;

> The Lark sitting upon his earthly bed; just as the morn
> Appears; listens silent; then springing from the waving Corn-field! Loud
> He leads the Choir of day! Trill, trill, trill, trill, trill,
> Mounting upon the wings of light into the Great expanse [26]

They are small brown birds, nothing much to look at but beautiful in their song and their behaviour. Rising from the cornfield or

---

[24] 'fructifying' in the *Two Part Prelude* 1798-9. Pt. 1 290; FT 16
  'vivifying' in the 1805 *Prelude*. Bk. XII. 259; FT 478
  'renovating' in the 1850 *Prelude* Bk. XII l. 210; FT 479
[25] *Prelude* 1805 xi 265; FT 478
[26] *Milton* ii 29-32; Erdman 130

from grass they climb higher and higher into the sky singing all the time until they are almost invisible and one just hears the voice. And then they float down to earth singing as they come. I am mentioning this partly because Blake doesn't need to. The lark was part of everyone's experience[27]. The moment was symbolic. Just at the place to where the lark mounts is a crystal gate; it is the entrance of the first heaven.

The moments that Blake draws our attention to in *Milton* have it in common that they are points at which time and Eternity touch, at which time attains to an Imaginative intensity that carries it over into the Infinite. Thought of in this way they are somewhat abstract. They make no suggestions as to the role of the individual. The central narrative of *Milton* however is impressive because it offers the descent of the hero (and that's Milton too) into consciously chosen 'self-annihilation'. Milton, though in heaven when first we see him, has been guilty while on earth of two major faults; firstly, of writing a poetry that imitates the classics and their celebration of war and, secondly, of failure to get on with his three wives and three daughters, seen collectively as the female principle Ololon. In Blake's highly imaginative poem Milton returns to earth to rid himself of the selfhood that has been responsible:

> I come in Self-annihilation and the grandeur of Inspiration
>
> To cast off Rational Demonstration by Faith in the Saviour,
>
> To cast off the rotten rags of Memory by Inspiration.

---

[27] JFW digresses: 'The nastiest aspect of this would be known to those who read John Clare. In a notebook he refers to the procession of carts bringing larks which have been netted to be eaten at the tables of the wealthy in London. And those carts go in every day at four o'clock in the morning!'

> To cast off Bacon, Locke and Newton from Albions covering
>
> To take off his filthy garments, and clothe him with Imagination
>
> To cast aside from Poetry, all that is not Inspiration
>
> That it no longer shall dare to mock with the aspersion of Madness
>
> Cast on the Inspired, by the tame high finisher of paltry Blots
>
> Indefinite, or paltry Rhymes; or paltry Harmonies...
>
> To cast off the idiot Questioner.....
>
> Who publishes doubt and calls it knowledge; whose
>
>   Science is Despair[28]

Blake concludes impressively:

> These are the destroyers of Jerusalem, these are the murderers
>
> Of Jesus, who deny the Faith and mock at Eternal life:
>
> Who pretend to Poetry that they may destroy Imagination;
>
> By imitation of Natures Images drawn from Remembrance. [29]

There are some complexities that need to be touched on, chiefly perhaps Albion and Jerusalem and their multiple roles. Nobody in Blakean myth is any one thing or belongs to any one mode of experience. It is quite easy to get used to and we see it

---

[28] *Milton* Plate 41 2-15; Erdman 142
[29] Ibid. 21-4.

clearly in the *Book of Urizen* which sets up that great Blakean myth at the beginning; Urizen is part of Eternity and therefore an Immortal. He is also a landscape and much else. Albion is England made of rocks and stones and trees; and mankind made of people; and the world which is more or less abstract; and is also the great humanity divine, at once God and Man. We can add more. Jerusalem is an idealised city, effectively heaven and the female counterpart or emanation of Albion into whom she will finally be reassimilated when we return to the original harmony (as Coleridge would like to do too).

Milton's speech is full of Blake's antipathies, above all rationalism and memory which are seen as the enemies of Imagination. And of course selfhood. It is one of the areas in which Blake is closest to Coleridge. What may be regarded as the first of the great Coleridgean definitions of Imagination from the early part of 'Religious Musings' belonging to 1794-5 takes the form of a denunciation of self:

> Made blind by lusts, disherited of soul,
>
> No common center Man, no common sire

('Religious Musings' contains true insights into Coleridge's thinking at the time; Lamb, Coleridge's fellow Unitarian, called the poem the greatest poem since Milton and *Paradise Lost*[30]. It is greater in some ways in that it has a greater subject):

> Knoweth! A sordid solitary thing,
>
> Mid countless brethren with a lonely heart

---

[30] 'the noblest poem in the language after the Paradise Lost and even that was not made the vehicle of such grand truths'. Lamb L i 94

> Thro' courts and cities the smooth Savage roams
>
> Feeling himself, his own low Self the whole;
>
> When he by sacred sympathy….

It is hard to find a better definition of the Blakean/Coleridgean Imagination than 'sacred sympathy':

> …..might make
>
> The whole ONE SELF! SELF, that no alien knows!
>
> SELF, far diffus'd as Fancy's wing can travel!
>
> SELF, spreading still! Oblivious of its own,
>
> Yet all of all possessing![31]

This passage is important to the Coleridge of 1798 and the background to 'The Ancient Mariner'. For 'Fancy's wing' we should read Imagination. The Fancy / Imagination distinction is not made by Coleridge at this period though it does seem to be hinted at by Blake. Man is the 'smooth Savage' as he roams not through wilds or communities in which he has a part to play (and that has its bearing on 'The Ancient Mariner') but through courts and cities, centres of power, loneliness, affluence, artificiality. The expression 'smooth Savage' is chosen for its apparent paradox. Savage is the French word *sauvage* meaning wild; to be 'smooth' is we assume to have lost one's wildness. There is another kind of savagery, Coleridge is saying, the savagery of being inappropriately smooth, of being selfish when one could be generous, closed off when one could be Imaginative. The 'smooth Savage' has it in his potential to achieve the great Romantic aim of

---

[31] 'Religious Musings' 147-57; STC I 181

making all one whole. To do so would require Imagination in its highest form, a 'sympathy' or feeling with what is 'sacred' in that it is an act of faith; 'sacred' in that it consecrates man's God-given powers to the harmony that is God's purpose.

'Annihilation' is a big word for Blake and in the prophetic books not uncommon. Milton's 'self-annihilation' means, as Blake was surely aware, two separate things – an annihilation that he himself carries out, and an annihilation of the self. That he should come too in the 'grandeur of inspiration' confirms that this is an imaginative act, one that can be performed only by a mind capable, as Shelley's is for instance in 'Mont Blanc', of standing outside itself. It is this aspect that connects the concept of 'self-annihilation' to the milder loss of consciousness dying into a life of the mind that we saw in 'Tintern Abbey', or that Andrew Marvell in the seventeenth century experienced in his garden as he felt the power of Imagination displace his sensual pleasure 'Annihilating all that's made / To a green thought in a green shade' (47-8) in about 1652.

In Blake, 'annihilation' in Milton's view of things, seems to have a good deal to do with getting rid of the wrong clothes. In Blake's nightmare metaphor, clothing is far from being superficial to be put on and taken off, replaced at will; it is powerful for good or ill, it takes over the inner man. Albion has been wearing 'filthy' clothes, morally 'filthy', and now may be clothed with Imagination. If we spell this out a little, rational demonstration (empiricism, the whole way of thinking of the previous one hundred and twenty years instituted by Blake's abhorrences 'Bacon Locke and Newton') is to be stripped off and replaced by Imagination. Blake's anger (he has been called mad by those whom he despises) is such that he makes no distinctions. First to come to mind are inferior painters who overfinish their work ('tame high finishers of paltry Blocks / Indefinite'). The last three words are a construction where the noun comes between two adjectives the second of which is Latinate and placed at the beginning of the line, a construction that all Romantics borrow from *Paradise Lost*. Coleridge uses the construction for instance in 'Frost at Midnight' with 'most believing' mind 'Presageful' and Wordsworth also in 'Tintern Abbey', 'the fretful stir / Unprofitable'. There is special appropriateness here as the fictive Milton of Blake's poem imitates the patterns of his once living predecessor. Those 'tame high finishers' along with rationalist philosophers, bad poets, bad musicians, painters of 'paltry blocks Indefinite' are 'destroyers of Jerusalem', 'murderers of Jesus'; they threaten the ultimate harmony that is another name for Imagination.

The passage is telling us why Blake has no use for what Coleridge terms the Secondary Imagination of the creative artist which is an 'echo' of the Primary, as Coleridge puts it, coinciding with 'the conscious will'[32]. Curiously, the author of 'Kubla Khan' thinks of creativity as 'conscious' and in doing so makes the Secondary Imagination seem very secondary. The Primary in its highest manifestation defeats consciousness bringing the individual to God in a 'repetition in the finite mind of the eternal act of creation in the infinite I AM'. However good the creative artist, his work, in Coleridge's view, is an imitation or analogy not a 'repetition' of the Eternal. This wouldn't do for Blake. The maker

---

[32] 'The primary Imagination I hold to be the living power and prime agent of all human perception, and as a repetition in the finite mind of the eternal act of creation in the infinite I AM. The secondary I consider as an echo of the former, coexisting with the conscious will, yet still as identical with the primary in the *kind* of its agency, and differing only in *degree*, and in the *mode* of its operation'. BL Chapter 13 p.304

of 'paltry blocks / Indefinite' is not merely a bad painter, he is a 'destroyer', as is anyone or anything that undermines Imagination – defined as the potential harmony of existence.

My fifth and last quotation is from *Jerusalem*.

Trembling I sit day and night, my friends are astonish'd at me.

Yet they forgive my wanderings, I rest not from my great

task!

To open the Eternal Worlds, to open the immortal Eyes

Of Man inwards into the Worlds of Thought: into Eternity

Ever expanding in the Bosom of God, the Human

Imagination[33]

Trembling at the immensity of his task as he sets out on the great epic that is to be the climax of his life's work, Blake astonishes us too. We should not have expected him to be aware of his friends' concern, much less of their indulgence. Yet here they are, comfortably forgiving what they see as the 'wanderings' of his thought. Then as now his final reference to 'the Bosom of God, the Human Imagination' might come as a surprise. But it is one of an extraordinary number of allusions in this later Blake period that make an outright claim for Imagination as divine. 'The human Imagination ... is the Divine Body of the Lord Jesus blessed forever' (this is the Bard speaking in *Milton* Plate 3[34]); 'O Human Imagination! O Divine Body I have Crucified,/ I have turned my back upon thee' (this is Albion speaking in *Jerusalem* Plate 24[35]).

---

[33] Blake; *Jerusalem*. Plate 5 ll.16-20; Erdman 147
[34] Plate 3 3-4; Erdman 96

'Babel mocks saying there is no God nor Son of God / That thou, O Human Imagination, O Divine Body, art all / A delusion'[36] (and that is Jerusalem herself speaking). The claim that human Imagination is the divine body of the Lord Jesus is one that would chime in with Coleridge's thinking on the Logos; he would like to be able to make the Blakean claim but as far as I am aware never does or never does in so many words. Blake is under no pressure such as Coleridge's to conform. He has no Anglican elder brother father-figure, no sense that he should be towing a line. He writes what he feels. Brief as they are we should see Blake's quoted lines from *Jerusalem* as among the great Romantic definitions of Imagination, scarcely less complex, powerful and lucid than Coleridge in *Biographia Literaria*. Reading them for themselves, ignoring the detail and yielding to the impressiveness of language we get a remarkably strong sense of meaning as we do with Coleridge's magnificent claim for the Primary Imagination, 'a repetition in the finite mind of the Eternal act of creation in the infinite I AM'. Both poets we gather are talking about an act that is God-like yet requiring a going inwards – a finding of the eternal within the transient – when we should expect the movement to be outwards and expansion beyond the human towards the ultimate that is out there. Space and time however for both of them have something of the quality of metaphor. To borrow a phrase from Keats, they 'tease us out of thought / As doth eternity'[37]. Blake and the Coleridge of the Primary Imagination deal in an ultimate reality, eternal truth, stretching language to say more than it conventionally can. Given the *marriage* of Heaven and Hell, and 'the doors of perception' that stand in need of cleansing, it is not greatly surprising that Blake's task here is to

---

[35] Plate 24 23-4 Erdman 169
[36] ibid Plate 60 56-8 Erdman 211
[37] Keats 'Ode on a Grecian Urn' 44-5; Allott 537

open the immortal eyes of man into eternity. The surprise comes when eternity is first equated with inward worlds of thought then said to be 'ever-expanding in the bosom of God'. It is a little more complex than quotations that assert in passing the identity of Imagination and the divine body. One is reminded of Wordsworth's subtle definition at the end of the 1805 *Prelude* of;

....a mighty mind,

...one that feeds upon infinity

That is exalted by an underpresence

The sense of God, or whatsoe'er is dim

Or vast in its own being.[38]

Blake has no doubt that the sense of God *is* that which is 'dim or vast' in our own being. Wordsworth is less certain; or perhaps one could say that for him it doesn't too much matter. What matters is that the sense either of God or of some inner greatness is a supreme imaginative act.

So what did the Fairy know? He knew that man could leave his man-forged manacles, step out of the fifth window into Eternity by performing the imaginative act of putting the 'stolen joys' behind him accepting his destiny. How did he know it? He knew it because tiny as he was he belonged to a world of pure Imagination.

---

[38] Wordsworth. *Prelude* 1805 XIII 69-73; FT 514

9 WORDSWORTHIAN TRANSFORMATIONS:

THE PITCHER AT THE FOUNTAIN[1]

As he stops to drink from Margaret's forsaken well, the Pedlar who tells the story of *The Ruined Cottage*, notices a spider's web hanging to the water's edge and not symbolising anything in particular. Margaret herself would have seen one often when she went to draw water for her family. It is the next detail to take the old man's eye that is important:

> Beside yon spring I stood,
>
> And eyed its waters till we seemed to feel
>
> One sadness, they and I. For them a bond
>
> Of brotherhood is broken; time has been
>
> When every day the touch of human hand
>
> Disturbed their stillness, and they ministered
>
> To human comfort. When I stooped to drink
>
> A spider's web hung to the water's edge,
>
> And on the wet and slimy foot-stone lay
>
> The useless fragment of a wooden bowl.[2]

---

[1] First delivered as a lecture to The Wordsworth Summer Conference 2003
[2] *The Ruined Cottage* i 82-91; MOH 35.

It is a beautiful piece of writing, an embodiment in a phrase that the Pedlar or Wordsworth has just used of the 'strong creative power of human passion'[3], feeling or passion rendered imaginative in its intensity. The Pedlar is shown as giving the waters of the well the sadness that they share. In an undidactic way we are being told how to read the poetry. But we are trusted on our own to respond to the presence of the great final symbol of the final chapter of *Ecclesiastes*:

> Remember now thy Creator in the days of thy youth, while the evil days come not.... Or ever the silver cord be loosed or the golden bowl be broken or the pitcher be broken at the fountain[4].....Then shall the dust return to the earth as it was; and the spirit shall return to God who gave it[5].

Hardly a reader of Wordsworth's day would not have known these lines by heart. Wordsworth has recreated the biblical sublime on a domestic level; naturalised it, one might say. Already in *Ecclesiastes* there is a movement beyond the grandeur of the silver cord, the golden bowl, things possessed by the few, to the humbleness of the pitcher on which everyone every day depended. It makes sense of course that where Wordsworth chose the pitcher Henry James would go for the golden bowl. Taking the hint from *Ecclesiastes*, Wordsworth binds the symbol into his narrative of day to day existence. Bowl and well, in addition to their poignant evoking of life cut off at its source, are revealed as having had a social function;

> Many a passenger,   [*passer-by*]
>
> Has blessed poor Margaret for her gentle looks

---

[3] ibid 78-9.
[4] KJV *Ecclesiastes* 12:6
[5] ibid 12:7

> When she upheld the cool refreshment drawn
>
> From that forsaken spring, and no one came
>
> But he was welcome, no one went away
>
> But that it seemed that she loved him.[6]

The last statement is curiously extreme. These are strangers passing Margaret's lonely cottage and asking to quench their thirst. In Wordsworth's religion of love that centres in community the bowl is almost a chalice, the giving of water almost a sacrament.

I am talking about transformations wrought by the 'strong creative power of human passion'; that is, Wordsworth's naturalising imagination. Another example from *The Ruined Cottage* occurs when the Pedlar tells the listening poet of one of the earlier visits to Margaret and her decaying cottage:

> I turned aside
>
> And strolled into her garden. It was changed.
>
> The unprofitable bindweed spread his bells
>
> From side to side, and with unwieldy wreathes
>
> Had dragged the rose from its sustaining wall
>
> And bent it down to earth. The border tufts,
>
> Daisy, and thrift, and lowly camomile,
>
> And thyme, had straggled out into the paths
>
> Which they were used to deck.[7]

---

[6] *The Ruined Cottage* i 98-103; MOH 36
[7] Ibid ii .312-20; MOH 42

Forgetful of Margaret, the 'calm oblivious tendencies / Of Nature'[8] have been at work. Flowers that she loved and tended are overgrown or straggling. More important is the image of the rose dragged from its sustaining wall which cannot but suggest to us Margaret's own situation parted from Robert by poverty and war. This time it is the grandeur of epic rather than the biblical sublime that has been transformed. Eve in *Paradise Lost* IX is to be seen stooping 'to support / Each flower of slender stalk'. She herself is then referred to specifically as the 'fairest unsupported flower / From her best prop so far'[9]. The process has been the same. The imagery that played its part in an immense conception of the Fall of Man finds itself evoking instead the pathos of a cottage woman. Eden has become the cottage garden.

Examples are everywhere but I have it in mind to bring out a few that seem especially Wordsworthian, those in 'The Thorn' and 'Lucy Gray'. Readers of 'The Thorn' seldom confess that they don't know what it is about. Wordsworth takes his dreadful Gothic source, Burger's *Des Pfarrer's Tochter von Taubenheim* published by William Taylor in 1796 as *The Lass of Fair Wone* ('wone' being a dwellingplace) and does what? These are the possibilities; he turns it into a murder mystery; or a story of village superstition; or a dramatic monologue revealing (but never describing) the character of the narrator, perhaps an old sea captain; or he turns it into an associationist poem (this is my

---

[8] Ibid ii 504-5; MOH 48

[9] When the serpent spies Eve in Eden, she is.....
> Veiled in a cloud of fragrance, where she stood,
> Half spied, so thick the roses bushing round
> About her glowed, oft stooping to support
> Each flower of slender stalk, whose head though gay
> Carnation, purple, azure, or specked with gold,
> Hung drooping unsustained, them she upstays
> Gently with myrtle band, mindless the while,
> Her self, though fairest unsupported flower,
> From her best prop so far, and storm so nigh.
>
> *Paradise Lost* ix 425-33. Fowler 463

own preference) in which the poet explores not murder but mental process, how the mind returns obsessionally to what De Quincey would call its 'involutes', 'concrete objects' unimportant in themselves to which emotions have attached themselves[10]. Interpretations are not exclusive. *The Thorn* can be all these things and others too. Among the oddest is the explanation that Wordsworth gives himself. Would anyone else look at an old thorn tree on a hilltop in a storm and say to himself, 'Cannot I by some invention do as much to make this thorn permanently an impressive object as the storm has made it to my eyes at this moment?'[11]

That Wordsworth did indeed think in this way seems to be corroborated by Coleridge's statement in Chapter XIV of *Biographia Literaria* on the two cardinal points of poetry much discussed at Alfoxden in Spring 1798 and leading, so we are told, to the creation of *Lyrical Ballads*. Cardinal point number one tends to bring Wordsworth to mind; 'the power of exciting the sympathy of the reader by a faithful adherence to the truth of nature'. Cardinal point number two brings Coleridge to mind but not excluding Wordsworth; 'the power of giving the interest of novelty by the modifying colours of imagination'[12]. More important is the strange fact that Coleridge, in looking for a bond between the two kinds of poetry that he and Wordsworth have become identified with, turns to the weather. 'The sudden charm', Coleridge continues, 'which accidents of light and shade, which moon-light or sun-set diffused over a known and familiar landscape, appeared to represent the practicability of combining

---

[10] 'I have been struck with the important truth that far more of our deepest thoughts and feelings pass to us through perplexed combinations of concrete objects, pass to us as *involutes* (if I may coin that word) in compound experiences incapable of being disentangled, that ever reach us directly, and in their own abstract shapes'. De Quincey; *Suspiria de Profundis*; Ward 130
[11] FN 14
[12] BL ii Chap 14 p.5

both'. Weather transforms landscape, showing, as it had in 'Frost at Midnight' a month or two before 'The Thorn' was written, a power analagous to the human imagination. In doing so, it offers both truth to nature and the interest of novelty. With 'The Rime of the Ancient Mariner' just completed, with Burger in the background, it is interesting to see Wordsworth in 'The Thorn' producing an imaginative poetry akin to the supernatural on the basis of an actual Gothic source. It is interesting too that he did not turn at once to the Gothic as his means of rendering permanent the thorn tree on the hill.

The two stanzas in the Alfoxden notebook describing 'The Thorn' are not as is often assumed a draft opening to the ballad, they are an attempt to render the tree permanently impressive through a poetry which has nothing to do with the Gothic or supernatural. Siting his poem on a 'summit where the stormy gale / Sweeps through the clouds from vale to vale', Wordsworth concentrates from the first on the thorn's pathos;

> A thorn there is which like a stone
>
> With jagged lichens is o'ergrown,
>
> A thorn that wants its thorny points
>
> A toothless thorn with knotted joints;
>
> Not higher than a two years child
>
> It stands upon that spot so wild;
>
> Of leaves it has repaired its loss
>
> With heavy tufts of dark green moss,
>
> Which from the ground in plenteous crop
>
> Creep upward to its very top[13]

The poet has got about as far as he is going to get offering mere description laced with sympathy. He needs a new element, a new direction. The fact that the *Lyrical Ballads* experiment was underway might lead him to choose narrative but there was no obvious reason why the horrors of *The Lass of Fair Wone* should come to mind as a means of rendering permanent the aged tree;

>Forth from her hair a silver pin
>
>With hasty hand she drew,
>
>And prest against its tender heart,
>
>And the sweet babe she slew.
>
>Erst when the act of blood was done,
>
>Her soul its guilt abhorr'd:
>
>'My Jesus! what has been my deed?
>
>Have mercy on me, Lord!'
>
>With bloody nails, beside the pond,
>
>Its shallow grave she tore:
>
>'There rest in God – there shame and want
>
>Thou can'st not suffer more!
>
>Me, vengeance waits! My poor, poor child,

---

[13] Draft of 'The Thorn'; P.W ii 240 footnote.

> Thy wound shall bleed afresh,
>
> When ravens from the gallows tear
>
> Thy mother's mouldering flesh!'
>
> Hard by the bower her gibbet stands;
>
> Her skull is still to show –
>
> It seems to eye the barren grave,
>
> Three spans in length below.
>
> That is the spot where grows no grass,
>
> Where falls no rain nor dew:
>
> Whence steals along the pond of toads
>
> A hovering fire so blue!
>
> And nightly, when the ravens come,
>
> Her ghost is seen to glide;
>
> Pursues and tries to quench the flame,
>
> And pines the pool beside.[14]

Wordsworth's clearly stated intention to find a way of making permanently impressive the thorn tree made briefly sublime by

---

[14] From *The Lass of Fair Wone* by Gottfried Burger translated by William Taylor 1796. *The Monthly Magazine* 1796 Vol. 1 p.223; *Penguin Romantic Poetry* 471

the storm surely implies that when he leaves behind his description of the tree and selects the story of the parson's daughter he has to some extent worked out how the material will suit his purpose. There was no obvious way to bring to bear on 'The Thorn' a story of seduction and infanticide – unless, of course, the tree could be a part of the murder! Hardly very likely considering its diminutive size and mass of knotted joints but it is briefly suggested nonetheless towards the end of Wordsworth's ballad:

> some will say
>
> She hanged her baby on the tree.

Wordsworth presumably expected his rendering permanent to work by a transformation of the Gothic. But that could not work in a way that is easily defined.

> High on a mountain's highest ridge,
>
> Where oft the stormy winter gale
>
> Cuts like a scythe, while through the clouds
>
> It sweeps from vale to vale;
>
> Not five yards from the mountain-path,
>
> This thorn you on your left espy;
>
> And to the left, three yards beyond,
>
> You see a little muddy pond
>
> Of water, never dry;
>
> I've measured it from side to side:
>
> 'Tis three feet long, and two feet wide.

And close beside this aged thorn

There is a fresh and lovely sight,

A beauteous heap, a hill of moss,

Just half a foot in height.

All lovely colours there you see,

All colours that were ever seen,

And mossy network too is there,

As if by hand of lady fair

The work had woven been,

And cups, the darlings of the eye,

So deep is their vermilion dye.

Ah me! what lovely tints are there!

Of olive-green and scarlet bright,

In spikes, in branches, and in stars,

Green, red, and pearly white.

This heap of earth o'ergrown with moss,

Which close beside the thorn you see,

So fresh in all its beauteous dyes,

Is like an infant's grave in size

As like as like can be:

But never, never any where,

An infant's grave was half so fair.

Now would you see this aged thorn,

This pond and beauteous hill of moss,

You must take care and chuse your time

The mountain when to cross.

For oft there sits, between the heap

That's like an infant's grave in size,

And that same pond of which I spoke,

A woman in a scarlet cloak,

And to herself she cries,

'Oh misery! oh misery!

Oh woe is me! oh misery!'[15]

Wordsworth finds in his source, and duly transforms, a 'grave', a 'pond', a 'tree', to be precise a gallows tree. With them and most needful of transformation is the parson's nameless daughter who, though hideously maltreated by lover and father, is guilty of the crime of which Martha Ray stands accused merely by local gossip and without substantial evidence. Burger's world is black and white save when it is blue of course to betoken the entry of a ghost! His most famous ballad, *Lenora*, offers us an

---

[15] 'The Thorn' iii-vi 22-66; Cornell LB 78-9

impatient lover damned from her own lips and carried off speedily to hell. *The Chase*, translated by the young Walter Scott, provides a competition of good and bad angels vying for the luckless human soul. *The Lass of Fair Wone* is no less crude in its morality. Every phase and stage is predictable – from the blasting of innocence, to unwanted pregnancy, to the reactions of the lover and the father, the desperate murder and unquestioned retribution. Rejecting the ghost, blue light, nightly ravens, pond of toads, Wordsworth for whatever purpose introduces into his ballad layers of imagery suggestive of infanticide. In some ways his poem is more, not less, Gothic than Burger's but it is Gothic of a different style. The grave, torn by the nails of the parson's daughter, is naturalised as a 'beauteous heap', a 'hill of moss' and should doubtless be seen as an anthill, common on the Quantocks, and covered with the red flowers of moss. 'Cups, the darlings of the eye' Wordsworth calls the flowers, and adds in a patent evoking of blood, 'So deep is their vermilion dye'. He then three times gratuitously tells us that the heap is 'like an infant's grave in size' or perhaps it is the narrator[16] and not Wordsworth who tells us these things, how should we know? Attempting to take seriously a plot that nowhere adds up, we find ourselves in the hands of an unreliable narrator assessing the witness of credulous villagers and we are confronted by a woman in a scarlet cloak who might as well be wearing a placard saying 'I am a murderess'. That she should turn out to have a cry as improbable as her cloak, 'Oh misery! oh misery! / Oh woe is me! oh misery!', suggests that Wordsworth knows his transformation to have little to do with truth to nature. As Coleridge comments in the 1811 Shakespeare Lectures, 'the grandest effects of poetry are where the imagination [is] called forth, not to produce a

---

[16] 'The poem of the Thorn, as the reader will soon discover, is not supposed to be spoken in the author's own person : the character of the loquacious narrator will sufficiently shew itself in the course of the story.' Advertisement to *Lyrical Ballads* 1798; Cornell LB 739

distinct form but a strong working of the mind...the result [being] what the poet wishes to impress, [namely, the substitution of] a grand feeling of the unimaginable for a mere image'[17]. Perhaps we should settle for 'The Thorn' as producing in its transforming of Burger a 'strong working of the mind', a sublime feeling of the unimaginable. We may, if we choose, read into it distinct forms, particular interpretations. But the essence of the poetry, and the source of the poet's pleasures as he writes, lies in the fact of the imaginative act of transformation. We see Wordsworth in 'The Thorn' rejoicing in the powerful incongruity of what he has done to make permanently impressive the spiky old tree.

> The speaker in 'Lucy Gray' remarks
>
> > Oft had I heard of Lucy Gray,
> >
> > And when I cross'd the Wild,
> >
> > I chanc'd to see at break of day
> >
> > The solitary Child[18].

As readers we are compelled to ask why he had heard of Lucy Gray and in what circumstances. Lucy it seems is different, can be talked and heard about. But for the moment we are far from knowing why. The poet sees her not just at any time but when he crosses 'the Wild'. Lulled by rhyme and rhythm we don't at first notice what a strange powerful thing it is to do. It is almost as if 'the Wild' was another mode or realm of experience. The poet chances to see Lucy, not to meet or talk with, but just to set eyes upon. At the end of the poem she will be heard as she sings her solitary song, but not yet. Like the girl on Penrith beacon[19] with the pitcher on her head, or like Mary Hutchinson in 'I travelled

---

[17] *The Collected Works of Samuel Taylor Coleridge*. Bollingen. Lecture 7 p.311
[18] 'Lucy Gray' 1-4; Cornell LB 170
[19] *Prelude* 1799 i 296-327; FT 16-17

among unknown men'[20], she is a lovely apparition, ghostlike, sent to be a moment's ornament. Seeing the solitary child, the poet is confirmed of her existence. Seeing her in the dawn accentuates her specialness, perhaps her solitude as well. She is a creature of the new day, a lonely one;

> No Mate, no comrade Lucy knew;
>
> She dwelt on a wild Moor,
>
> The sweetest Thing that ever grew
>
> Beside a human door! (5-8)

'Mate' seems odd. For a moment the word transforms the solitary child to an animal, a true inhabitant of 'the Wild'. But then we recall the boy taken from his 'mates' in the lines added to 'There was a Boy'. On second thoughts perhaps the point that Wordsworth is making is that she is not *of* the wild moor, she dwells there. She is, he tells us, affectionately 'the sweetest Thing'. Like 'mate', the use of 'thing' pulls in two directions, at once taking away some of Lucy's humanity and bringing it back again as we recall the 'thinking things' of 'Tintern Abbey'[21] written three months before. Language continues to be gently mysterious. Lucy grows 'beside', not within, a door. It is characterised itself as 'human' where she seems more like a tree or a beautiful shrub. As if to confirm this 'otherness' the poet's thoughts turn to the 'Fawn at play' which is like the hare on the green, whose descendant will run 'races in her mirth' in 'The Leech-Gatherer'[22]. Like the blackbird who sings when he will in

---

[20] PW ii 30; Cornell *LB* 821
[21] A motion and a spirit, that impels
All thinking things, all objects of all thought,
And rolls through all things. 'Tintern Abbey' 101-3; Cornell LB 119
[22] All things that love the sun are out of doors;
The sky rejoices in the morning's birth;
The grass is bright with rain-drops; – on the moors

'The Fountain'[23], these creatures are beautiful and free. But a threat hangs over them whether they know it or not. The 'yet' in 'You yet may spy the Faun at play' (9) hints surely at the ominous. One day there may not be room even for the faun and the hare. It is a shock as we read on:

> But the sweet face of Lucy Gray
>
> Will never more be seen.   (11-12)

but a shock that has been prepared for. She has just been seen. Why, we are bound to ask, will her face not be visible again? The poem has started with her appearance in the dawn and seemed to be going to be about it. It is not a question that will ever be answered. Wordsworth finishes his introduction, almost a twelve line poem in its own right, with the teasing thought of Lucy as having somehow relinquished even the slender hold on existence that has been permitted to her. And suddenly we find her there before our eyes, fully human, being talked to quite ordinarily and by a father who is anxious about quite ordinary things – snowstorms and firewood and a wife who will need a lamp to get her home. Standing out in all this normality is the detail of the moon:

> 'To-night will be a stormy night,
>
> You to the Town must go,
>
> And take a lantern, Child, to light

The Hare is running races in her mirth;
And with her feet she from the plashy earth
Raises a mist; which, glittering in the sun,
Runs with her all the way, wherever she doth run.
    'Resolution and Independence' 8-14; Cornell Poems 2 Vols 123-4

[23] The blackbird in the summer trees,
The lark upon the hill,
Let loose their carols when they please,
Are quiet when they will. 'The Fountain' 37-40; Cornell LB 216

> Your Mother thro' the snow.'
>
> 'That, Father! will I gladly do,
>
> 'Tis scarcely afternoon –
>
> The Minster-clock has just struck two,
>
> And yonder is the Moon.' (13-20

Moons are important to Wordsworth and he is curiously concerned with whether people have seen them or not. Johnny Foy[24], whom Lucy a little resembles as she sets out on her errand of mercy to a town she will never reach, has been in the moonlight from eight o'clock till five but probably never noticed. Lucy will spend the more terrifying version of Johnny's night but meanwhile is singled out because she does see the moon. Talking to Crabb Robinson in 1816 Wordsworth goes out of his way to stress that she is unlike both town and country girls in noticing[25]. It is a mark of her solitude, her difference.

How many people have 'rais'd [a] hook / And 'snapp'd a faggot-band'? ('At this the Father rais'd his hook / And snapp'd a faggot band' 21-2). The hook is a bill hook, its heavy blade ten inches or so long ending in a curved point that gives the hook its

---

[24] Now Johnny all night long had heard
  The owls in tuneful concert strive;
  No doubt too he the moon had seen
  For in the moonlight he had been
  From eight o'clock till five. 'The Idiot Boy' 441-5; Cornell LB 104

[25] Crabb Robinson in his diary for 11th Sept 1816, following a conversation with Wordsworth, states that in 'Lucy Gray' Wordsworth's 'object was to exhibit poetically entire *solitude*, and he represents his child as observing the day-moon, which no town or village girl would ever notice'. *Henry Crabb Robinson on Books and their Writers* ed. Edith J. Morley, 3 vols 1938 i 190

name. The faggot is a bunch of hazels, six or seven feet long and used as winter fire wood if they haven't already been made while still green into gates and hurdles for penning lowland sheep. Upland sheep as we all know from *Michael* have stone sheepfolds. The guarantee that Wordsworth knew all this is in the word 'snapp'd'. The 'band' consists of the hazel twisted round the faggot's midriff which in time dries out and can then be snapped by the bill or beak of the billhook. This has relevance because we need to be able to see this poetry of ordinariness just as we need to be able to see Lucy bounding like the young 'roe' of 'Tintern Abbey', who was Wordsworth's earlier self, kicking the snow with 'wanton stroke' (26) up into the air. The storm comes on 'before its time' (29) just as labour-pangs, in a sort of natural treachery, come on before their time. Lucy climbs hill after hill, all exuberance gone. The parents go shouting 'far and wide' and for a moment the poem turns into the tragic ballad that we should have expected and that Wordsworth can write so well if he chooses. Nothing could be sadder or more perfect than the stanzas that cross the landscape taking the parents to the terrible end of their search:

> Then downward from the steep hill's edge
>
> They track'd the footmarks small;
>
> And through the broken hawthorn-hedge,
>
> And by the long stone-wall;
>
>
> And then an open field they cross'd,
>
> The marks were still the same;
>
> They track'd them on, nor ever lost,

> And to the Bridge they came.
>
> They follow'd from the snowy bank
>
> Those footmarks, one by one,
>
> Into the middle of the plank,
>
> And further there were none. (45-56)

Wordsworth is not 'clinging to the palpable' in Coleridge's disloyal and demeaning phrase[26]. He is as always validating his trust in emotion by tying it to place, to scene details of a landscape: in 'And through the broken hawthorn-hedge / And by the long stone-wall' we are reminded of the 'single sheep', the 'hawthorn' bush and old stone 'wall' of *The Prelude* spot of time[27], also written at Goslar in 1798-9. The poem has come to its natural conclusion just as *The Ruined Cottage* had come to its natural end in the thought of Margaret as 'last human tenant of

---

[26] 'He (Coleridge) lamented that Wordsworth was not prone enough to believe in the traditional superstitions of the place, and that there was a something corporeal, a *matter-of-factness*, a clinging to the palpable, or often to the petty, in his poetry, in consequence.' Hazlitt; *My First Acquaintance with Poets*. Wu (1) ix 104

[27]   There was a crag
   An eminence, which from the meeting-point
   Of two highways ascending overlooked
   At least a long half-mile of those two roads,
   By each of which the expected steeds might come –
   The choice uncertain. Thither I repaired
   Up to the highest summit. 'Twas a day
   Stormy, and rough, and wild, and on the grass
   I sat halfsheltered by a naked wall.
   Upon my right hand was a single sheep,
   A whistling hawthorn on my left, and there,
   Those two companions at my side, I watched
   With eyes intensely straining, as the mist
   Gave intermitting prospects of the wood
   And plain beneath. *Prelude* 1799. i. 335-349. FT 17.

the house's 'ruined walls' (492). But Wordsworth has not finished. No more than in *The Ruined Cottage* is he concerned merely with sadness:

> Yet some maintain that to this day
>
> She is a living Child,
>
> That you may see sweet Lucy Gray
>
> Upon the lonesome Wild.
>
>
> O'er rough and smooth she trips along
>
> And never looks behind;
>
> And sings a solitary song
>
> That whistles in the wind. (57-64)

Who then are these 'some' and what price their maintainings? The poet has, as we know from the opening lines, seen sweet Lucy Gray himself, met her in the wild. For good measure he has also told us that her sweet face 'Will nevermore be seen'. Can he now be among those who think her to be alive? Or can we perhaps see her 'sweet' face *without* her being 'a living child'? Are we being told that if we crossed the wild, now the 'lonesome' wild, as the poet crosses it, we shall see Lucy as he does in an act of imagination? She will no more speak to us than Martha Ray or the cottage woman with her pitcher and she cannot look behind (62). But we may participate in her existence that is in some sense the 'solitary song' just as the 'solitary song' is in some sense the poem. So transformations again and again; a playing with different modes of existence such as we see so beautifully explored in 'Three Years She Grew' where Lucy grows to maturity before our eyes, reared to stately height though dying in fact, as we learn at the end of the poem, at the age of three.

But this is to forget the great transforming act which is the poem itself – a transformation that is confident and deliberate and even to some extent explained. The poem, Wordsworth told Isabella Fenwick in 1842,

> 'was founded on a circumstance told me by my Sister, of a little girl, who not far from Halifax in Yorkshire was bewildered in a snow-storm. Her footsteps were traced by her parents to the middle of the lock of a canal, and no other vestige of her, backward or forward, could be traced. The body however was found in the canal'[28].

In working on 'The Thorn' he had had for his source a lurid and unacceptable account of human suffering which required to be transformed if it was to be used at all. For 'Lucy Gray' he had, in the words of *The Prelude* a 'tragic fact[s] of rural history'[29], unadorned but appalling, waiting for its inherent dignity to be recognised as poetry. Few would guess if they knew merely the incident itself the extent to which here too the source would be transformed. 'The way in which the incident was treated', Wordsworth writes looking back over the period in which Romanticism has burgeoned and died away, 'and the

---

[28] FN 1

[29] following the account of the drowned man of Esthwaite and immediately before the spots of time passage in the *Two Part Prelude* Wordsworth writes;
　　　I might advert
To numerous accidents in flood or field,
Quarry or moor, or mid the winter snows,
Distresses and disasters, tragic facts
Of rural history that impressed my mind
With images to which in following years
Far other feelings were attached – with forms
That yet exist with independent life,
And like their archetypes, know no decay.
　　There are in our existence spots of time　*Prelude* 1799 i 279ff. FT 15

spiritualising of the character might furnish hints for contrasting the imaginative influences which I have endeavoured to throw over common life with Crabbe's matter of fact style of treating subjects of the same kind'[30]. Few of us would care to define the 'spiritualising of the character'; but the concept means all to Wordsworth himself. By the imagination the mere fact is connected with that infinity without which there is no poetry, or no Wordsworthian poetry. Lucy has been disconnected from humanity, connected with infinity at a single step. It is not that we are confused as to whether she is alive or dead; she lives on in a world of imagination that transcends even her own very moving ballad story, a world in which she cannot look behind but makes her own strange contribution as the 'solitary song / That whistles in the wind'.

'The Immortality Ode' is my final example of Wordsworthian transformation and is, for me, the greatest lyric poem in the language. It has its faults, chiefly in stanza vii with the dreadful child 'among his new-born blisses'. But the grandeur of its concepts and its rhythms is astonishing. Memories of past visionary strength 'Uphold us, cherish us, and [have power to] make / Our noisy years seem moments in the being / Of the eternal silence'[31]. Imagine a poet in the last hundred years thinking in such terms, let alone writing with comparable magnificence! Poet and critic alike have been terrified of the 'spiritualising' that Wordsworth above all values:

> There was a time when meadow, grove, and stream,
>
> The earth, and every common sight,

---

[30] FN 1
[31] 'Ode' 154-6; Cornell: Poems in 2 Vols 276

> To me did seem
>
> Apparelled in celestial light
>
> The glory and the freshness of a dream.   (1-5)

Transformation by the 'celestial light' is beautifully accomplished in the use of 'apparelled', found as a verb nowhere else in Wordsworth and as a noun four times only, though 'arrayed' is common and 'clothed' more so. 'Apparelled' shares with 'arrayed' the biblical ring so often enhancing Wordsworth's grander, deeper moments but is more musical, more strange and powerful in its juxtaposition to the 'common sight'. I wish to pass over the great central transformation wrought by Wordsworth in the poem in his use of the myth of pre-existence and concentrate on the great transformations of stanza ix:

> O joy! that in our embers
>
> Is something that doth live,
>
> That nature yet remembers
>
> What was so fugitive!
>
> The thought of our past years in me doth breed
>
> Perpetual benedictions: not indeed
>
> For that which is most worthy to be blest;
>
> Delight and liberty, the simple creed
>
> Of Childhood, whether fluttering or at rest,
>
> With new-born hope for ever in his breast: –
>
> Not for these I raise

>   The song of thanks and praise;
>
>   But for those obstinate questionings
>
>   Of sense and outward things,
>
>   Fallings from us, vanishings;
>
>   Blank misgivings of a Creature
>
> Moving about in worlds not realiz'd,
>
> High instincts, before which our mortal Nature
>
> Did tremble like a guilty thing surpriz'd;
>
>   But for those first affections,
>
>   Those shadowy recollections,
>
>   Which, be they what they may,
>
> Are yet the fountain light of all our day,
>
> Are yet a master light of all our seeing;
>
>   Uphold us, cherish us, and make
>
> Our noisy years seem moments in the being
>
> Of the eternal Silence:

Note how this extraordinary poetry moves, clause after clause, line after line, despite the fact that we have yet to reach the end of the opening sentence:

>   truths that wake
>
>   To perish never;
>
> Which neither listlessness, nor mad endeavour,

> Nor Man nor Boy,
>
> Nor all that is at enmity with joy
>
> Can utterly abolish or destroy! (132-163)

At first we have not so much transformation as paradox, the refusal to bless that which is most worthy to be blessed, childhood associated with delight, liberty and new-born hope (good Wordsworthian companions) and offered us in what is surely the subdued natural image of a young bird hopeful of food and 'fluttering' as the parent lands on the nest. It comes as a surprise that such things should be so sternly rejected. But a transformation is taking place. Simple childhood is not merely innocent but ignorant too of life's mysterious weight of pain and fear. In 'Tintern Abbey' 1798 'the burthen of the mystery...is lightened'; in 'The Ode' 1804 it can't and shouldn't be. 'Seeing into the life of things' will not now be enough; pain and fear must be understood, acknowledged as central to the education that has made the poet what he is. What are the 'obstinate questionings', 'the fallings from us', 'vanishings'? And what is a 'world unrealised'? The Fenwick note is useful in which boy Wordsworth is described grasping at physical things to rescue himself from an abyss of idealism and convince himself of the existence of his material surroundings:

> I was often unable to think of external things as having external existence, and I communed with all that I saw as something not apart from but inherent in my own immaterial nature. Many times while going to school have I grasped at a wall or tree to recall myself from this abyss of idealism to the reality'[32].

But Wordsworth was not speaking solely for himself because, as

---

[32] FN 61

in 'Tintern Abbbey', 'the affections gently lead *us* on'; he is speaking for the rest of us too. In some sense the answer seems to be that what is falling from us is security, but that would make the 'fallings' and 'vanishings' identical and I don't think Wordsworth thinks they are.

It is significant that Wordsworth has told us about 'fallings from us' once before and in a poem that he was reworking in February 1804 in the same month that he was writing the 'Ode', the 1799 *Prelude*. The boy-poet's situation at the end of the boat-stealing episode is not the same of course but the affinities are interesting both in what is said and in the manner of putting it over. The child there is chased across Ullswater in the moonlight by a huge cliff 'as if with voluntary power instinct'

> and after I had seen
>
> That spectacle, for many days my brain
>
> Worked with a dim and undetermined sense
>
> Of unknown modes of being. In my thoughts
>
> There was a darkness – call it solitude,
>
> Or blank desertion. No familiar shapes
>
> Of hourly objects, images of trees,
>
> Of sea or sky, no colours of green fields,
>
> But huge and mighty forms that do not live
>
> Like living men moved slowly through my mind
>
> By day, and were the trouble of my dreams.[33]

---

[33] *Prelude* 1799 i 119-129; FT 11

Pursued by the 'huge and mighty forms' (that ought to 'live / Like living men' 127-8, considering their behaviour striding up after the child, but don't because they are half mountain) the child is deserted (note the connection of 'blank desertion' here and 'blank misgivings' in the 'Ode') by what Wordsworth elsewhere brilliantly calls 'the ballast of familiar life'[34]. The hourly objects (trees, sea, sky, green fields) fall from him leaving him subjected to unknown creations of his own mind, appalling creations, merciless and not to be defined by any language or concept that the child possesses. And this is what the poet gives thanks for in a preference to a simple childhood, or childhood as others have seen it.

As we read either *The Prelude* passage or the 'Ode' our ideas of childhood are transformed. No-one had ever thought like this and few do now two hundred years later despite the benefits of modern psychology. But there is further transformation to come as Wordsworth moves on, to our surprise, however well we know the poetry, from 'Blank misgivings of a Creature / Moving about in worlds not realiz'd' into 'High instincts before which our mortal Nature / Did tremble like a guilty thing surpriz'd'. Hamlet's father, who is in Wordsworth's mind, was not a mortal thing. But he was surprised; and he was guilty. But what kind of 'high instincts' could inflict guilt on a terrified child who feels deserted by all which has made him safe? Presumably ones that in some sense go too far. All that we have talked about comes apparently for Wordsworth under the heading of 'first affections', primal emotions, and 'shadowy recollections / Which, be they what they may (I am always so grateful that the poet himself is prepared to admit to *not* knowing the answer) Are yet the fountain light of all our day, / Are yet a master light of all our seeing / Uphold us, cherish'.....and we come back to and 'make / Our noisy years

---

[34] *Prelude* 1805 vii 603; FT 286

seem moments in the being / Of the eternal Silence'. Again, the 1799 *Prelude* is in Wordsworth's mind. 'All these were spectacles and sounds [he writes at the end of the spots of time passage] to which / I often would repair, and thence would drink / As at a fountain'[35]; a fountain at the time was a stream, a brook, a beck. Wordsworth drinks reassurance maybe inspiration from the fountain light of the 'Ode' as from *The Prelude* fountain. It is just that the imagery of the *Ode* concerns itself typically with light;

> And I do not doubt,
>
> That in this later time, when storm and rain
>
> Beat on my roof at midnight, or by day
>
> When I am in the woods, unknown to me
>
> The workings of my spirit thence are brought.[36]

It is a milder giving of thanks than that in the 'Ode', but thanks are being given nonetheless for the capacity of the mind to feed upon itself; to feed upon the past associatively, whether or not there is conscious memory or association which leads back to pain and fear. In the case of the *Prelude* it leads back to the father's death and the child's terrible sense that God has 'corrected [his] desires'[37]. So the poetry is, as we should expect with Wordsworth, about education through associationism that strengthens the present in feeding on the past. If simple childhood whether 'fluttering' or 'at rest' offers the underlying image of a fledgling in a nest, the concept of 'first affections' and 'shadowy recollections' as upholding us and cherishing must take us to the mother's arms. But even she, important as she is to Wordsworth, cannot explain why or how they should 'make / Our

---

[35] *Prelude* 1799 i 368-70; FT 18
[36] Ibid. 370-4.
[37] Ibid. 360

noisy years seem moments in the being / Of the eternal Silence'. At one level their meaning is in their effect. Wordsworth is being deliberately, powerfully imprecise. Our 'noisy years' beautifully evoke both childhood as a central them of the 'Ode' and man's whole unquiet life as seen in contrast to the 'eternal silence'. What then is the 'eternal silence'? Is it primal? Is it existence before man began to make his noises? Or does it take him into account? And why the *being / Of the eternal silence'*? It is immensely important in the structure of the lines; if omitted only the flatness of 'moments in…the eternal silence' remains. Does the 'eternal silence' mean existence or duration? Should we hear it as having some implication of life – a tiny bit godlike, a being that is in the earth and the air?

One final transformation. After transforming our notions of childhood, Wordsworth transforms pain and fear into positive forces in 'High instincts' and comes finally to be talking in purely numinous terms. Whatever associations we find in 'the being / Of the eternal silence', it has lifted the poetry into a quite different realm of experience;

> Hence, in a season of calm weather,
>
> Though inland far we be,
>
> Our Souls have sight of that immortal sea
>
> Which brought us hither,
>
> Can in a moment travel thither
>
> And see the Children sport upon the shore
>
> And hear the mighty waters rolling evermore.
>
> (164-70)

10 BLAKE : THE FIRST BOOK OF URIZEN[1]

It is rather typical of Blake that there is not another book. Since he is so mischievous, he may never have intended one! So much of Blake we do not understand. So why lecture on him? Because he is an extraordinarily powerful member of what we quite erroneously think of as a group of Romantic writers. They weren't a group and didn't consider themselves one. But they do have things in common which are perhaps the 'zeitgeist' rather than anything else. Blake is the most difficult of them. We should not expect to understand everything. For nine years I used to run a Blake reading group in Oxford modelled on the painting of the Forth Bridge; when we got to the end we had to begin all over again. We started at the beginning with *Poetic Sketches* 1783, worked through to the great climax of *Jerusalem* engraved around 1818 or 1820. With meetings every week during term-time the cycle took three years. Members of the group came and went. All were or became quietly obsessed as one had to be if one was to enjoy reading out loud poetry that frequently seems incomprehensible, written two hundred years ago in a strange idiom by a man reputed to be mad. I doubt if we ever came close to knowing the major Blake texts. What we learned was something more general about how to read.

With other writers it would be fairly straightforward, a

---
[1] First delivered as a lecture to The Wordsworth Summer Conference 2004

question of understanding well or ill, attempting to make correct interpretations. With Blake it is a question of assessing probabilities. In his more complex poems we seldom know for certain what he means, what he intended. In so far as we come to understand the difficult passages, it is through parallels and recognitions; themes, situations, names, phrases, individual words that we have met before, crop up as we read giving us a sense that we may for the moment know where we are. It doesn't help of course that Blake despises consistency or that he is not above teasing his readers. The following remarkable passage in *The Marriage of Heaven and Hell* starts without any batting of an eyelid:

> The Prophets Isaiah and Ezekiel dined with me, and I asked them how they dared so roundly to assert that God spake to them. [2]

No-one else would have written that. But what sort of ground are we left with when we talk about him and the relationship with the divine?

Buried in all this is the question of how to value Blake, or how *we* should do so. With the *Songs of Innocence* (1789) and *Experience* (1794) rhymes, rhythms, images, moments of arresting satire and exquisite storytelling permit us to talk in terms of beauty and skill. These are the things that we normally and rightly value. But Blake often prevents our doing so. We are watching a great master at work. The *Songs of Innocence* and *Experience* are the lyric Blake. He may be difficult at times but it seems he wishes to carry us along with him. Problems come when he turns his back on rhyme especially in the long lines of the prophecies, borrowed

---

[2] *The Marriage of Heaven and Hell* Plate 12: Erdman 38.

from Ossian, that sometimes look more like prose. Here is a writer who is more prophet than poet. One who is making fewer and fewer concessions to the mere pleasure of his audience.

The First Book of Urizen (1794) seems to me to be the great cross-roads poem. For some reason the poem is extremely pleasurable. Blake has moved on from his early lyric self but, as he builds his great myth of The Fall, he excites one with the sheer power of his writing, despite the poem's remaining through repeated readings obstinately itself and difficult. Chronologically and thematically, *Urizen* forms a link between the *Songs of Experience* and the earliest of the prophecies, beginning with a short missing version of *Vala* or *The Four Zoas* written around 1797. We see a series of evolutions: evolution of the character (for want of a better word, which in this context is an inaccurate term) of Urizen, the hero (similarly inaccurate) and the 'primeval Priest' (Pl.2.1); evolution of Blake's great central myth of The Fall into Creation, the starting point of the prophecies; evolution within the myth both of the human form and of the globe of earth as we know it; evolution of sexual difference and procreation; evolution of 'The Net of Religion'(Pl.25.22). And one could go on.

Urizen has cropped up as early as the 1790 *Visions of the Daughters of Albion* and the 1791 *Song of Liberty*. He even makes a guest appearance in the *Songs of Experience* drafted in 1792. In all these he is, to use an expression in *Paradise Lost*, the 'great forbidder'[3] and not much more. It is when he comes to have a book of his own in 1794 that he takes on the stature of myth. It is clear now that we are dealing with a shape-shifter, not of the classical protean sort but a rather new kind. And we are not receiving a lot of help from the writer in diagnosing this condition:

---

[3] *Paradise Lost* ix 815. Fowler 486

> Of the primeval Priests assum'd power,
>
> When Eternals spurn'd back his religion;
>
> And gave him a place in the north,
>
> Obscure, shadowy, void, solitary.
>
> Eternals I hear your call gladly,
>
> Dictate swift winged words, and fear not
>
> To unfold your dark visions of torment. (Pl.2.1-7)

These difficult verses are offered us by way of a 'Preludium', and in some sense a help! Blake's 'prefaces', 'arguments', 'preludiums' have a way of being doubtfully useful! His seven innocent-seeming lines raise far more questions than they answer. In what sense is Urizen the 'primeval Priest'? Why or from what source does he have either 'power' or 'religion'? Do the 'Eternals', whoever they may be, object to religion in general or only to his? What authority have they to send him off to solitude in 'the north'? Should we be hearing a reference to *Paradise Lost* as they do so? If so, how far should an association of Urizen and Satan be taken? And so on!

Blake's own position is interesting as he tells the Eternals – presumably in some sense his superiors – that they need not worry about dictating to him 'dark visions of torment' (whose 'torment' and who will the tormentors prove to be?). This is to assume that we are being offered a narrative sequence inside time or something like it. But if we think about it, the fall of Urizen, 'primeval Priest', must be taking place outside time;

before time, if that is not too paradoxical. Milton had had similar problems in *Paradise Lost* but followed the logic of *Genesis* in making the Fall a part of human history. Blake goes a stage further back citing it where it should surely be in eternity, effectively within the mind of God. As the poem opens we are confronted with the news that Urizen, 'so nam'd / That solitary one in Immensity' (Pl.3.42-3), is 'brooding', has become selfish and split himself off from his fellow Eternals who collectively represent the divine mind. This is a good basis for looking at this kind of prophetic Blake. We have Urizen as reason, a component of the divine mind, a component of eternity, who becomes broody and separated.

> Lo, a shadow of horror is risen
>
> In Eternity! Unknown, unprolific!
>
> Self-closd, all-repelling:　　　　　(Pl.3.1-3)

To be 'unprolific' is to be unvital, ungiving. Urizen is, as his punning name suggests, the embodiment of reason (so we might be pronouncing him 'your reason'; some interpret this 'horizon' but I think it unlikely). In wrenching himself away he wrenches apart the oneness of eternity and scars himself in the process. It is never clear how far Blake regards the Eternals as maimed by his fall. But the self-wounding is irreversible. Urizen becomes chaotic taking on as he falls many different shapes and aspects. We have to live with this in reading Blake. He is at one moment landscape – 'desolate mountains' (Pl.3.11), strangely endued with the power of language; at another, priest or prophet laying down a brazen new Mosaic law; at a third he liquefies – 'hiding in surging / Sulphureous fluid his phantasies' (Pl.10.13-14). He has enormous energies and is even in some sense creative.

But the process of division which he has initiated is out of control, spirals downward and onward and cannot at this stage in Blake's thinking be reversed. From the moment when Urizen, elsewhere emerging as a sun-god, rises upon the scene not as a horror but as the 'shadow of horror' (Pl. 3.1), Blake's language, though vivid, is conspicuously negative. We hear of vacuums and voids and discussion between the Eternals as to whether the brooding, secret, unspecific power is truly Urizen. Worse is to come. Urizen is not only 'Self-closd, all-repelling' (Pl.3.3), he is splitting up before our eyes. His fellow Eternals look on bemused. (It is one of the attractive things about the other Eternals; they may be maimed and showing that they are not complete, which is true as Urizen should be a part of them, but they have this sense of being bemused.)

> What Demon
>
> Hath form'd this abominable void

this is the Eternals speaking

> This soul-shudd'ring vacuum? – Some said
>
> 'It is Urizen', But unknown, abstracted,
>
> Brooding secret, the dark power hid. (Pl.3.3-6)

These lines and sentences disintegrate on examination. "Some said / 'It is Urizen'"; here are the Eternals talking about a fellow Eternal, a fellow part of the divine wholeness and thinking about it in terms of a being, almost a character. Then there is 'But unknown, abstracted,...the dark power hid'; but how did he hide if he was 'unknown'? How was he known to be doing it? Blake's language is constantly shifting, offering great power, great interest, much pleasure and yet refusing to sit still. Then the memorable statement at Plate 3 line 8:

> Times on times he divided

and division here (as it would be for Coleridge, but not quite to the same degree for Wordsworth) is important because wholeness, oneness, is one of the things that the Romantics have or wish to have in common.

The central drama of Blake's poem is the struggle to contain Urizen, prevent his 'dividing and dividing' (Pl.13.57). To bind his changes the Eternals choose among their number the blacksmith, Los, who resembles Vulcan in his trade but is allied to the poet himself and referred to consistently as 'the eternal Prophet' (Pl.13.35). There is an opposition between Los, the eternal prophet, and Urizen, reason. That is vastly too simple but it makes some sort of sense. Los uses metal rivets in his binding but we need to read with an eye for larger significancies. Imagination in Los is being ranged against reason, its traditional opponent, in Urizen, fallen though he is.

Before we are aware of such things however, we see Urizen both under attack from the black fires of the Eternals' rage and experiencing the horrors of a war within. As himself, he fights the Eternals. And as an Eternal, he fights himself. Either way the nature of his existence is confusing:

> changes appear'd
>
> In his desolate mountains, rifted furious
>
> By the black winds of perturbation

> For he strove in battles dire
>
> In unseen conflictions, with shapes
>
> Bred from his forsaken wilderness,
>
> Of beast, bird, fish, serpent and element
>
> Combustion, blast, vapour and cloud.   (Pl.3.10-17)

Already, a mere seventeen lines into Blake's poem, we are struggling to form a coherent idea of what is going on. Who has stirred those surprising 'black winds of perturbation'? One thinks of the sun, 'black but shining'[4], of *The Marriage of Heaven and Hell*. What precisely, or imprecisely, is Urizen's 'forsaken wilderness'? And what of the 'shapes' that breed there and seem in their lack of substance to parallel the definitions of Urizen as 'shadow'? If we are to read Urizen's 'unseen conflictions' as unseen because internal, in what sense or form has he internalised beasts, birds, fishes that cannot logically yet exist? Can what we think of as living creatures perhaps, in this strange context, be regarded as of the same nature as 'Combustion, blast, vapour and cloud'? Blake's vision at this moment seems odd enough to embrace almost any conjunction or paradox. Urizen is 'clos'd', 'unknown', 'shut in the deep' for 'age on ages' (Pl.3.24-5) yet at the same time significantly 'brooding' in the active sense.

Next we see him marshalling his combat troops…'cold horrors silent…ten thousands of thunders' (Pl.3.27-8)…equipped apparently with chariots:

> …the rolling of wheels,

---

[4] *Marriage of Heaven and Hell* A Memorable Fancy; Erdman 41.

> As of swelling seas, sound in his clouds,
>
> In his hills of stor'd snows, in his mountains
>
> Of hail and ice; voices of terror
>
> Are heard, like thunders of autumn,
>
> When the cloud blazes over the harvests.(Pl.3.30-5)

As 'the cloud blazes over the harvests', we experience sudden relief. Here there is normality, something we have all actually seen. The image supposedly takes us back to 'voices of terror' and 'mountains of hail and ice' but its presence throws into relief the opening words of Chapter II:

> Earth was not: nor globes of attraction
>
> The will of the Immortal expanded
>
> Or contracted his all flexible senses.
>
> Death was not, but eternal life sprung

No earth, no gravity, no death! Urizen though fallen is in fine fettle! Eternal life is unimpaired. So *where* are we? *When* are we? Why does Blake emphasize that Urizen has still the 'all flexible senses' (Pl.3.38) associated with eternal life when he seems in so many ways now to be distanced from eternity? They are not questions for which one is likely to find answers but there is a sense in which they have to be asked.

Within a context that is outside time, Blake has written a narrative that has, or appears to have, a linear progression.

> The sound of a trumpet the heavens

> Awoke and vast clouds of blood roll'd
>
> Round the dim rocks of Urizen,   (Pl.3.40-3)

What could more clearly suggest progression than a 'trumpet'? Waking the heavens, this one sounds not as a reveille but a call to battle. Yet like everything else in this stage of the poem it exists not so much in pre-existence (which would be Wordsworth) as in the Blakean technical impossibility of before time:

> Shrill the trumpet: and myriads of Eternity,
>
> *Plate 4*
>
> Muster around the bleak desarts,
>
> Now fill'd with clouds, darkness and waters
>
> That roll'd perplex'd, labring and utter'd
>
> Words articulate

Waters 'roll'd perplex'd', labour and utter words: they apparently have language! The Wordsworthian parallel is 'Black drizzling crags that spoke by the wayside / As if a voice were in them' from the Simplon Pass passage in the *Prelude*[5]. It suggests how the world of imagination in which Blake is working is divorced from the ordinary. Wordsworth's poetry at that point is at a high of Imagination as he descends into the ravine of Gondo. But Wordsworth compared to Blake is a very ordinary, comprehensible plane of experience. It is not just that as a visionary painter Blake *sees* his imagery though that is very important (red 'clouds of blood', for instance, swirling round Urizen's black rocks) but that he moves instinctively from one

---

[5] *The Prelude* 1805 vi. 563-4; FT 242

imaginative realm into another. Waters, already humanized in their perplexity and labouring, prove to be 'articulate' and to have been Urizen speaking, not as a landscape, but in the role in which he has been first announced, the 'primeval Priest'.

The poetry becomes for the first time openly satirical:

> From the depths of dark solitude. From
>
> The eternal abode in my holiness,...

As Priest, Urizen is boaster, law-giver and hypocrite!

> Hidden set apart in my stern counsels

a wonderful piece of self-regard

> Reserv'd for the days of futurity,
>
> I have sought for a joy without pain,
>
> For a solid without fluctuation
>
> Why will you die O Eternals?
>
> Why live in unquenchable burnings?   (Pl.4.6-13)

In these last four lines the 'primeval Priest' is speaking in the Urizenic mode of hexameters. More important are the terms of Urizen's challenge to the Eternals. Why are they bringing death on themselves, or dooming themselves otherwise to live in 'unquenchable' fire? What is it that prompts the truculent questions? Death, we have been told, does not yet exist. It is not in the nature of Eternals to die. Something might perhaps be made of Urizen's claim to knowledge of the 'days of futurity'. Is he in his holiness predicting a catastrophic future state? With their suggestion of hell-fire, 'unquenchable burnings' certainly sound like a threat!

'Stretch'd o'er the void' (Pl.4.18) the 'primeval Priest' emerges in a parodic version of Milton's Holy Spirit brooding over chaos[6]. It is one of the great images of Romantic poetry often repeated but here in a particularly odd form. Urizen proclaims:

> strong I repell'd
>
> The vast waves, and arose on the waters
>
> A wide world of solid obstruction.   (Pl.4.21-3)

Did Urizen himself arise 'on the waters' as 'a wide world of...obstruction', a material world? Or should we assume a passive construction and insert the word 'there' – and *there* arose' on the waters a solid world? Maybe it doesn't matter a great deal. But in a poem where it is so often difficult to find even one meaning, it seems a waste to have two and be unable to decide between them!

Urizen suits the Priest's role and he is beginning to come into his own;

> Lo! I unfold my darkness: and on
>
> This rock, place with strong hand the Book
>
> Of eternal brass, written in my solitude.
>
> Laws of peace, of love, of unity:

---

[6] And chiefly thou O Spirit / Dove-like sat'st brooding on the vast abyss / And madest it pregnant: *Paradise Lost* I 17-22; Fowler 43-4

Of pity, compassion, forgiveness.

Let each chuse one habitation:

His ancient infinite mansion:

One command, one joy, one desire,

One curse, one weight, one measure

One King, one God, one Law.   (Pl.4.31-40)

It will soon be revealed that the 'flames of eternal fury' (Pl.5.2) are dark. But I take it that Urizen's unfolding the darkness instead of the light is chiefly Blake being naughty, a follow-on from the parody and the playful inversions of *The Marriage of Heaven and Hell*. Urizen is Moses now – but Moses with the power of having got there first. Effectively he has just created the seven deadly sins that will be the great weapons of priestcraft – 'terrible monsters Sin-bred / Which the bosoms of all inhabit' (Pl.4.28-9), or will inhabit when the 'primeval Priest' has laid down his law. Who they 'all' can be whose bosoms are capable of sin is not clear. The Eternals can summon 'myriads' to do battle in their cause and Urizen can match them but these fighters who spring up as if they were dragons' teeth cannot be human beings and no less than Eternals who might be responsive to the seven deadly sins. The modulation of 'peace', 'love' and 'unity' (Pl.4.34) at the opening of Urizen's speech into the horror of 'One curse, one weight, one measure, / One King, one God, one Law' (Pl.4.39-40) at the end is so gently achieved that we might for a moment be carried into the trap of supposing this to be an early statement of the great Romantic theme of oneness. A voice at the back of us though is saying insistently 'One Law for the Lion and Ox is Oppression'.[7]

> The Eternals can take no more:
>
>> The voice ended, they saw his pale visage
>>
>> Emerge from the darkness; his hand
>>
>> On the rock of eternity unclasping
>>
>> The Book of brass. Rage siez'd the strong
>
> (Pl.4.41-5)

This is to be the moment of non-time, and in non-space, that severs Earth from Eternity. Very obscurely the severing is bound up with the new existence of sin:

> Rage, fury, intense indignation
>
> In cataracts of fire blood and gall,
>
> In whirlwinds of sulphurous smoke:
>
> And enormous forms of energy;
>
> All the seven deadly sins of the soul
>
> *Plate 5*
>
> In living creations appear'd
>
> In the flames of eternal fury.
>
>
> Sund'ring, dark'ning, thund'ring!

Blake is enjoying himself through internal rhymes and pleasurable

---

[7] *The Marriage of Heaven and Hell* Plate 24; Erdman 44

metres:

> Rent away with a terrible crash
>
> Eternity roll'd wide apart,
>
> Wide asunder rolling (Pl.5.4-6)

Rage at Urizen setting himself up as a law-giver seizes the Eternals, 'the strong' ('Rage seiz'd the strong'). But there is no obvious explanation as to how or where the deadly sins have grown to be 'enormous forms of energy' (Pl.4.48). Blake does not suggest it but have they perhaps been nurtured by Urizen as a means of controlling his new dependency of Earth? Eternity has been marvellously torn apart:

> Leaving ruinous fragments of life
>
> Hanging frowning cliffs and all between
>
> An ocean of voidness unfathomable. (Pl.5.11)

There is no answer to the question 'what sort of life do these 'Ruinous fragments' belong to?' The poem is full of questions that might as well not be asked.

Under attack from the black flames of the Eternals' rage, Urizen enjoys a state akin to death as he undergoes the first of three major falls in the poem which shape existence as we know it. But first he attempts to hide;

> In fierce anguish and quenchless flames
>
> To the desarts and rocks He ran raging
>
> To hide, but He could not: (Pl.5.19-21)

Then 'combining' (Pl.5.21), summoning up the strength diffused through his self-begotten armies, he digs and piles mountains:

> He dug mountains and hills in vast strength
>
> He piled them in incessant labour,
>
> In howlings and pangs and fierce madness
>
> Long periods in burning fires labouring
>
> Till hoary, and age-broke, and aged,
>
> In despair and the shadows of death.   (Pl.5.22-7)

Urizen it seems loses his immortal flexibility as Milton's Lucifer loses his light – only gradually. Neither can die. But Urizen passes through the phases of ageing humanity as he creates his last astonishing defence against the raging Eternals. Not a pile of mountains this time but the globe itself and with it the human heart:

> ….a roof, vast petrific around,
>
> On all sides He fram'd: like a womb;
>
> Where thousands of rivers in veins
>
> Of blood pour down the mountains to cool
>
> The eternal fires beating without
>
> From Eternals;   (Pl.5.28-33)

Even by Blake's standards, there is genius in this vision of thousands of rivers in veins of blood pouring down the mountains. The poem has alternated in seeing Urizen as landscape and as character, or something like it. But here there is especially imaginative vision. Standing on the shore of the infinite ocean, the Eternals see the vast world of Urizen appear like a 'black globe' (Pl.5.33), 'like a human heart, strugling and beating' (Pl.5.36).

Enter Los, blacksmith and prophet, sent by his fellow Eternals to contain Urizen, bind his changes, stop his 'dividing and dividing';

> And Los round the dark globe of Urizen,
>
> Kept watch for Eternals to confine,
>
> The obscure separation alone;
>
> For Eternity stood wide apart,
>
> *Plate 6*
>
> As the stars are apart from the earth.

Creative, though petrific, Urizen has made or turned into – perhaps *and* turned into – the earth. His fall, seen in many different ways but always divisive, has proved to be Creation. What has seemed to be a complex narrative contracts to a single cosmic event. Los weeps,

> cursing his lot; for in anguish,
>
> Urizen was rent from his side;   (Pl.6.3-4)

There is a sort of sympathy with Los from the start. He has an impossible task; he is set by his fellow Eternals to contain that which cannot be contained and which leads to his own physical pain.

Urizen meanwhile is laid in a 'stony sleep / Unorganiz'd, rent from Eternity' (Pl.6.7). Watching as always, the Eternals are perplexed:

> What is this? Death
>
> Urizen is a clod of clay.   (Pl.6.9-10)

Still 'flexible' as an unfallen Immortal, Los heals but Urizen doesn't. But though he can be death-like, he cannot be dead. One moment, if moments there be, he lies 'in a dreamless night' (Pl.7.6), the next he is again the 'surging sulphureous / Perturbed Immortal, mad ranging' and frightening Los with a 'hurtling' of bones (Pl.8.2-4).

> And Urizen (so his eternal name)
>
> His prolific delight obscurd more and more
>
> In dark secresy hiding in surgeing
>
> Sulphureous fluid his phantasies.
>
> The Eternal Prophet heavd the dark bellows,
>
> And turn'd restless the tongs; and the hammer
>
> Incessant beat; forging chains new and new,
>
> Numb'ring with links. hours, days and years
>
>   (Pl.10.11-18)

This is the work of Los.

Separated from Eternity, Urizen and with him the world that he makes (and in some sense becomes) must logically be or become subject to time. As blacksmith, Los binds Urizen with the chain of 'hours, days & years'. As Imagination, he contains reason beating it at its own unimaginative game:

> Restless turn'd the immortal inchain'd
>
> Heaving dolorous! anguish'd! unbearable
>
> Till a roof shaggy wild inclos'd
>
> In an orb, his fountain of thought.   (Pl.10.31-34)

The second major fall in Blake's poem, hinted at in the likeness to a heart, is productive of the human form – as the first is of the human world. Los binds every change in Urizen with rivets of iron and brass. Blake offers the conflict to us in a vividly imaginative parody of the seven days of creation:

> In a horrible dreamful slumber;
>
> Like the linked infernal chain;
>
> A vast Spine writh'd in torment
>
> Upon the winds; shooting pain'd   (Pl.10.35-38)

A spine writhing in torment upon the winds of a world that does not yet exist but already has pain!

> Ribs, like a bending cavern
>
> And bones of solidness, froze
>
> Over all his nerves of joy.
>
> And a first Age passed over,
>
> And a state of dismal woe.   (Pl.10.39-43)

As the spine writhes 'upon the winds', somewhere in unspecific space, we are invited to see also the linked infernal chain of 'hours, days and years', the chain of time writhing too. It is a reminder of the surreal visual power of this poetry, just as the bones freezing in their solidness over the nerves of joy are a reminder of its pain.

Blake is doing something wholly new, wholly unlikely, formulating successfully in words a myth that as painter he can see. Age one in this enjoyable imaginative sequence of the poem creates for Urizen and mankind the spine and bending cavern of the ribs; age two creates the heart, veins and arteries; age three the eyes, 'two little orbs... fixed in two little caves' (Pl.11.13-14); age four, the ears, developing unexpectedly among 'pangs of hope...Two Ears in close volutions' (19-21) (whose 'pangs' one wonders?); age five offers us the 'nostrils'; age six, the stomach ('the craving Hungry Cavern'), throat and tongue. And Age Seven, which ought to have been a rest, offers us the legs and arms;

>Enraged and stifled with torment
>
>He threw his right Arm to the north
>
>His left Arm to the south
>
>Shooting out in anguish deep,
>
>And his Feet stampd the nether Abyss
>
>In trembling and howling and dismay.
>
>And a seventh Age passed over:
>
>And a state of dismal woe.   (Pl.13.11-19)

The arms are thrown! They must logically be inside the body but telescopic so that a good throw will bring them out!

Los shrinks from his task, the hammer falls from his hand. It seems though that his fires have been watching him, though to us this sounds ridiculous. These are the fires that he stokes as a blacksmith. Ashamed, they now hide 'their strong limbs in smoke' (Pl.13.23). We can if we wish see the strong limbs as flame and their behaviour as metaphor. But why be so banal when Blake gives them life?

Narrative at this stage of *Urizen* seems fairly comprehensible, as we witness the third of the great falls, the fall into sexual division. This time it is Los who falls, divided by his own pity before the death image of Urizen:

> He saw Urizen deadly black,
>
> In his chains bound, and Pity began,
>
>
> In anguish dividing and dividing
>
> For pity divides the soul   (Pl.13.50-53)

Sympathy is feeling with, compassion is feeling for, pity is feeling from above, feeling for someone or something in one's own differentness. Experiencing division, Los becomes fully or merely human. And, in a way that is not so easily explained but which has something to do with Creation and Eve in *Genesis* and *Paradise Lost*, Los brings to life the otherness that is a part of him: the female principle:

> At length, in tears and cries imbodied,
>
> A female form trembling and pale

> Waves before his deathly face
>
> All Eternity shudder'd at sight
>
> Of the first female now separate.   (Pl.18.6-10)

There is something comical in the Eternals' reaction:

> 'Spread a tent, with strong curtains around them
>
> Let cords and stakes bind in the Void,
>
> That Eternals may no more behold them!'
>
> (Pl.19.2-4)

Many of the writer's problems in *Urizen* have been to do with getting 'cords and stakes [to] bind in the Void'; they have to be dependably lasting and yet they bind in a nothingness. Blake is getting narrative to make sense where there is no material world. In this case the tent, though it will be effective, is not being built quickly enough. In no time the Eternals see, and we see, man begetting his likeness on his own divided image.

With sexual difference comes procreation and with that the fall is perpetuated. Each generation will now mark a further stage away from original harmony. Blake has created a pattern from which there is no logical way out. The great epics that follow, all starting from the concept of a fallen world, will have it as their mission to find a means of reversing the downward spiral, achieving a redemptive myth. Enitharmon, never again called Pity, becomes pregnant, feels as Blake inelegantly puts it, 'a Worm within her womb', waiting 'to be moulded into existence' (Pl.19.20 and 23). Nor is she alone. It is one of the complexities of this late stage of the poem that Enitharmon is not merely an individual but representative of the natural world. As she gives birth to Orc, many forms of fish, bird and beast that have no logical right to exist give birth too. Orc himself *digs* his way to the surface as if to make the point that at some level his mother is Nature:

> Delving earth in his resistless way;
>
> Howling, the Child with fierce flames
>
> Issu'd from Enitharmon. (Pl.19.44-6)

Another fall has been completed.

> The Eternals, closed the tent
>
> They beat down the stakes the cords
>
> *Plate 20*
>
> Stretch'd for a work of eternity;
>
> No more Los beheld Eternity.

With little of the drama and great imaginative poetry of Urizen's fall, Los too falls.

Oedipal jealousy of Los for his son is a feature of this late stage of the poem;

> They took Orc to the top of a mountain.
>
> O how Enitharmon wept!
>
> They chain'd his young limbs to the rock
>
> With the Chain of Jealousy

> Beneath Urizens deathful shadow (Pl.20.1-5)

The chain tightens every day as a girdle and is burst at night, forming in the process link after link of an iron chain. As we should expect, it turns out to be Urizen who is presiding. Not content with chaining down his son, Los (as ever part myth, part prophet) encircles Enitharmon with fires of prophecy from the sight of Urizen and Orc. Enitharmon we are told in the poem's last reference to her, or for that matter to Orc and Los, bears an enormous race. By one logic, mankind is descended from her as it is from Eve; by another, humans are the children of Urizen's fall, created as he himself takes human form. The confusion, or complexity, is never sorted out. Instead Blake shows Urizen in his poem's final phase (Chapters VIII and IX) exploring his dens, accustoming himself to his fallen role, justifying in a rather squalid way his title of 'primeval Priest'. His world has never settled down; it teems with bits, fragments:

> Frightening; faithless; fawning
>
> Portions of life; similitudes
>
> Of a foot, or a hand, or a head (Pl.23.3-5)

bits that sound as if they are too incomplete to be dangerous and yet behave like piranhas. It is the state of his children though that sickens him and the knowledge of his responsibility as parent and law-giver:

> he curs'd
>
> Both sons and daughters; for he saw
>
> That no flesh nor spirit could keep

His iron laws one moment.   (Pl.23.23-6)

Thoughts of 'The Ox in the slaughter house …. / The Dog at the wintry door' (Pl.25.1-2) bring pity at last from Urizen himself and with it the realisation, unfortunately accurate for us all, that life lives 'upon death' (Pl.23.27).

The last bequest he has for his children before he disappears from the scene is the gruesome 'Net of Religion' so suited to humanity that its cords and meshes are knotted like to the human heart:

> And where-ever he wandered in sorrows
>
> Upon the aged heavens
>
> A cold shadow follow'd behind him
>
> Like a spider's web, moist, cold, and dim
>
> Drawing out from his sorrowing soul   (Pl.25.7-11)

And the last message that Blake has for us after we see Urizen's race shaping up for existence in a final parody of Creation is a laconic quatrain aimed at those of his contemporaries in 1794 who have been drawn into 'The Net of Religion' (Pl.25.22):

> And their children wept, and built
>
> Tombs in the desolate places,
>
> And form'd laws of prudence, and called them
>
> The eternal laws of God.   (Pl.28.4-7)

And so we come back to the thought of 'understanding' Urizen. I don't suppose that anybody but Blake ever has. Maybe we should ask him to supper and ask the prophets Isaiah and Ezekiel to help us in the matter!

ABOUT THE AUTHOR

Jonathan Fletcher Wordsworth (1932-2006) was Professor of English Literature at the University of Oxford, an internationally acknowledged expert in the field of Romantic Literature and a charismatic and influential critic, scholar and teacher. Educated at Westminster School and Brasenose College Oxford he became a Fellow firstly at Exeter College and then St. Catherine's. He was the great-great-great nephew of William Wordsworth and great-great grandson of Christopher Wordsworth, poet and Master of Trinity College Cambridge and Bishop of Lincoln. He was Chairman of the Wordsworth Trust 1976-2002 and President from 2002 till his death. He was a commanding academic presence at the Wordsworth Summer Conference (which began in 1970 as the brainchild of his cousin Richard) and at the Wordsworth Winter School held annually in Grasmere and the place where the lectures contained in this book were given. Towards the end of his life he was Director and Convenor of both conferences.

He wrote *The Music of Humanity* in 1969 which importantly recovered the poem now known as 'The Ruined Cottage' 1797-8 from the manuscripts and which also contains 'the best analysis of Wordsworth's intellectual relationship with Coleridge'. His magnum opus *The Borders of Vision* followed in 1982 and is an authoritative study of Wordsworth's poetry. He wished to make primary eighteenth and nineteenth century sources easily available to the modern reader and edited over 180 titles in his 'Revolution and Romanticism' series published by Woodstock Books. The introductions to these volumes were characteristically succinct and demonstrated his mastery of the period. In collected form they comprised three further volumes of his scholarship: *The Bright Work Grows* (1997) on women writers, *Ancestral Voices* (1991) and *Visionary Gleam* (1996). He co-edited *William Wordsworth and the Age of English Romanticism* which accompanied a major Romanticism exhibition held in Britain and America. As testament to his conviction that early poetic drafts rather than later revised editions demonstrated more clearly the "original intentions" of the poet, he published *The Two-Part Prelude* and then *The Prelude: The Four Texts*. He co-edited the Norton edition of *The Prelude* with Stephen Gill and M.H. Abrams and was an advisory editor with M. H. Abrams and Geoffrey Hartman of the most ambitious and scholarly editions of Wordsworth's work to date for Cornell University Press. With Jessica Wordsworth, he edited *The New Penguin Book of Romantic Poetry* (2003).

Made in the USA
Charleston, SC
27 January 2015